Recollections of
the Siege of Kut & After

Recollections of
the Siege of Kut & After

Two Accounts by Indian Army Officers during
the First World War in Mesopotamia

ILLUSTRATED

Besieged in Kut and After

Charles H. Barber

A Kut Prisoner

H. C. W. Bishop

LEONAUR

Recollections of the Siege of Kut & After
Two Accounts by Indian Army Officers during the First World War in Mesopotamia
Besieged in Kut and After
by Charles H. Barber
A Kut Prisoner
by H. C. W. Bishop

ILLUSTRATED

FIRST EDITION

First published under the titles
Besieged in Kut and After
and
A Kut Prisoner

Leonaur is an imprint of Oakpast Ltd
Copyright in this form © 2018 Oakpast Ltd

ISBN: 978-1-78282-784-9 (hardcover)
ISBN: 978-1-78282-785-6 (softcover)

http://www.leonaur.com

Contents

Besieged in Kut and After

Contents

CHAPTER 1

The River Journey Busra to Amarah

Ten months of monotonous overwork at the Base, finishing up with an appalling hot weather amongst the floods, had made us all soul-weary and "fed up" with life in general, so that the prospect of moving nearer to the Front and the glorious uncertainty of the future higher up the old, old river were doubly welcome.

Mobilising our men and material, packing up all the extras we could get hold of, and handing over our responsibilities to others, were a wonderful tonic to our stale and tired brains; whilst over all lay the sense of coming events, of the imminence of another battle, the anticipation of which sent the blood coursing more swiftly and sentiently through our veins, bringing with it a feeling of elation and of the joy of life.

Guns and horses, mules and men, carts and stores were being pushed up in boat after boat, barge upon barge; whilst we at the hospital, watching them go by, went with them in our hearts, and with our lips grumbled at our own inactivity and chafed at our delay. But some of us, at least, were soon to press hard on their heels, with the chance of sharing in whatever was going forward. A game or two of strenuous football on the dusty parade-ground of the old Turkish barracks was a welcome relaxation in those last days of waiting. Little did we guess that in a few short weeks half the gallant regiment we played with would be lying with loosened knees on the field of Ctesiphon. . . .

When all our stuff was packed and piled ready for loading, we waited with such patience as we could muster for the word to move and the transport to take us. Soon the former came, but the latter hung fire. All available transport was being used for troops and guns. The turn of the medicals would come when a few odd square yards of deck-space fell vacant. But at last a "whole steamer" of microscopic size, big enough for about one-third of our requirements, was provided. This we boarded with some of our personnel and less of our equipment and started away merrily on the new jaunt. Could we

GENERAL MAP OF

Asiatic Turkey

have foreseen what was to come, and all the horrors of Kut that lay before us, we should have commenced our journey with very different feelings. How different was to be the return of a small fraction of our party nearly a year later, and with what an experience behind us!

As it was, our departure was invested with all the glamour of a launch into the unknown; a fresh chapter of our part in the great adventure was opening.

At ten o'clock on a bright morning we cast off from the little wooden jetty with a nod and a hand-shake with old associates and started away up the splendid reach of the river which stretches between Busra and Kurna.

Lined on both sides by deep groves of graceful palms down to the water's edge, the broad majestic river presented a fine sight. The palms formed a beautiful monochrome study, from the light bright green of the upper fronds, reflecting the brilliant sunlight, to the dark and sombre hues of the shaded aisles beneath. This underworld of the palm groves, especially when the floods are high enough to cover entirely the ground beneath, forms a beautiful picture.

It is a vast and beautiful cathedral, with its thousands of columns of sepia brown boles supporting a Gothic roof of luscious green. The trunks are arranged in parallel rows, which thus form innumerable cloisters and aisles stretching away in all directions until they are lost in the distant background of velvety green. Here and there rays of sunlight pierce the rich canopy, and show up in a thousand reflections the warm brown smoothness of the liquid floor that is spread like polished marble beneath. A cathedral! Nay, rather a gorgeous hall of audience beloved of the Eastern monarch. 'Twere easy to people it with its natural complement of courtiers and slaves, its ambassadors and merchants, its beggars and its suppliants at the throne of a mighty despot.

Passing from dreams to realities, we wonder at and try to calculate the wealth represented by these millions of generous date-bearing trees, which for over a hundred miles line both sides of the Shatt-el-Arab to a depth of a thousand yards. If each tree produce ten shillings' worth of dates *per annum* for seventy years, and there are so many million of trees, what revenue will be derived from the Busra Vilayet?

We have become fond of the palm. She is Mesopotamia, so far as we have seen it—we have watched her and her mate quiescent during the winter, blossoming forth with flowers and new foliage in the spring, have noted the process of fertilisation guided and controlled by her human owners; watched the formation of the fruit whilst her huge and graceful leaves spread themselves in their richness and pride; and finally, have awaited with ever-increasing curiosity the ripening of the generous fruit hanging in great golden bunches from her neck. Borne down with the weight and wealth of the fruit, exhausted by their wonderful effort, these god-sent trees lose their gloss and colour; their lower leaves wither and brown, they look worn and bedraggled, they retire to rest for another winter, and care not how their human taskmasters dispose of their progeny.

They have done their work; they have earned their rest. Their fruit does not, however, represent their only usefulness. The lighter parts of the old frond are used for making matting, which forms the floors and the walls of many a poor dwelling, whilst the stem of the leaf, tough and strong, serves the hundred purposes to which stout sticks are put—the base of the old leaf is the staple firewood, and the trunks of the old trees are seen in many a rustic bridge over irrigation channels, and form the props or beams of many a house. No part of the palm is lost, nothing is wasted.

We reached Kurna after dark. Passing by the mouth of the mighty Euphrates, we anchored off the middle of the little town. We could see nothing but a subdued light here and there below the dim outline of the house roofs. A hail and an answer, a few short orders, and we take up our final position for the night. Are we near the Garden of Eden? What will it look like by the light of day? We pass a miserable night, for the sand-fly is in his myriads and neglecteth not his opportunity of taking his fill of the blood of the soldier-men who sprawl on the upper deck. I can quite imagine that the sand-fly was one of the first of the exterior pests to attack our first parents when they were driven forth, and that Adam at least made a remark that can easily be understood by those who have made the acquaintance of the little beast.

But joy cometh in the morning, and soon after the sun was up we were ashore with the object of climbing the look-out tower and so getting a bird's-eye view of the country round and of the confluence of the two ancient rivers. The tower, built by the R.E., was 180 feet high, and the climbing of it by ladders served as a good appetite-raiser for breakfast.

From its top, which was once hit by a shell, a splendid panorama of the surrounding country is spread before one. To the south-east the stately Shatt-el-Arab, with its palm-covered banks, stretches away into the haze to Busra; to the west the Euphrates, the very name of which makes one pause and dream for a moment amongst the fascinations of

Biblical history, winds away towards Nasiryeh and the shallow lake. At one's feet lies the mud village of Kurna, and the Tigris with its boat-bridge and the site of the Turkish boom, which we broke with our ships a few short months ago; across the river another clump of palms; all else, desert, which begins abruptly at the fringe of the palm groves and stretches away as far as the eye can reach.

To the north the Tigris wanders along like a silver streak, through illimitable barrenness of sand and marsh, to the distant horizon, or is lost in a flickering mirage. Take away these little ribbons of life-giving water, and nothing is left—nothing, nothing. Easily can one understand the Oriental's love of a garden, a retreat, green and well watered, filled with delicious fruit, perfumed with the sweet odours of a thousand flowers, where trickling water, clear as crystal, lulls one's senses to languorous repose; a shady refuge walled around, and protected both from the cruelty of the blistering sun and from the irritation of the blinding dust. Small wonder that his ideal of a happy dwelling should be the very antithesis of his sun-baked desert country.

Descending to earth, I went in search of Lancelot, and then for breakfast to the sylvan quarters of some friends who were stationed here. Eaten up by sand-flies and plagued by mosquitoes in their reed huts amongst the palms and village houses, they had dragged on a weary existence through the long months of a wicked hot weather and were heartily sick of it. Busra is bad in the hot weather, but Kurna is probably the worst spot on the river—always moist, save when the "*Shamal*" blows well, the heat may be anything up to 123° for weeks. Combine this with insect pests and a monotonous existence, and you have a terrestrial hell wherein life has no charms.

The huts and hospital wards and barracks were constructed of walls of dried reeds from the marshes, in crossed layers or in bundles, roofed over with the same material, which afforded good protection from the sun. A large number of sick had been accommodated in these at one time, but they were now nearly empty.

Breakfast over, we boarded our little stern-wheeler, and watched another "*mahela*" being made fast to our remaining free side. This carried a surveying party under Major L—— of the R.E., who had put a roof on it and turned the waist of it into a tolerably comfortable residence, and we were glad to get on board now and again to talk and smoke. Thus, squeezed between two heavy *mahelas*, our gallant little craft struggled gamely on, and made about three knots against the stream. The time passed pleasantly enough. It was good to sit well forward on the little bridge and enjoy our idleness and the desert air.

Palm-trees were soon left behind, and the landscape for miles offered nothing better than a few scraggy crops on the river banks. Away from the banks the ground sloped gently downwards and fell into widespread areas of reeds and marsh. An occasional flight of duck was met with, and sometimes a few teal would settle on the water ahead of us, only to get up again on our approach and carefully keep out of range. Humans were scarce, but from time to time we came upon a watch-tower built four-square of mud-dried bricks, whilst beside it nestled a few reed huts or rude cloth tents of a family or two of miserable nomads, or of the watchman's people, with their brats and their ponies, their dogs and chickens. Here and there, as you go up the river, you see the tomb of some holy man whose monument it is—some village Jacob or local prophet. Their invariable and only form is that of a dome surmounting a square platform or plinth, the whole built upon a low mound, and made of the same material and of the same tint as the surrounding dust-coloured silt. By its side is sometimes a lean-to or mud hut, with its tiny doorway, wherein may live the caretaker of the shrine.

Though a little hot at midday, the weather in this mid-October was delightfully clear and bright, and the breeze we made was enough to keep away the fly and other biting beasts.

Sketching and dozing were the order of the day, and we felt we could do with a large dose of such an existence. The course of the river is extraordinarily tortuous, winding to right and to left—now going northward, and now bending back in an almost complete loop to the south—mile after mile, and the scene does not change. Dotted about on the plain—some going in one direction, some in another—the graceful sails of large native cargo-boats are noiselessly moving hither and thither in all directions, like wherries on the Norfolk Broads; but for all one can see of the river beyond the nearest bend, or of the boats themselves, they might very well be a squadron of land yachts engaged in a peaceful regatta race.

Far away on the horizon can just be made out the smoke of a distant steamer curling up into the misty blue. Soon we shall meet it, and perhaps get news of the recent battle. Just at sunset we approached Ezra's famous tomb. Standing on the right bank, amidst a clump of palms, its turquoise-blue dome reflecting the glory of the setting sun, it formed as charming a picture as one could wish to see. Coming down the river a year later, I observed a huge rough notice-

17

TURKISH GUNBOAT MARMORICE WHEN THE NAVY HAD
DONE WITH IT. ON THE TIGRIS, 1915.

WATCH-TOWER AND REED HUTS ON BANK OF THE TIGRIS.

board that had been put up quite near the base of the venerable pile, bearing some necessary directions relating to navigation. It seemed to desecrate the ancient sanctity of the holy place.

An hour above the prophet's tomb, we anchored for the night close to the steamer whose smoke we had espied earlier in the day. She had on board a couple of hundred or so wounded from the Battle of Kut of a week ago and was towing a couple of barges containing 400 Turkish prisoners. From her officers on board we got tales of the fight, and, alas! the names of fallen comrades. With the *medico* in charge, an old friend, we strolled round his Hospital Ship and consulted over one or two bad cases that he was anxious about. His patients were tucked in for the night and seemed cheery and comfortable. A few were on camp-beds; the rest were lying on mattresses or blankets on the deck and seemed to be well covered up. I remember being struck by the sense of completeness and care that overspread the broad upper deck, and the air of snug repose that seemed, in spite of their situation a hundred miles from anywhere, to lie over the lines of recumbent figures.

The lights were shaded, and many of the patients were already asleep, as, with careful steps and lowered voices, we moved in and out amongst the groups of wounded. The lap, lap of the stream round the paddle-boxes, the howl of the desert jackal, and the general incongruity of our surroundings faded away, and save for the absence of the gentle nurse, we might have been doing a night round in a London Hospital.

The *padre* gave me sad news of a special chum who had been dangerously wounded and had been asking for me; but he had been put on the preceding ship, and so we had missed each other.

We were well off the mark at dawn next day, and all went well and as monotonously as usual until midday, when we met a large paddle-boat well-grounded on the mud. We had been in sight of her for hours, and guessed her trouble, and could see her making desperate efforts to get off the offending sandbank. As ill luck would have it, she wrenched herself free just as we were about to pass her, with the result that we collided and got badly mixed up. The free language and forcible remonstrance of the P. boat's skipper were quite lost upon our own captain, who was an Arab of no linguistic attainments. We had to slip our two *mahelas* and impotently watch them float away downstream on the wrong side of our unwieldy antagonist. We just got by ourselves, and forthwith tied up at the bank for the next four hours until we could rescue our helpless boats.

The river here is narrow and its submerged sandbanks many. With no way on it, the P. boat and its heavy barges became an unmanageable mass of wood and iron, and it was not long before it swung round so much that the bows of the starboard barge stuck on one bank and the stern of the port one on the other bank, thus blocking the fairway completely. For a time, we watched the unfortunate skipper resume his efforts to get clear, ringing the changes on paddles and kedge, donkey-engine and cable, or man-haulage from the banks—a tiring business, and one calculated to try the temper of the calmest sailor. Lancelot and I strolled off in different directions, I to inspect a tomb in the vicinity. In doing so, my wanderings took me beyond a slight rise in the ground, which hid me from my faithful staff, whom I met an hour later come out to look for me, armed *cap-à-pie* and anxious as to my whereabouts.

That night we reached the village of Q—— S——, where was a telegraph station and a detachment of Indian infantry as guard. The Arabs here were none too peaceably disposed, and marauders were like to be met with, so we turned in feeling quite prepared to be unpleasantly awakened. Sure enough, in the middle of the night a shot rang out, then another, and another—a dozen in all. They appeared to come from the bank close by, but nothing more happened, and we were just settling down again when the splash of oars was heard, and a boat came alongside. Out of the darkness a Tommy's clear voice hailed—"Is there an officer on board?" We assured him that there was, and he then proceeded to inform us that one of their number had run amok and chased them all out of their quarters.

"'E went mad, sir, all of a sudden, collared all our rifles, and came for us with the butt—swore 'e'd do for us, and would shoot anybody who came near the place—'e's firin away now at everything 'e sees,—what are we to do, sir?"

"What upset him?" we ask.

"Well, sir, 'e got 'old o' two bottles o' whisky, and because we wouldn't drink with 'im, bein' teetotalers, 'e drank the lot himself and went ravin' mad."

This solved the problem, and when the three homeless ones averred that they could double up with the Indian guard for the night, Major L—— advised them to leave the maniac alone and let the spirit do its work. This it did, for quiet soon reigned, and at six o'clock the next morning the culprit was sober and denied all knowledge of his night's frolic.

A Street in Kut.

On the Tigris. A river paddle-boat and two barges
laden with Turkish prisoners, &c.

Resuming our journey, we soon landed to stretch our legs, and keeping pace with our boats we walked up such birds as there were, and bagged a couple of brace of black partridge, which made a welcome addition to the pot.

Reaching Amarah just before sunset, we heard to our joy that we were to proceed at once to Kut.

Chapter 2

Amarah to Kut

Amarah, with its ten or twelve thousand inhabitants, is a well-built town, situated for the most part on the left bank. With its forests of *mahela* masts on both sides of the broad river, its palms and gardens, and its long, straight row of handsome houses on the river front, the view of the place as you approach it from the S.E. is a pleasing one.

The houses are two-storeyed, surmounted by a flat roof, with its usual flimsy-looking encircling wall. Most of them have large and handsome bay windows, projecting from the first floor, and made of carved or latticed wood, with generously designed cornices. These first-floor rooms are large and airy, and form ideal quarters, except in the hottest weather.

The Bazar is large and roomy, with a lofty, gabled roof. Save for the absence of glass, it reminded one of our own arcades, though it comprises a whole street. At the river end are a couple of good shops, where European stores are to be had. The late *Sultan*, it is said, took a special interest in the designing and erection of this town, in which he was personally interested. It is but fifty years old; its population is a mixture of Moslems, Sabaeans, Jews, and R.C.'s; it exports grain, and lies at one end of a trade route to Persia.

At Amarah we remained that night and all the next morning. Dropping Major L—— and his survey party, we took on another *mahela* with two more *medicos* and their kit, and a few tents for ourselves on loan from another section of our own hospital already established here. Also, we bought stores and food, and had a look round generally. The Arab inhabitants were respectful and seemed anxious to placate our people; the R.E. were very busy with barracks and hospitals.

Off again at midday, we reached Kamait an hour after sunset and anchored. Here our friend the sand-fly was in force and defeated our sleep badly, so we landed early, and keeping pace with our boat, we bagged a brace of partridges and a hare and forgot the miseries of the night. We saw many huge flights of duck and some sand-grouse, but

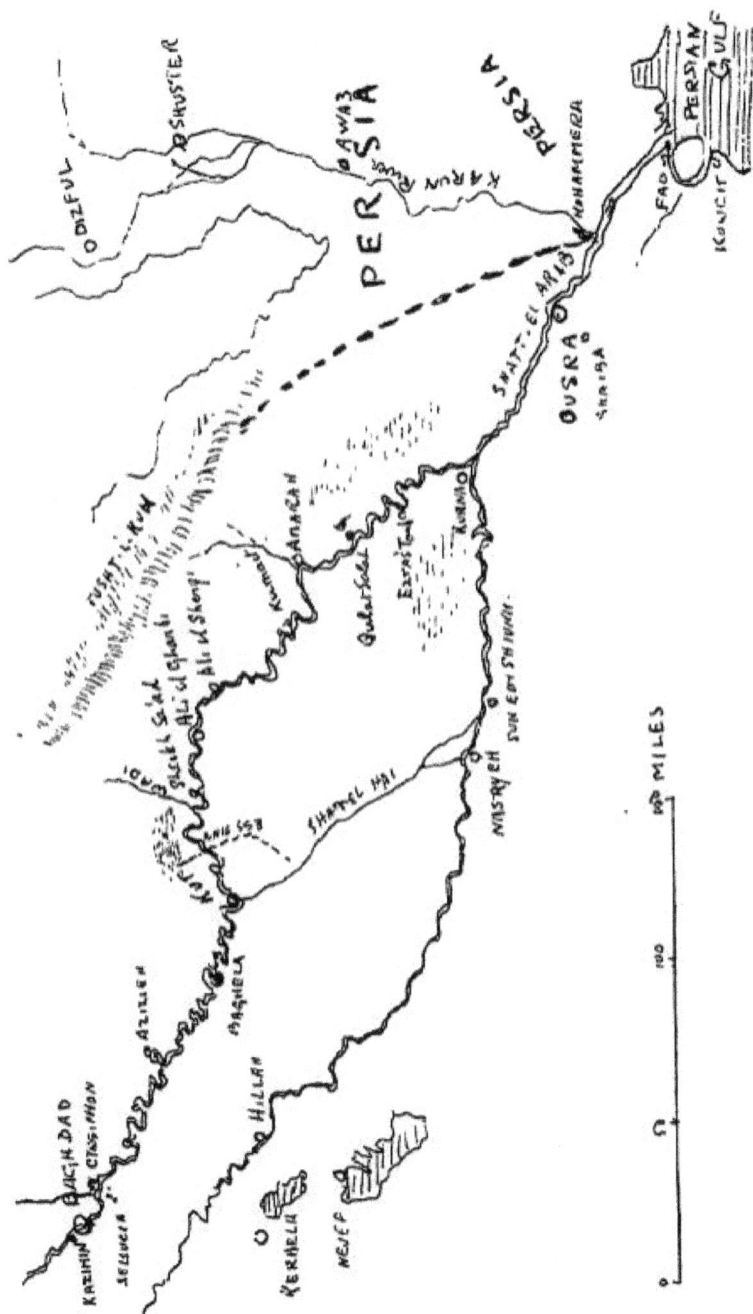

THE TIGRIS TO BAGHDAD

none came within range. The country remained most uninteresting, and a few groups of nomads, with their flocks of sheep or a herd of camels, were the only relief in a scene of barren desolation.

That night we anchored, most unwisely, within a mile or so of a large herd of these prehistoric beasts. Amongst them were many white camels, which look uglier even than the ordinary sand-coloured ones, if that were possible. Unwise were we, for the smell of the animals, perhaps aided and abetted by that of their equally dirty human attendants, permeates and poisons the sweet desert air for a distance of a couple of miles at least—and there is nothing else like the stink of an "*oont.*"

Next morning, we reached Ali-el-Gharbi, where we found established a strong perimeter camp held by a few companies of the Blankabad Infantry. The "intelligence" officer here cheered us by the information that persistent Bazar rumours had it that a goodly force of Arabs, with a couple of guns, was manoeuvring in the neighbourhood. As these gentlemen had cut up and burnt a large convoy a few days before, it was suggested that we might have trouble. We were therefore advised to fortify our craft as best we could and "clear for action." As our guard consisted of a lance corporal and six men, all jungly recruits, this was indeed merry news! but, in the absence of more precise details, there was nothing for it but to get on. We spent the next few hours in putting up breastworks of bundles of tents and hospital boxes and bales, the while we stationed a look out on the awning above the bridge, which just enabled him to see over the high banks in this portion of the river and get a good view of the surrounding country. Hereabouts the river approaches its nearest to the Pusht-i-Kuh, the western bulwarks of Persia. Bare and brown and barren, and thirty miles away, these rugged hills are often ravishingly beautiful in their delicate pink at sunrise, or in their hazy mauve and purple gloom at even, when their charms appear as though partly hidden by a diaphanous garment of milky white.

We were not molested, and at nightfall we fell in with a P. boat stuck on the mud, and so anchored close by her for company. At dawn we spent a couple of hours helping to get her off, and then proceeded on our way. Soon we passed Sheikh Sa'ad, a place destined often to be in our thoughts in the near future, and also many a burnt and sunken *mahela*, half submerged near the banks, eloquent tributes to the work of the marauding Arab force. These wrecks stretched at intervals for miles up the river, and it required no very strong imagination to pic-

FORTIFYING THE POOP OF ONE OF OUR MAHELAS WITH BUNDLES
OF TENTS, &C., OCT. 1915.

THE VILLAGE OF SHEIKH SA'AD, RIVER TIGRIS.

ture the gallant little running fight of the escort against a cruel and ruthless enemy in overwhelming odds.

But we are nearly at the end of our long, lonely voyage, for next day, soon after sunrise, we make out the solitary minaret and the patch of palms that mean Kut. Another hour, and our siren uttering its thick and discordant request for the boat bridge to be opened for us to pass through. Just above it we tie up to the bank and await the pilot who shall guide us along the tortuous channels that lie between us and the town. The place seems quite near, so that two of us make a bee-line for the camp, which we can see pitched a little away from it, to find out where we are to dump ourselves down when we do get in. The pilot soon arrives, but it takes us many hours to round the great bend of the river and get to our moorings, and we have but time to land a few stores before darkness sets in.

CHAPTER 3

Kut Before the Battle of Ctesiphon

Our first impression of Kut was not a pleasing one. Approaching it from the east, almost the first thing that caught the eye was a gibbet—always a gruesome-looking object—and on the dirty, untidy portion of the bank around it, backed by an irregular row of squalid-looking, mud-coloured houses, lay a heterogeneous collection of oil tins, a decrepit native boat, some old Turkish carts, a rubbish-heap, and a wireless station, with a tent or two for the operators: a veritable East End. We slept on board, and with the dawn a gang of Turkish prisoners was brought down to help us unload and take our stuff to our hospital site a mile away. This was to the north-west of the town and separated from the river by a grove of palm-trees. Evidences of previous enemy occupation in the shape of bits of old rag, bits of bone, and old tins, were in plenty, and the flies were flourishing both here and elsewhere; but its aspect was soon changed, and tents were erected.

The S. M.O. was anxious to hand over to us 200 or 300 sick that were clogging his held ambulances, so we did our best to "get a move on." In the evening the three of us who were fit went over to the Tessex Brigade camp and heard tales of the recent fight and talk of the coming advance. Our fourth colleague, the "wet bob," remained in his tent with a fever, which we feared was typhoid, and we sent him down to Busra a few days later. Most of the division, we heard, had already gone on and encamped at Azizieh, fifty miles ahead, waiting for more troops and munitions, and in touch with the enemy. Kut itself was in a state of great activity, turning itself as rapidly as the water-borne traffic could allow it into an advanced base, and sorting, forwarding, hurrying on ammunition, stores, and equipment of all sorts.

All the principal houses were occupied by the busy gilded staff. Generals there seemed to be in plenty, who were soon to take an unnatural interest in the building of our new hospital, which lay on the road between the town and the camp, and so came in for very frequent visits by the Brass Hats. Our big Base Hospital tents called forth much comment, and it was not long before it was impressed upon us that such valuable canvas would not be allowed to remain so near the Front. Orders were soon received to have them struck and replaced by huts, so within ten days or so we were taking down our carefully dressed rows of tents and watching the ubiquitous R.E. put up generously designed erections of wood and matting. The work went steadily on, and for the next four or five weeks we had a busy but peaceful time.

Every other day or so a convoy of sick and wounded would arrive from Azizieh, and from time to time we sent one down the river, each time depleting our scanty staff. Our own full complement of personnel and equipment rolled up in due course, and the hospital and its work pursued the even tenor of its way. We enjoyed the planning and erection of the different parts of the two hospitals, their wards and storerooms, Operating rooms and dispensaries, kitchens and bathing places, isolation wards and offices.

Troops and hospitals came steadily through us on their way to join the division at Azizieh, and as time went on the activity on the wharves feverishly increased; work went on all night by the aid of huge flares on the river bank, which was crowded with perspiring *coolies*, panting backwards and forwards between huge collections of stores and the iron barges by the bank, shouting S. & T. sergeants, and worried officers, the whole constituting a thrilling but weird and ghostly picture, dimly seen through the dusty atmosphere.

One night those gallant Punjabis, so keen on football at Busra, reached Kut, full of excitement, fearful that they might be too late for the great fight to come. One of them, Captain T——, lay in hiding in his berth with a temperature of 105°, from an attack of malaria, and trembling with apprehension lest he should be landed and left behind. How greatly I wished he had been, when I saw his poor body laid aside for burial on his return journey a fortnight later!

But they went on and were not too late, and they walked up to the barbed wire as if on manoeuvres; but only some of them got back.

In those days, for relaxation, we would take a gun and stroll out for an hour to bag a few sand-grouse. Of these dovelike birds there are very large numbers; one could sometimes get them within 100 yards of camp and could always be sure of a few. At times they fly about in such huge flocks that the noise of their wings and, even more, their peculiar cry, can be heard for great distances. Some good shooting can be had when they are flying down wind, for then they travel at a great pace. They are best got in the morning, when they are flying around between 8 and 11 o'clock. Or we would explore the town itself. "Kut of the Amir" is situated on the left bank of the Tigris and built for the most part on the south and southwestern part of a very complete loop of the river. East and west of it lie gardens and palm groves; opposite it, on the other bank, is the small mud village of "Woolpress."

In peace time Kut (pronounced Koot) is the seat of a small military post, and it ships much grain.

The town itself contains some 5000 inhabitants, mostly Arabs. The majority of the people are Mussulmans; but there are also Jews, Sabians, and Nestorian Christians. The town consists of an extended river front, perhaps half a mile in length; and back from this and running roughly at right angles to the stream lie a series of streets at various intervals and running more or less parallel to each other. Cross-streets between these are few and far between and very irregular. On the left, as you face the town from the river, is the Turkish "*Serai*," with its roomy barrack square, its Headquarters offices, and its flagstaff. Just behind it stands the mosque and the lofty minaret, famous for its graceful proportions and topped by its turquoise dome.

To the right of the *serai* lie the bazars, the lower and lesser one parallel to the river, the main one at right angles to this. Both are covered in by matting spread over wooden rafters, but are very inferior to those at Amarah. In the hot weather these sheltered arcades prove a welcome refuge from the fierce rays of the sun, but in winter they are dark and foul, squalid and dirty. On each side of the bazar street is a raised plinth and a row of cubicles, in which the owners squat behind their piles of wares. At night each cubicle is closed by folding wooden doors, which are securely fastened by clumsy iron-padlocked staples, and a night watchman patrols the deserted market, or sits and doses as the fancy takes him.

Farther to the right, houses and *khans* stretch away to the garden at the eastern end, whilst between the houses and the river lies a strip of bare, uneven bank, that serves all the purposes of a wharf.

Scattered about here and there, but mostly towards the western end, are a few good two-storey houses, well-built of brick. Each is built four-square around an inner court, upon which open verandahed rooms and the winding stairway to the roof. In the middle of the flagged courtyard is a small drain-hole leading to a large cess-pit underneath, which in very wet weather sometimes gets over-full and is not oversweet. The poorer houses are merely larger or smaller hovels, built of mud or mud-dried brick, aided by a few poles and pieces of matting. Often several are built around a single courtyard or area, surrounded by an encircling wall, within which are generally an odd palm tree or two, a drain and a mud oven, common to the community. Here the women sit winnowing or grinding their corn, cooking their "*kabaabs*," which resemble thick pancakes, or playing with their grubby and nearly naked children.

Later on, when the siege was in full swing, most of these contained at least one underground dug-out, into which the poor wretches crowded during the worst bombardments. Many of the "short cuts" that were made between the parallel streets passed through these poorer quarters and enabled one to see something of the family life of these descendants of Ishmael.

With an average depth of a quarter of a mile from the river, the town on the north side ends irregularly on the open plain between the arms of the great loop of the river. Here, in the immediate vicinity of the town, lies a tract of uneven dusty ground covered with the village refuse, rubbish-heaps, dead dogs, and scores of living ones. Just beyond this zone of smelly no man's land one stumbles on a straggling graveyard, where lie the marks of those returned to dust. A few hundred yards farther stand up in bold relief a line of brick kilns, like Martello towers set to watch over the little town, and only too soon to be used for this purpose on our own behalf.

November was yet young when the riparian activity reached its climax, the generalissimo and his gilded staff departed in a blaze of glory, and Kut was left, it seemed, to desolation and to us. The quiet of the place was painful. The brigade had left, and but a few companies of infantry and half a dozen guns remained, though small batches of troops and cavalry continued to come through. Also, a new and large hospital arrived, with tents enough for 500, and proceeded to settle down beside us. Work on the new fort by the ferry near the boat-bridge proceeded steadily, and our hospital grew as near perfection

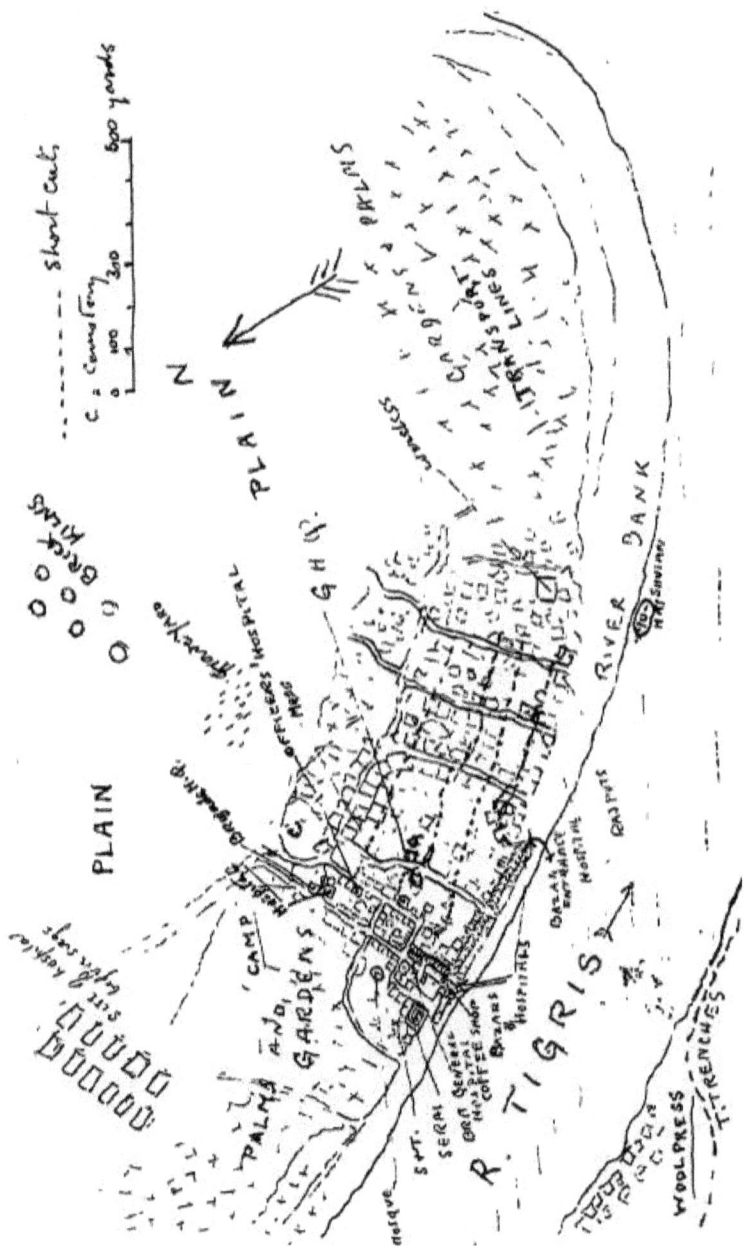

PLAN OF KUT

as we could make it with the materials and labour at our command. Our surgeon-general had seen it and approved, but we hoped it would never be put to a severe test—five or six hundred wounded might perhaps call for accommodation temporarily, but we little expected thousands.

In view of the uncertain attitude of a force of Beni Lam Arabs a few miles away under the hills, we also put in a good deal of work in preparing perimeter breastworks and small trenches around our hospital as part of a local defence scheme, which at one time appeared likely to assume prime importance.

For the rest, we dealt with our convoys, speculated on the date of the coming battle, and waited with a none too sanguine impatience for news of the result.

CHAPTER 4

Kut, After Ctesiphon

Boom! boom! boom! Faintly the sound of distant guns was borne to us on the north wind. It was the 2nd of December, and, tired and hungry, we were sitting down to a late breakfast and talking inconsequently, when the unmistakable sound made us sit up and stare at each other. "By God! those are guns, F——," said one, and we were up and outside the tent in a second, listening for a repetition of the ominous sound. *Boom! boom!* Yes, there was no doubt about it, and all the tales and rumours of disaster we had been hearing at intervals for the past ten days suddenly seemed to take concrete form, and the ghastly truth of it all was borne in upon us. We conjured up visions of our struggling, retreating troops being pressed by a relentless foe, and having to fight hard to keep him off.

Boom! boom! they must be eight or ten miles away yet. God! what sort of a time have they had for the last sixty miles if they are still being so pressed within a mile or two of Kut, where they mean to stand? Such the unspoken question that rises unbidden to our lips, and we seem to realise in a flash something of the past ten days' horror through which the old 6th Division has passed.

For a dreadful week we have been struggling to cope with the streams of wounded that have been poured in on us in shipload after shipload. Night and day, have we all been working to tend and to pass on thousands of poor devils, masses of crumpled humanity, until our very souls are sick within us, but nothing has so brought home to us the plight of the struggling army as has this booming of the distant guns.

31

Never shall I forget those days before the siege when the spectre of disaster walked the air and troubled our dreams, nor the way in which we first heard that anything was wrong.

Soon after the army commander had left us to join the division, we had begun to conjecture when the fight would take place. "It will be today," we would say. But the morrow would come and still no battle. Then one day, at last, news came that it had commenced; that our gallant fellows had driven the enemy out of his position; that he was being pursued. All seemed going well, and we thought of Christmas in Sinbad's City. But the next day a silence, an ominous absence of news—"had they gone on? were they in Baghdad?" But no, next day a whispered rumour, like a breath of icy cold wind, struck us dumb, and made us shiver as with an ague. Thus, it ran:

> The enemy has retaken the position; there has been a night attack—heavy casualties—the division is retreating on Azizieh!

Surely 'tis merely a rumour—such cannot happen to us, to those splendid troops who have done so much! But the rumour is insistent, and presently is strengthened by orders over the wire to us to prepare for large numbers of wounded. Ill news travels fast; again that icy wind; "the army is retiring." Again word from our Medical Head— "have evacuated 3500"—the past perfect tense! where the devil shall we put them? We will send some of the boats straight through to Amarah! But the M.T.O. thinks otherwise—only one boat out of six may go through, so all the wounded on the rest must be disembarked and taken to hospital! How we can expand accommodation for 900 into that of 4000 is now the problem. We must have more tents, and tents we get, and start pitching them for dear life. Our staffs respond to our call and work with a will, and our sections grow to the size of a complete unit, whilst the newly-arrived Stationary Hospital becomes a forest of canvas.

Soon the rush comes, and we are strained to the utmost; boat after boat is unloaded; fetch and carry, accommodate and feed, examine and tend and treat, is the order of the day,—we do our best. Offers of aid by fatigues, or of carts, or in any way they can serve us, are sent in by our friends of the regiment and the battery, whilst a portion of a stranded field ambulance gives of its best. Major Dashwood of the F.A. is everywhere at once, arranging, encouraging, day and night. A huge two-decked derelict barge is commandeered, strewn with S. and T. hay, and hundreds of the slighter cases bedded down therein. Captain

Martel establishes a huge "coffee stall" on the bank near the *serai*, and with soup and hot milk cheers the hearts of those that are ready to perish. It is a nightmare, a week one hopes never to repeat. On one of the boats one finds a deck-load of officers, amongst them many familiar faces looking worn and pained; some of them are of those who hurried through Kut a few days ago, "fearing to be late."

"And what of the others, old man?" we ask.

"Oh! it's dreadful, F——, there are only two of us left; Billy's gone, Jack died yesterday, T—— and M—— this morning. Watson was killed just before the barbed wire."

"I? Oh, I had just cut a couple of strands when I was bowled over."

We get to work again with a lump in the throat and curse all war and violence and the man who started it. The second day we send away a sick convoy down the river, and with them goes the army commander and his staff; but the day following we get another shock, for rumour hath it that the convoy is held up by Arabs and cannot get through.

Two companies are despatched to help, but twenty-four hours later they return, convoy and all. The same day we hear there is every chance of Kut being attacked by the Arab force which still hovers about, and we improve our defences and arm all who can hold a rifle. The last day of November brings us news that Townshend has detached a brigade, which is hurrying down to Kut, and our convoy, taking all wounded it possibly can, once more essays the passage of the river to Amarah. This time we hear no more, and they get through; but next day, at the urgent request of those who know most, we load every available craft with every patient we can send and feel that we are on the eve of big events.

The atmosphere is pessimistic—another rumour brings the disquieting news that the detached brigade has been recalled to Townshend—what does this mean? Is it the beginning of the end, the forerunner of a tragedy? Or will they pull through?

But now the army, or what is left of it, is nearly here; we are hearing the guns. The "defence officer" runs in and tells us to fall in every man who can stand, and we await events with breathless interest. The guns are silent now, and an hour of suspense passes; but presently out of the dusty distance emerges the head of the retreating column, and we heave a sigh of relief. First of all, arrives a mounted officer, bedraggled and overwrought, and craves some food. The while he eats voraciously, his excited tongue gives to us his own picture of the past fast–moving events.

Overwrought and unstrung, he almost babbles his momentous story, and we realise something of the strain our fellows have just undergone. We forthwith set every available cook cooking as he never cooked before, whereby we may help to feed our weary comrades as soon as they arrive. And they soon begin to do so. Guns, cavalry, transport-carts, and stragglers, group by group, appear, dusty and weary, yet cheery withal, and not downhearted. Their ground is allotted, and they are soon sitting about resting and having a snack of food or soup, which we all hasten to give them.

We of Kut are not sorry to see them. For days past we have been existing in lively expectation of being attacked and having to turn to every man-jack of us, sick or sound, to defend ourselves for our lives' sake, for the Arabs give no quarter.

Now, so do numbers cheer one, we feel safe again, though we know we must be besieged in this horrible little mud town; and with Pepys we exclaim, "and what shall be the end of it, God knows!"

Another chum arrives, dog tired and dirty; he has no kit save that on his back. Can I give him breakfast and a shirt? Why not a hot bath first, say I?

"My dear chap," he gasps, "you save my life; I haven't had my clothes off for ten days!"

One after another they roll up, and we are glad to keep our mess-tent and kitchen busy feeding them. They have had practically nothing for three days, and they are ravenous.

Only a portion of the army, with baggage and waggons, reached Kut on the 2nd December. The main body bivouacked for the night a few miles outside, and marched in unmolested and unruffled on the 3rd, and there was a day's peace. It had been a magnificent effort, that splendid retreat on top of a hard-fought battle, and all honour is due to those who made it. Next day digging began in earnest along a line previously prepared from the fort near the ferry, and across the neck of the loop to its western arm.

Fortunately, the Turk was dead beat, and not at all ready to worry us, so that the work went on uninterruptedly for two or three days. In the evening of the 4th, and during the night, there was a good deal of sniping; the bullets came whizzing over and through our tents, and one unlucky wounded man was again hit in hospital. Some of them seemed to come from the town, and doubtless did so, for it is the way of the Arab to kick those who seem to be getting the worst of it.

TOWNSHEND'S TROOPS JUST ARRIVING IN KUT AFTER THE
RETIRAL FROM CTESIPHON. SOME INDIAN SOLDIERS RESTING ON
THEIR CAMPING GROUND.

HEAD OF COLUMN OF TOWNSHEND'S ARMY ARRIVING IN KUT,
DECEMBER 2, 1915.

CHAPTER 5

The Town Invested, December 5, 1915

On the 5th December the siege began in earnest, and the enemy was soon busy sending his shrapnel screaming over the western palm grove. As our hospital camp lay just beyond it, we came in for a goodly share of its attentions, and our A.D.M.S. began to look about for another site. That evening our cavalry were sent away: they stole out at night, and got through the incomplete cordon that was drawing in around us; but with their departure the door was shut, and we knew ourselves invested and cut off from the outside world.

On the 6th the shelling of our camp increased, and it became evident we should have to move. One sweet messenger of death burst over the "wet bob's" tent, and lumps of its case tore through his tent, smashed his box, and landed in his little dug-out. Fortunately, he was not in residence at the time, but it made him think; whilst my Indian servant, who was standing by, presently woke up to find himself running round in circles, whereat, when he had recovered, he was intensely amused. Those of us who had never been under shell fire before were inclined to take it very coolly at first. But after being nearly hit once or twice, we developed a healthy respect for an approaching shell, and ceased to take unnecessary risks.

So, the Bazar was emptied of its wares and its occupants in double-quick time, and every available sweeper turned on to clean it up. That night, at 8 o'clock, we commenced to move our hospital—lock, stock, patients, and staff—and by 5 a.m. next morning we were installed in our new quarters and had left forever the buildings we had erected with so much thought and labour. In a very short time they had been razed to the ground and used for firewood.

Moving house in the dead of night was a weird experience. Fatigues were out of the question, so, with the help of a few S. and T. carts, we did it ourselves. Backwards and forwards, stumbling along over uneven and scarcely known roads and streets in the pitchy darkness, we struggled through the work and wrestled with our heavy stores and equipment. Patients went first. Giving orders that those who could walk should do so, and start at eight o'clock, and that the rest should be carried, we ate a hasty dinner before taking part in the proceedings. Great was my surprise to find, a few minutes later, that all but a very few of my 300 had discovered their ability to move unaided and had legged it away to the new refuge. The very few had either broken legs or were semi-moribund. Necessity is sometimes the mother of locomotion.

But we soon discovered that we had quitted the frying-pan merely to fall into the fire. It will be remembered that one portion of the Bazar runs along the river bank, whilst the other lies at right angles to it. Close by, on the bank, was one of the few possible sites for our guns, and three or four were soon established within a few yards of us. The Turks soon did their utmost to knock these out, and as a natural consequence scored a good many hits on the hospital. Within a very few days we had several casualties, both amongst the wounded and our staff, and our own escapes were narrow and numerous. We realised to our dismay that our Hospital was by no means one of the safest places in Kut, but it was secure from most rifle fire, and there was nowhere else to go, so we had to stick it.

We ourselves got quarters in a tiny Arab house a few yards away and made ourselves comfortable enough as things went in those days. Other hospitals were no better off. The Field Ambulances found accommodation in various parts of the town, but none could avoid the enemy's shells, and all suffered casualties from time to time. But during the first two days in our new quarters the artillery duel was of an intermittent and desultory character, and we spent our time "consolidating our position." Everybody was cheery and intensely busy; the trenches grew in depth and the parapets in height; gun emplacements were prepared, and parties of the enemy moving about within range were shelled, just to show them that we were not downhearted.

"Woolpress" village across the river was occupied, and its fortification by trench digging and so forth rapidly proceeded with. It was still possible in these first days to go out on the river bank without the certainty of getting sniped—but this immunity did not last long, and five long months were to pass before one could again take the air by the old Tigris. At the river end of the Bazar a little general store shop still existed with open doors, and all day long had a crowd of eager purchasers, mostly Tommies, around it. Such looked ahead and thought the time might come when a few extra stores would make a big difference. We secured a few for our own mess, but there came a time when we cursed ourselves bitterly for not exercising more forethought and laying in a larger stock whilst it was still available.

The little store was sold out in a couple of days, and it never opened its shutters again, for the last time I saw it all that remained was a ragged heap of bricks.

MINARET AND GATEWAY OF MOSQUE, KUT, 1915

On the 9th the Turks got busy and shelled us considerably, and some stretcher-bearers and a *"bhistie"* were killed in the hospitals. There was a tussle for the boat-bridge, which we held by a detachment on the far side and a force on the hither. Two officers were killed and lost, and the gallant general of the Blank Brigade made a noble effort to retrieve them that will not be forgotten by those who were there. We heard something of the story—how that alone he rushed across the bridge when he saw his youngsters fall and endeavoured himself to carry back the one he could reach. That same night a heroic sapper and another swam the river, in itself no mean feat, and blew up the bridge from the far side, under the very noses of the enemy. This was a performance that more than merited the V.C., but, since poor Kut was never relieved, the deed is lost in unjust oblivion.

On the following day, old man Turk made five separate attacks on our line, but was beaten off with loss each time, and the shelling of the town grew steadily fiercer.

In the hospitals half a dozen were killed and several wounded. Many of the townspeople were hit—men, women, and children. So sad was it to see the poor little creatures suffering from ghastly wounds! One little maid was led in to us, actually walking, with a huge shell-wound in the lower part of her back that had wrenched away skin and flesh and bone—yet she lived to become a hospital favourite and was cured and playing with her companions by the end of March.

Sunrise on the 11th brought with it another fierce attack. In the midst of the pandemonium of shrieking shell and clattering rifle fire, the *"muezzin,"* the call to prayer of the steadfast Mussulman, rose clear and sweet from high up the minaret, above the din of human strife. One's thoughts turned heavenward and one wondered if *le bon Dieu* were noticing this ignoble squabble amongst the pigmies down below—and, if he noticed, cared!

The hospital again came in for its share; a few were wounded and the roof was set on fire, and we were coming to look upon that sort of thing as part of the day's work. But we had plenty to do without that, for casualties steadily rolled in and kept us hard at our own peculiar and saddening job.

Day by day our foes attacked, and daily did they bombard the wretched town. We had a bad morning on the 13th, for many *"whizz-bangs"* found their billet in our devoted hospital. One in particular I remember, for it burst close to my office door and wounded four of my hospital staff, two of whom soon died, and could ill be spared. A violent burst was followed by a choking cloud of fumes and of bricks and dust, through which it was difficult to find the poor moaning "*bhistie*" who lay huddled up with half his side blown away. We lifted him carefully and laid him aside out of the line that gun was firing on, and soon his spirit fled.

Another shell landed in our little dispensary and smashed half our bottles, and yet another came hurtling through the wall of one of the cubicles and showered its bricks and mortar all over the three poor devils who were lying there. One of these, an Indian sergeant with a broken leg, had the same leg broken again, besides a torn scalp and other wounds. To have our patients thus knocked about made us wild; it did not seem fair for them to have to go through a second mending. My office appearing to act as a magnet, it seemed to me a good idea to move it; but my little clerk, feeling comfortable and secure in his corner, with a thick wall on one danger side and bales of hay on another, was loath to leave, so I gave in; but when a day or two later another whizzbang burst on the threshold, I had to insist on transferring it to a healthier spot. Had I not done so, I had not lived to write this, for soon afterwards a "windy Lizzie" landed plumb on the roof and burst within into a thousand pieces.

But we were full of hope and expectation of our early relief. As early as the 8th did our general, in whom we all had sublime faith, send round his first circular to let us know that reinforcements were expected at Sheikh Sa'ad in the following week, and we presumed they would soon make their way up to us, though we gave them till Christmas or a little longer. Six weeks, we thought, would be the outside limit. But the end of the six weeks was to come and to bring with it the first of a long series of disappointments, which were by far the hardest parts of the siege to bear.

CHAPTER 6

December 14th to 23rd, 1915

The next week was full enough of unpleasant incidents, and the weather steadily grew colder. In the early part of it our hospital suffered a sad and serious loss in the deaths of three of our wounded staff, and our Bazar roof was again set on fire by shells. I myself had another narrow escape but suffered nothing more than a temporary bronchitis from the fumes. Such little accidents were, however, sufficient to enable one to imagine the agony of the "gassed" in Europe, and we thanked God that Abdul had none of that villainous variety of projectile. One day a group of warrant officers, who were lunching together in their dug-out, was scattered, and killed or maimed by a "windy Lizzie" that landed fairly on the roof and burst amongst them inside.

One, more lucky than the rest, was killed outright; two others, or what remained of them, died very soon; but the rest we managed to patch up. Shells are gross and clumsy things, and the wounds they make are terrible. The poor human body has no chance. They bash it, they tear it and mangle it; they wrench away brutally great chunks of it, and leave a battered quivering thing, which to look upon gives one almost physical pain. They are indelicate and beastly in their blind, blundering rage. To the surgeon, such indiscriminate violence is intensely abhorrent; the clumsy damage to the beautiful, perfected human organism makes his professional spirit wince, and the ruthless disregard of anatomical detail, and the smashing up of nicely balanced interdependent organs, rouses his ire. He sees and pities the poor suffering man—but more, he imagines and weeps for the hidden molecular shock to the ultimate particles of that bone, muscle, nerve, and brain that but a moment before were instinct with pulsating and marvellous life.

At such moments as these the "doctor man "curses all war and the economic necessities that bring it about, and he wonders at all the farcical talk and controversy over explosive and dumdum bullets whilst the effects of shell fire are tolerated without a murmur. Often, he wishes it were his lot to see more of the excitement and glory of the game, and less of the soul-sickening sights that, in their cumulative effects, weary him to death and sometimes threaten to overwhelm him with depression. Of hard work and innumerable surgical operations there was of course more than enough, and the siege was many days old before we could snatch a few minutes for a "breather" away from the "wards."

When I did so it was to take a hurried stroll through the town and around part of its outskirts to the north with the incorrigible Major Dashwood of the Punjab Brigade Ambulance, whose chief delight it was in these days to prowl around finding out all the danger zones in the immediate neighbourhood, and then to hale his friends away thither and point them out by personal demonstration.

It was a dreary sight just outside the loop-holed walls of the last houses and gardens. In the foreground a flotsam and jetsam of debris, rubbish, a dead horse or mule or two with their legs in the air, an old cart, and a row of gun-limbers sheltering under a wall; in the middle distance the brick kilns, like giant truncated sugar-loaves, standing out boldly above the surrounding plain, and to their left a slight ridge, marking the site of our middle line of trenches. Around the foot of the kilns could be seen a mound or two, and some irregularities in the ground indicating some of our gun-pits, to improve which the gunners were working hard.

Two or three of the kilns had been turned into observation towers, and the heads and telescopes of the watchers could just be seen silhouetted above their rims. Yonder, a mile and a half away, the outline of the fort stood out slightly on the skyline, and between us and it no sign of life was visible—a sense of desolation brooded over the deserted flat—but the crackling of rifles, the bursting of shells, and the ping of bullets as they passed overhead, or the sharp "pat" of one as it landed on a wall, were conclusive evidence of the activities of the rival forces that had gone to ground. And so back to our little mess of four in a small Arab house in A1 Street, there to meet other one or two who have come in to smoke a pipe and exchange the latest "gup."

'Tis said, we hear, in the Bazar that some of the enemy are trekking away northward. Good news! say we, but why? Are the Russians getting a move on at Kermanshah, or is it a mere canard? The latter, of course, is the truth; but, like drowning men, we eagerly catch at any straw, and at any rate it serves as food for the endless discussions on the prospects of our relief. But in these days, there was little time for talk and discussion, or for aught but hard work. The hospital was full, and casualties steadily came along, either from the shelling or the continuous sniping or from the attacks on the trenches.

Usually at night there was a violent fusillade of rifle fire, and day by day the Turks sapped closer.

The general frequently visited the hospitals, but invariably found us busy in our operating theatre, mending some poor unfortunate, and so passed along. He would smile with the Indians and chat with Tommy, and cheer him up with his own splendid optimism, and everyone felt the better for his visits.

The general's dog appeared to have a rooted objection to shells. I was walking with him one day along one of the streets when presently over came a 4-inch and burst with a clatter nearby; the little terrier didn't wait for permission, but, much to his master's annoyance and disgust, whisked round, and incontinently skedaddled for home as fast as his legs would carry him, and this habit he could by no means be broken of.

On the 18th our mess was reduced to three, for "Lancelot" went sick and to hospital for a few days, but medical society is a co-operative one by instinct, and there was no lack of offers of help to make up for his loss. The same day witnessed that brilliant little sortie from the trenches by some of our men at the fort, which resulted in the bayoneting of a good thirty Turks, and the taking of a few prisoners, with little or no loss to ourselves.

Within a week of Christmas, we began to dwell on thoughts of home. What were they thinking of Kut? Did they know yet that we were beleaguered, and were they worrying about us? God forbid! Should we be relieved by Christmas? Some thought so, but the most likely conjecture seemed to be January 10—another three weeks!

Hearing one day that there were a lot of letters of sorts at the post-office still undelivered, Dashwood and I wended our way thither to see. Doleful and dreary were the postmen and their stifled charge; it was bad luck indeed to be boxed up and find themselves out of a job. A few shells and an unhealthy number of snipers' bullets had rendered their first floor office, which looked out on the river bank, a most undesirable residence, and there was a goodly litter of unclaimed letters and parcels, mostly addressed to our friends outside, or to those who had already joined the great majority. A parcel of cigarettes was a welcome find, but we got no letters, and went away with our hopes dashed, and a grouch against the fate that interfered with the last mail that should have reached us before the investment.

At dawn on the 20th we awoke to the scream of a shell passing close over the mess and the sound of a brisk fusillade. It resulted in the usual bunch of casualties; two or three were killed in one of the field ambulances, and our water pump hose-pipe was riddled by shrapnel.

One poor devil of a servant sitting cleaning plates for his master's breakfast got in the way of a shell and lost both his legs, and his life soon afterwards. Someone in some little Indian village would wait in vain for his return, till his name became but a memory of the time when the *sahib-log* went mad.

Succeeding this outburst came a period of comparative calm, which led up to the great storm on the 24th and was devoid of incident save for an issue of "strawberry" jam in our ration and for the opening of the wireless for private cables. There was, of course, a rush to send messages, and the good-tempered staff-major, who had lightly undertaken the job of receiving them, found he had let himself in for more work than he bargained for.

But the capacity of the wireless was limited, and it had to be used with care, so that it took many days for some of the wires to get away. What a blessing that wireless was! Thereby we scored heavily over the besieged of the old days; for though the enemy cordon was drawn tight and all material communication was cut off, yet they could not stop our talking to the outside world, and brief news of the progress of Armageddon, of the doings of our people, of the Relieving Force, and of home affairs, continued to find its way in.

So, we got our Reuters—an abbreviated edition, it is true, but still Reuters—and copies were supplied on any old pieces of paper to heads of units, and were posted up at G.H.Q. They made a great difference to us, for they enabled us to follow the world's events, properly discounted, to feel ourselves less cut off from all that mattered, and to keep alive the expectancy of early relief.

We of the medical world were faced with an added anxiety, for that bugbear of surgeons, Tetanus, raised its ugly head in a few isolated cases. Confined as we were in a dirty Eastern town, unable to get access to the fresh air, with a lot of animals and with a limited supply of antitoxin, the possibility of a serious extension of this dread disease caused us some unhappy hours. Fortunately, our A.D.M.S., with his usual forethought, had already some time before wired for more of the precious fluid to come by aeroplane. The cases remained limited to a few, and to our relief the danger passed.

CHAPTER 7

December 24th to 31st, 1915

After a night of incessant firing, Christmas Eve was ushered in by a furious onslaught on the fort and an intense bombardment of the town, which continued throughout the whole day. A whole division of Turks swarmed around the fort, and the fighting was fast and furious for hours.

The fort, situated on the extreme right of our line across the peninsula, close to the river and at the western end of the Mohammed Abdul Hassan bend, was an enclosure some 150 yards square, at a guess, surrounded by a thick ten-foot-high mud wall. This was loopholed in every direction, and at one angle it projected 20 yards or so to form a bastion. On the internal surface of the walls were fire-steps, and shelters, or barracks, for the garrison. To these were added trenches, traverses, and dugouts of all sorts and directions. Outside a good deal of barbed wire had been set up, but the enemy had sapped pretty close.

Frequent bombardments of the tiny place had knocked it about a good deal, and the violent shelling on Christmas Eve played sad havoc with the walls. But in spite of it all, the gallant garrison put up a great fight, and held the place for England. The Turks did their best to rush it, and came on gallantly in swarms, struggling over the rough ground, stumbling through and over the wire, and being shot down in hundreds. They reached and took the bastion. Clambering over such walls as were left, they drove our men back and through the second line of defence that had been built across the base of the projection. This was all they could manage, and they were not allowed to stay there for long. A few hours later the gallant Blank and Downshires counter-attacked and drove them out, and no enemy ever set foot therein again until the end of the siege. Abdul had lost very heavily indeed, and he never attempted a similar attack in force. Our own casualties during that fateful 24th were of course considerable, though but a fraction of those sustained by the attacking Turks, which were numbered in thousands.

We in the town had our own particular trouble in the form of a very heavy bombardment, which spoilt the architectural beauties of the place very considerably. The hospitals, as usual, came in for a goodly share. Two sergeants in one hospital and three stretcher-bearers in another were killed and several were wounded, but none was hurt in our own. Amongst other losses in the town that day were three officers whom we could ill spare. Our popular senior gunner was standing with two others on H.Q. roof watching the play of the guns. As luck would have it, a Turkish shell fell right in the middle of the group. Captain Begg was killed outright, the colonel's leg and elbow were broken, and G——t was also hit.

In both cases the wounds were to prove fatal. In characteristic fashion the great-hearted colonel refused to be carried below, but, with the aid of a comrade's shoulder, hopped down the winding stair despite the agony of his dangling leg.

His death a few days later cast a gloom over us all, for his genial, hearty spirit was a greatly valued asset.

It was a memorable Christmas Eve, and one none of us is likely easily to forget it. We were ourselves desperately busy. Fortunately, Lancelot was back at work again, and "Trixie" and the "wet bob" got through a tremendous amount. The "wet bob" had been unfortunate enough to get back from Busra after his illness just in time to be caught for the siege—a bit of bad luck he is now, I doubt not, bitterly

45

regretting amongst the hills of Asia Minor.

Christmas Day dawned quiet and peaceful, and remained so throughout. No gun was fired, and scarcely a rifle shot disturbed the almost uncanny silence.

Was it due to exhaustion, or were both sides, we asked ourselves, loath to desecrate by violence the birthday of the Saviour of mankind, the great Prophet of Peace? Be that as it may, the day was calm and extraordinarily restful, and the *padre* held his two services without interruption. For the Medicals, of course, there was no rest, and we could get to neither of them. For us of the healing art the aftermath of strife means an abundance of work. It is for us to mitigate, as far as in us lies, the pitiable suffering, and to reconstruct to the best of our power some of the damaged fabric from the brawl of the yesterday.

For our Christmas dinner we had carefully nurtured a duck, bought in the very early days; and Lancelot having likewise carefully preserved a birthday plum pudding sent him by a fond mother, produced it to match the bird, "so all merrie" after a strenuous day. Our thoughts flew homeward. What were they doing in the old country?—surely at times thinking of beleaguered little Kut, and the boys it contained. Doubtless as we sat around our deal table, covered by a hospital sheet, in a smudgy, squalid Arab cottage, and raised our glasses in silent toast to those we loved, they were doing the same in the cosy rooms of the dear homeland. We had planned a very different celebration of the feast. "Christmas in Baghdad" was often on our lips in the autumn, and visions had been conjured up of festive boards in the old *Caliph's* capital. But the reality was "Christmas in Kut," and a very different one at that; and as for Baghdad, our chances of seeing it had gone by the board.

"For," said we, "when we are relieved they'll give us a rest, and we shall go down the river, whilst the other fellows go up and get the glory, and the flesh-pots of Sinbad's city."

But we were wrong again! We were to see Baghdad without the fleshpots, and they were destined for many hard knocks.

The 26th was also quiet. The enemy was seen to be moving his guns. Why, we could only conjecture; probably because of the threatening aspect of the weather: the sky was overcast, and rain would render his movements difficult or impossible.

The 28th saw a special order published to let us know that the Relief Force would start from Ali Gharbi on January the 3rd, and a counterblast in the rumour that the Turks were receiving reinforcements. That night was, I remember, rendered hideous by a lot of blind shelling on the part of our enemy. Lying exposed to shell fire at night is an unpleasant business, and mud brick walls seem but a poor protection against a hurtling 50-lb. missile. You try to doze off but are intermittently awakened by the *"sizzing"* scream of an approaching *"obus."* You cock up an interested ear to judge whether you are exactly in the line of its flight or not, and if you are, and you have no dug-out, you await its fall with still greater interest, which is equalled by your relief when it bursts clear or lands with a *"wump"* in a neighbouring mud hut. The next evening, we had a mild practical demonstration of what happens when you *are* exactly in the line. I had turned in early with bad *"growing pains"* and a temperature. The others sat in the mess-room close by, with a couple of visitors. A *"whizz bang"* came hissing through our mud wall, through the roof of our servants' quarters, scattering segments right and left, and filling our little courtyard and our rooms with its poisonous fumes.

We were out in a second to investigate the damage—they thought it was I who must be done in, but the only casualty was one of the slaves with a bullet in his thigh. Our visitors postponed the telling of their yarns and removed to a healthier spot. These *"whizz-bangs"* are annoying little beasts; they give no warning of their coming and are on you before you have a chance to move.

Very different was the mode of approach of a new kind of missile our friends over the way sent at us a week or two later. This took the form of a huge, spherical, bronze cannon-ball, about 15 inches in diameter, filled with bullets the size of walnuts. From a short range of a couple of thousand yards or less, it came buzzing over from the far side of the river, for all the world like a huge beetle. It burst on percussion with a loud bang into a thousand fragments, the larger of which could be followed with ease by the naked eye as they sailed through the air like cricket balls.

From collected pieces of the casing, which was of solid bronze and about an inch in thickness, it was possible to reconstruct the whole sphere, and to imagine the sort of engine of destruction it was fired from. Probably it was some ancient cannon or mortar dug out from a century-old sleep in Baghdad; it was used perhaps in the city's successful defence against the mighty Nadir Shah, near two hundred years ago.

The last few days of the old year passed fairly quietly, save for bursts of firing in the trenches from time to time, a morning and evening "hate," and the everlasting sniping. This accursed sniping took its steady toll of life in the streets of the town and from amongst the watercarriers, who ran down to the edge of the bank at night—and these were mostly women; from our working parties and from all others who went to and fro; and lastly, and so sadly, from the children as they played. Our own snipers were as constantly at work. They were posted at all points of vantage, mostly on housetops, and by their efforts kept the enemy's fire within reasonable limits.

New Year's Eve found our own little group none too cheery. We were dog-tired: myself peevish and irritable with fever and muscular rheumatism, three of our colleagues sick, and our hospitals filled to overflowing.

It was getting colder than ever, and pneumonia was becoming serious amongst the troops.

But good news of the Russians filtered through and cheered us up—how they were at Kermanshah and pressing on to harry the Osmanli. Our own people also, it seemed, must be nearly ready; another week or so and we should be joining hands with them, and our confinement would be ended. So, does hope spring eternal in the human breast—but sometimes, as one expressed it, something goes wrong with the springs!

However, we were seldom depressed. Our third member, "Trixie," was invariably cheerful, and his sunny smile and unfailing good-humour were an invaluable asset to us when the novelty of being besieged wore off and the days grew longer. Our No. 4, like Martha, was troubled about many things, and had little use for sieges.

CHAPTER 8

January 1st to 17th, 1916

The New Year opened quietly but was scarcely two days old when a virulent bombardment suddenly started late in the afternoon. As luck would have it, our hospital seemed to be specially signalled out for punishment at the hands of some guns placed in a new position straight across the river, to the left of Woolpress village and the liquorice factory. Shell after shell burst in our little grain-selling courtyard behind our main Bazar. Around this covered-in yard were arranged several beds and opening out of it were little dark hovels which we had turned into wards with from two to six beds in each. The little round hole in the roof of each we had enlarged for light and air.

These formed the Indian officers' wards, after their previous ward in the old coffee-shop by the river, which also formerly accommodated our hospital office, had been evacuated. But in spite of it all no one was seriously hurt, though two men had a most marvellous escape. One "*whizz-bang*" burst in the doorway of the smallest "ward," in which they were lying, and one of the two had his head within a foot of the door. Though untouched by the shell fragments, his clothes, bed, and blankets were riddled by the iron segments, and the drums of both his ears were burst! The other man, similarly, was not touched, but his water-bottle and belts hanging near his head were smashed to bits.

Our guns, of course, replied, and added to the din. Within half an hour the enemy's fire slackened and died away, but they had managed to plunk in a couple of hundred messages of hate before they were got under.

On the 3rd we got the first shower of rain, which was to cause us so much discomfort in the near future. It was very cold, and fuel was getting very scarce, but our greatest trouble at this time was the myriads of lice that infested clothes and bedding. Our wretched patients would sit for hours picking them off their blankets and shirts, or rather killing them *in situ*, choosing, if possible, a patch of sunlight to do it in, though this was difficult to find in our covered-in Bazar. We ourselves, too, became, from constant practice, quite expert in the arts of spotting and catching them. The plague of lice lasted until the beginning of spring, when they almost uncannily disappeared with the coming of the warmth.

But hard on their heels marched, or rather jumped, an army of *pulices irritantes*, which, though less numerous than their pale-bodied predecessors, far exceeded them in their agility and biting powers. But it is the way of the East ever to provide each season with its special pest wherewith to irritate and chide its human guests. If it be not lice, then it's fleas, and if not fleas, then mosquitoes; failing mosquitoes, or in addition thereto, the sand-fly is provided. If a much-prayed-for wind springs up and blows them away, it brings with it a dust-storm and chokes you, or it blows so swiftly over a sun-baked desert that it scorches you and heats you till your head is like to burst.

And if for some unaccountable reason none of these pests is in the ascendant, there is always the snake, the centipede, or the scorpion to fall back upon. And over and above all is the common fly, to whom, I suppose, in his myriads, pride of place should be given, for his numbers in the East sometimes are almost incredible to those who have not experienced him, and his persistence wears one out. Never have I felt more grateful to any nation, I think, than to the Japanese when I came across the clockwork fly-catcher which they have introduced. It is good to watch its syrup-smeared cylinder revolving inexorably and taking to their inevitable death thousands of your buzzing enemies.

About this date, too, our fresh meat, of an ordinary kind, gave out, and "bully" became the order of the day. All these things, however, lost their importance, and were overshadowed by the suspense in which we were held for the next week or two regarding the movements of the Relieving Force. Younghusband's Brigade was supposed to have started from Ali-el-Gharbi (el Gharbi = the west), and we hoped soon to hear of it farther up. Day by day we had seen column after column of Turks going down to Sinn, and doubtless beyond, to meet our fellows, and we knew there must be many thousands of them down there dug in and awaiting our onslaught.

We knew, too, they had strengthened their Ess Sinn position, but we never doubted the ability of the Relieving Force to get through and were quite prepared to see Aylmer and Townshend shaking hands in the time-honoured way, and according to Cocker, before another ten days had gone by. They told us, too, of greetings from Russia's grand duke to our army commander, and his expressed hope of meeting him soon in person. Reuters meanwhile talked of some sort of compulsion at home, and of the thousands of bachelors still outside the colours, and also, worse luck, of the sinking of the *Persia*, doubtless with mails for us on board.

Lancelot now fell sick again and reduced our mess to three; but the fiery Hepaton, whose quarters were unpleasantly near some of the guns, spent much of his time with us. Poor friend Lambert continued to run a temperature and developed a lingering typhoidal illness which was to lead him to a much-lamented death. But the work went on; when one dropped out, those who were left took on his job. One came to realise that no man is essential; one knew that if he had to lay down his burden and join the great majority, another would take it up and carry on until his turn, may be, came too. Life is immortal, its holders are but temporary.

This first week saw the death of that very gallant gunner colonel, the genial Irishman whom the whole force loved. In solemn procession we laid him to rest to the fitting sound of guns and snipers' rifles, which mingled their cruel voices with the *padre's* solemn tones.

For the cemetery a small field or garden near the outskirts of the town had been set apart. It was enclosed by a low mud wall, and it contained a few scattered palm-trees. Beneath their shade soon grew a rapidly spreading forest of small wooden crosses, and the *padres* were never at rest. At the gap in the wall that served as a gate a sentry was placed to guard the sanctity of the place, and to preserve these crosses from the attentions of the village robbers.

The loneliness of those we left there always impressed me. I thought of the time to come when Kut would no longer be a bone of contention, nor be garrisoned by British troops. Then we should be obliged to leave them, these many good fellows, to sleep their long sleep away from their native heath and those that loved them; to turn to dust in alien soil and amongst a hostile people. . . .

One evening Trixie and I strolled forth to look up our Punjabi friends of "soccer" fame. We found them doing their "week in" in a palm grove on the outskirts of the town. Passing the sentry by the hole in the wall, we came upon their camp. But it resembled a rabbit-warren more than aught else. The whole enclosure was a mass of underground dug-outs, separated by narrow surface paths along which a few of the men were moving about in pursuance of their lawful occasions, but most of them were just coming up out of their holes, booted and spurred and about to fall in.

The colonel we found in the underground mess—a fairly capacious cavern, with a roof of corrugated iron and sandbags, supported by wooden props. He and a subaltern were the only two left of the original crowd that had brought up a fine regiment two short months ago. We had but time to drink him "good luck" before he was off with his men to take their turn in the trenches.

"We're going into the middle line," he said; "worse luck! for they're not half so comfy and safe as the first line; we get all the 'overs' in the middle and lose a good many men. So, we do here from snipers' bullets, which are continually dropping amongst us."

Late at night on the 5th there was suddenly a terrific burst of firing—rifle, star-shell, bomb, and gun—so that we thought they must have launched another heavy attack on the first line. It lasted for an hour, and a good many shells were sent into the town also, and then died away. Next morning it appeared that no attack had "materialised." They had either got the "wind up," or merely wished to show us that there were plenty of them still there, in spite of the thousands that had trekked downriver to deal with Aylmer.

These nocturnal bursts of firing were events of frequent occurrence, for the two lines of trenches were now very close to each other—twenty or thirty yards in some places—and both sides were always on the *qui vive*. The Turks often loosed off many thousands of rounds for no apparent reason. Sometimes we replied, but always with one eye on our stock of ammunition.

On the 10th the town suffered another severe "evening hate," and my new office again narrowly escaped destruction; but the 40-pounder proved to be a "dud," and buried itself in the Hospital Quarter-guard opposite. Later on, when doing a night round after "lights out," I came across three of the guard calmly sleeping over the precious missile, fatefully ignoring, as is the way of these children of the un-changing East, the chance of its changing its mind and blowing them to bits. I carefully preserved one of these "duds" for some days, in the hope of getting a gunner to draw its fang, but they weren't for it, and advised its speedy removal to the river. So, this, to my regret, had to be done, and at the dead of a dark night it was consigned to a watery grave. But the 9th brought us great news, and the town was all agog. The R.F., the Relieving Force, had beaten the enemy at Sheikh Sa'ad, so the report said, the Turks were retreating, and our people were pur-suing them, albeit "slowly," owing to the bad going.

Although we had had rain and we knew what silt soil was like when it is wet, yet we didn't altogether like that word "slowly"; it sug-gested "fatigue" and difficulties. And when the evening came and with it a rumour that we were to be put on "half rations," our optimism got a shock and we felt that the success was not an unqualified one. Next day there was no news, and the weather was vile. It was damp and wet and cold; the roads, or rather unmade lanes, were indescribably muddy and sloppy, and one slipped, splashed, and slithered rather than walked. There was no fuel save for the barest necessities, the sky was overcast, and the outlook grey and miserable.

Our "Lancelot" fell sick again, this time with an illness that was to keep him away from us for nearly three months, and poor Lam-bert was worse. Huddled up in our thickest clothes, we considered and reconsidered our prospects, conjectured and guessed at what was happening down below; surmised and supposed, and, generally, went through the first of those periods of trying suspense which we were later to become so familiar with from their frequent repetition.

Restless and stiff, I took a walk to the "East End" by the "A" short cut, to exchange a word with Gasbard and the "Fat Boy" of the Ra-jputs, who were quartered down there, and to gain their roof, like Sister Anne, and look around.

Of these alleyways or "short cuts" through the town from east to west, four or five had been made. They were labelled alphabetically. Each one had its appropriate letter stuck up on a board at corners or difficult turns, to keep one to the right track. "A" road passed along the southwest or riverside Bazar throughout its length, and then dived through a maze of *"khans,"* stables, private houses, and passages, until it ended in the palm grove in the S.E. of the town. It was the weirdest road. The *khan*, or inn, was a dirty yard surrounded by a verandah, from which led off rooms or stables as the needs of the moment demanded. Crossing it, you cut across the corner of a small hovel which in these days was used to stable a friendly old flea-bitten Arab pony, whose unhappy death in April, under the orders of the Food Controller, we all lamented. Leaving the stable, you passed through a nondescript court or into the courtyard of the R.E. Headquarters, where, if you nosed about, you would find yourself amongst the bomb-makers, with their jam-tins and old nails; the mortar manufacturers, the makers of Roman catapults and other improvised engines of destruction, of scaling-ladders and carpentry of all sorts, and a hundred other evidences of the sleepless activity of the engineers.

Leaving them you passed through an open piece of ground shielded from transfluvial snipers by a wall, and full of elaborate dug-outs prepared by the pioneers. Thence the road dipped to cross a weak spot and avoid the attentions of the enemy on the far bank. Up again to ground-level, you passed through some Tommies' quarters, and then dived below one of the main streets. Climbing up on the far side of this you found yourself in the chambers of some Turkish baths, domed and vaulted like a cathedral crypt, and nearly as dark, but now fitfully illuminated by the crude oil lights, or the cooking fires of the Hindu bearers who lived there. Another dip beneath another road brought you to the living-rooms of a house occupied by the Rajputs, and near your journey's end, for across the next street lay the mess and those you came to see.

And so up to the flat roof, by the usual winding stair in the wall of the usual courtyard. The house-top was some twenty-five feet square, and around three sides of it was a four foot brick wall. On the fourth or eastern side, a palisade of sheet zinc of the same height had been erected, with a few sandbags around its loophole. The walls were loopholed at intervals of three yards or so, for the convenience of our snipers and observers. Two or three snipers were always on duty here. Each sat on a brick or two close by his loophole, with his eye glued to a telescope. Within reach of his hand he had spare ammunition, and by his side lay an accumulating heap of empty cartridge cases. From time to time the short "*plock*" of a rifle rang out, as one or other of them spotted an exposed head in the trenches opposite and loosed off at it.

This particular roof was one of the highest in the place and commanded a good view of the rest of the town and of the river and the country round about. Immediately below, on the river side, lazed the few "*mahelas*" that still remained in our hands, and straight across the stream was the mouth of the Shatt-el-Hai, that connecting link between Tigris and Euphrates, which it joins near Suk esh-Shiukh, where resides the spiritual head of those followers of John the Baptist, the Sabaeans.

At this time of the year "the Hai" is nearly dry, but with the coming of the rains it fills up and is navigable for large native craft for some months, or until the snow-water flood has died away.

On either side of its mouth, and extending along the bank of the main river nearly to "Woolpress" or the liquorice factory village, could be made out the Turkish trenches. In them we could just see the Turks and Arabs as they moved about and passed by small gaps in their parapet.

Farther up lay the village, occupying a quarter of a mile or so of bank opposite the west end of Kut, and consisting of a hundred or so flat-roofed mud houses and the factory chimney. Beyond it, again, bare river-bank and more trenches. Away to the west, on the skyline, could easily be seen the great white camp of the Turks at Shamran, as well as the masts and funnels of two or three of their boats, including the smart-looking monitor *Firefly*, with its tall "wireless" mast, which we lost at Ctesiphon,

Between their camp and the Sinn ridge on the right bank ran a raised road, and traffic along it could usually be seen; sometimes a camel train, sometimes a straggling column of wounded coming from down below, but always something.

To the north east the curving river pursued its tortuous way to Megasis Fort and beyond, whilst thirty miles or so away the snow-clad peaks of the Pusht-i-Kuh stood out, milky pink in the evening sunset. Northwards we looked down on a heterogeneous collection of flat house-tops of all shapes and sizes, with here and there a watcher gazing earnestly through a telescope, or an Arab woman busied with domestic duties. Out beyond them, in the middle distance, our gun-pits and the brick kilns, and farther still, the open and deserted plain stretching away to our front line and the fort.

All this through the loopholes, for it did not do to show a head above the wall; the enemy snipers at 500 yards made far too pretty practice at anything showing above the top. But it was good to sit up there for a bit and vie with the sparrows and sand-grouse in their enjoyment of God's good air. Gasbard, too, was a wit of no mean parts, and often wiled away a pleasant hour with his fairy stories and comic anecdotes, so that the roof became a popular resort and a welcome refuge from the *ennui* of the daily round. Often "of an evening," as the weeks went by and the days grew warmer, did we sit there watching the evening hate and the Turks' attempts to hit the guns on the bank below us.

The 11th passed silently, but on the 12th a message told us that it had been a big action at Sheikh Sa'ad; that the enemy had lost 4500 men and two guns, as well as prisoners and deserters, and that we were following them up. But in the usual way our own losses were left to the imagination, and we guessed they were not inconsiderable. General Nixon, the message continued, had relinquished the army command through ill health. However, the news that our people had given the Turk a good hard knock cheered us greatly, and one man even drew upon his imagination so far as to see shells bursting over the Ess Sinn position.

The 14th brought us more particulars of the great defeat and retreat of the enemy, and the over sanguine ones saw the smoke of our ships in the distant east.

All day long a straggling column of the enemy's camels and men passed by, just out of range, on the right bank, on their way up to Shamran. They appeared to be wounded, and, so, very tangible evidence of a big "strafe" somewhere. Late in the afternoon a column of some 5000 Turks, with guns, was descried in the east, going north west, so we persuaded ourselves that our deliverance was near, though the Turks, as an antidote, hurled a lot of their spherical shells at us just to show that they were not downhearted. We were all very cheery, and "Relief" was on every one's lips—what mattered it that the rations had sunk to a half and the cruse of oil had failed?

An order came out, too, that no Arab was allowed outside his house after 5 p.m., on pain of being shot at sight, and the whole garrison was standing to arms. So, the air was tense with excitement, and we waited with what patience we could command for the next development. But the 15th was silent, and that force of 5000 Turks came down again on the other side of the river. On the 16th it leaked out that our people were only just this side of Wady, had lost a good many in a second battle, and were not likely to get on; and the next day the official blow fell.

D.H.Q, issued a *communiqué* to the effect that, owing to the losses and bad weather, the Relieving Force could not get on, and the troops were exhorted to patience against the arrival of more reinforcements. So, we reluctantly came to the conclusion that the end was not in sight, and that it was up to us to go on sticking it for yet a week or two. With a sigh of disappointment and a muttered "damn!" we turned each to his job and "carried on."

CHAPTER 9

January 18th to 26th

The siege, so far as we were concerned, now entered on a second stage. The exhilaration bred of the novelty of being invested had by now worn off and was succeeded for a time by the dull ache of disappointment at the failure of our people to relieve us after six weeks, and by a period of enhanced discomfort. Our unbounded faith in their capacity to help us was somewhat shaken, and although we felt quite certain of relief in the near future, yet the knowledge that it was possible for a British Relieving Force to do less than the anxiety of a besieged one had marked out for it to do, served to render our enforced confinement more irritating.

As early as the 10th January rations went down to about two-thirds, though we had not yet started on the battery bulls or the horses. Fuel had become scarce. All the wooden settees, so dear to the coffeeshop *habitués* of Iraq, had been chopped up and burnt, and all the wooden doors of the quondam shops in the Bazar were being pulled down to share the same fate. The usual wood ration now consisted of bits of liquorice root or furze bush or of old doors and beams. Oil was coming to an end, and candles and *ghi* were beginning to be used for illumination purposes.

On the 13th we were on half rations—bully, rice, butter, jam, dates, and bread,—we might have done worse! and fortunately could not see into the future.

The same day the brick plinths of the Bazar were pulled up and taken away for making defences. Since the Bazar had to be used as a public road, the increased floor-space this gave us was a distinct gain.

That afternoon was typical of many. After the usual round of hospital duties—office work, correspondence, rations, rounds of visits, dressings, and operations—we had gone over for tea, and the Turk started his evening "hate." As so often happened, a bad case of abdominal wound soon had us back again, and we had to operate in the midst of the "pother." Several shells dropped round about us as we worked, and one just behind us landed fairly inside one of the little "wards" of the next-door hospital and killed three patients. Amongst the hiss of our "primus" stove, the sizzle of the steaming steriliser, the clatter of the instruments in enamelled trays, and the smell of the chloroform, the dull thuds of shells as they dropped or burst amidst the walls of the houses, and the tremors of the ground we stood on from their frequent concussions, formed a strange accompaniment to our work in the little mud-walled theatre. We were never sorry when these hates finished, and we could feel that, short of a night exacerbation, we might expect peace for at least a few hours.

But from a professional point of view the siege gave the surgeon a rare opportunity of getting his patients very soon after they were hit, of treating them before complications set in, and of watching their progress and the effect of his treatment upon them, instead of having, as is almost always the lot of the military doctor, to send them along to the Base for someone else to look after.

The next few days it rained steadily, and the lanes of Kut became indescribably filthy. The hospital main Bazar street became a stream; many of the wards leaked, and the patients were miserable and cold. The trenches were abominable, and the Tommies were in some cases up to their waists in liquid mud. The 21st beat all records up to date, and it rained unceasingly. Everybody and everything were wet through, and the roads became troughs of mud. It was a pitiable sight to watch the efforts of the mule transport carts struggling through these quagmires on a dark night—one often wondered how on earth they ever got to their destinations. The river rose to within a few inches of the top of the bank, and our men were washed out of the front-line trenches. But the Turks were in worse case, and had to evacuate their first, second, and third, and so to retire a thousand yards. Our fellows suffered several casualties through having to get up out of their flooded trenches. The poor lads came in wet and perished with cold, mud-bespattered and dishevelled.

Our own operations were carried on under difficulties, and the rain dripped through our skylight and down our necks. One unfortunate *sowar*, I remember, came in mortally wounded. He had been hit whilst helping to dig the grave of a comrade who had just been killed. Such is the irony of fate; but what atrocious luck!

The floods set us wondering if the Turks would be washed out of their positions down below, and if the promised assault by the Relieving Force would come off; but though distant guns were heard at dawn, and again at intervals during the day, we were left in ignorance as to the result.

A visit to the housetop gave a splendid view of the swollen river and of the extensive floods. The Hai had become a considerable stream, winding away to meet our people at Nasiriyeh, and the enemy's ships stood out boldly high above the Turkish camp.

The 23rd was a Sunday, and in the evening one went to church. The services were held in an upper room in the "*serai*," and in that part of it nearest the river. The room was quite small but could overflow into the *padre's* private room next door, and so accommodate some fifty people. At one end was a plain table covered by an improvised altar-cloth and a simple ornament or two, the body of the room occupied by a few benches, and by the altar our surpliced *padre*.—A simple church indeed, but far more impressive than many a mighty cathedral. For, mingled with the priest's solemn tones as he read the prayers for peace were the boom of the enemy's guns and the crack of his snipers' rifles, and it was easier perhaps amidst such surroundings to draw near to the God of Battles and the Prince of Peace.

That day we got in a wounded Turk from the trenches. He was a fine-looking, hefty fellow, phlegmatic and stoical like the rest of his kind. They are men of robust physique, broad and burly, and of splendid vitality.

In this particular their allies the Arabs vie with them. They take a lot of killing, and, when wounded, recover rapidly from wounds and answer readily to the surgeon's efforts.

The 23rd saw a further reduction in rations, and bread seemed to be giving out; but we dined friend Hepaton that night, and in his honour broached our last bottle of green gooseberries.

On the 25th the heads of departments met in solemn conclave to consider the state of our supplies; and on the 26th our suspense regarding the doings of the R.F. was ended for some time, for the general issued a lengthy *communiqué* on the subject and took at the same time the opportunity of explaining to us all his strategy of the past few weeks. He thought, perhaps, that such was due to the gallant division he had led for so long, it ran:

The Relieving Force under General Aylmer, has been unsuccessful in its efforts to dislodge the Turks entrenched on the left bank of the river some fourteen miles below the position at Ess Sinn, where we defeated them in September last. . . . Our Relieving Force suffered severe loss and had very bad weather to contend against; they are entrenched close to the Turkish position.

More reinforcements are on the way upriver, and I confidently expect to be relieved some day during the first half of the month of February.

I desire all ranks to know why I decided to make a stand at Kut during our retirement from Ctesiphon. It was because, as long as we hold Kut, the Turks cannot get their ships, barges, stores, and munitions past this place, and so cannot move down to attack Amarah, and thus we are holding up the whole of the Turkish advance. It also gives time for our reinforcements to come upriver from Busra, and so restore success to our arms.

It gives time to our allies the Russians, who are now overrunning Persia, to move towards Baghdad, which a large force is now doing. I had a personal message from General Baratoff, in command of the Russian Expeditionary Force in Persia, telling me of his admiration of what you men of the Sixth Division and troops attached have done in the past few months, and telling me of his own progress on the road from Kermanshah towards Baghdad.

By standing at Kut I maintain the territory we have won in the past year at the expense of much blood, commencing with your glorious victory at Shaiba, and thus we maintain the campaign as a glorious one, instead of letting disaster pursue its course down to Amarah, and perhaps beyond.

I have ample food for eighty-four days, and that is not counting the 3000 animals which can be eaten. When I defended Chitral some twenty years ago we lived well on 'atta' and horse-flesh; but, as I repeat, I expect confidently to be relieved in the first half of the month of February.

Our duty stands out clear and simple. It is our duty to our Empire, to our beloved King and country, to stand here and hold up the Turkish advance as we are doing now, and with the help of all, heart and soul to me together, we will make this defence to be remembered in history as a glorious one. All in India and

England are watching us now and are proud of the splendid courage you have shown; and I tell you, let all remember the glorious defence of Plevna, for that is what is in my mind.

I am absolutely calm and confident as to the result. The Turk, though good behind a trench, is of little value in the attack. They have tried it once, and their losses in one night in their attempt on the fort were 2000 alone.

They have already had very heavy losses from General Aylmer's musketry and guns, and I have no doubt they have had enough. I have done my duty. You know the result, and whether I was right or not; and your name will go down to history as the heroes of Ctesiphon, for heroes you proved yourselves in the battle. I, perhaps by right, should not have told you of the above; but I feel I owe it to you all to speak straight and openly and take you into my confidence, for, God knows, I felt our heavy losses and the sufferings of my poor, brave wounded, and shall remember it as long as I live; and I may truly say that no general I know of has been more loyally obeyed and served than I have been in command of the Sixth Division.

These words are long, I am afraid, but I speak straight from the heart, and you will see that I have thrown all officialdom overboard. We will succeed—mark my words!—but save your ammunition as if it were gold!

Thus, spake Townshend, and all were pleased with the confidence he placed in them. The talk of "eighty-four days' ample rations" was rather a bombshell—we were already down to half, and the prospect it held out to us was not an inviting one. But Reuters told us of the Russians' pressure at Erzerum, and the weather improved. Though we had no vegetables, we were not yet hungry, and all were very fit.

CHAPTER 10

February 1st to 22nd, 1916

With the indefinite postponement of our relief, we settled down with grim determination to last out, and to "wait and see."

February brought us novelty in the form of aeroplanes.

Our friends they threw us papers; our foes they dropped us bombs. But they provided interest and kept us from getting dull. There was always the speculation as to whether an approaching aeroplane was a friend or an enemy. Our people were in the field first and had it all their own way for a fortnight before "Fritz" appeared. The first thing our airmen dropped was a parcel said to contain much-needed rifle "pull-throughs." Afterwards they dropped a few messages, some rupees for the F.T.C.O., and an occasional bundle of papers.

The general and some of the gilded staff received a few letters from time to time, and the S. and T. and one or two others who happened to have friends amongst the flying men also got a batch, but the ordinary man got none. He groused bitterly in consequence as time went on, for it never seemed to strike them down below that we were simply pining for news from our people at home. Daily they came up to see if we were still there, sailed about above us for a bit, and as often went back and left us never a letter. We argued that there must be many letters for us all lying at Amarah and thought the least they could do would be to bring us a small mail now and then.

But it was not to be, and so most of us went without news for many months. In my own case it was eleven, which is a long time. However, they dropped us millstones for grinding our corn, for which we were devoutly thankful, and which were absolutely invaluable. The necessary machinery for setting up a mill was found in or near the fort. There it was dismantled, and although the difficulties in transporting it from there to the town, across the open, were almost insuperable, the R.E.'s and the flying men overcame them in some wonderful manner, and soon a full-fledged flour-mill was grinding away merrily to the music of its belts and pistons.

Corn for its maw was none too plentiful. Albeit a large quantity had recently been unexpectedly discovered, yet more was wanted if we were to hold out. Supplemented by the invaluable aid of Bodd of Lynch's and of old Tom Baxter and Sassoon, thorough house to house search was made and more was discovered and bought, but the townspeople were cunning and their hiding-places many. Our own hospital provided a good example. One day some "government agents" came round and deliberately began to make a hole in the end wall of one of our little wards, and lo! beyond it was a considerable chamber full to the brim with large tins of "*ghee*" or clarified butter. More than three hundred of these four-gallon canisters there were. They had been *cached* by the simple process of "walling up" one end of a long and narrow hovel.

"*Ghee*" is dear to the heart of the Indian, and this new stock was a godsend. Nearby were also two more dens half filled with dirty barley, which was so very dirty and mixed with so much mud and sand, and of such very poor quality, that at first it was looked upon as unfit for food, but there came a time towards the end when even this was roped in and turned into "bread."

Abdul's first effort at bombing was made on the 13th—a most suitable date—when to our surprise and chagrin an aeroplane of his flew over us three times and dropped a dozen or more bombs. We didn't like it. Cooped up in a small mud town we felt rather like rats in a trap, and very helpless against this new form of frightfulness. Your bomb comes down with a vicious scream and bursts with a nasty flame and an equally unpleasant bang. Sometimes you can watch its flight if the sun catches it and is reflected from its brazen top, and you become expert in deciding whether you are standing in the same vertical plane as is occupied by the aviator.

Alarm gongs, consisting of suspended shell cases, were soon erected on the housetops in different parts of the town, and look-out men stationed beside them to give us timely warning of the approach of hostile craft. All who could do so were enjoined to get under cover whenever this occurred. Some crawled into dug-outs and some climbed on to roofs, but the favourite places both for safety and observation were the numerous arched-over passages beneath the first floors of the larger houses. Here would collect excited groups of "townees," chattering and straining their necks to watch the evolutions of the common enemy.

Sick men in the Officers' Hospital, who couldn't walk, had to be carried below from the first floor to a safer retreat till the danger passed. It was a nuisance, this bombing, and we all heartily cursed it.

Those early days of February were bitterly cold. Once or twice at night the thermometer registered eight degrees or more of frost. Our little mud roof was white with hoar frost as morning after morning I ran upstairs for fresh air and to note the crop of bullets and shrapnel that had landed thereon during the preceding twenty-four hours.

But they were bright days, and one longed to get outside for exercise in the clear bracing air. Thanks to the floods and the consequent retirement of the Turks to 1000 yards or more from our own line on the north side, it became possible for a few days to walk out in the open and stretch our legs. But stray bullets were always flying about, and the practice of walking above ground had very soon to be stopped officially. Thus, one day we took a walk out to the Pioneers' camp, near the middle line. Partly we wound our way along a communication trench, partly we walked "overland" to avoid the mud.

It was good to be out of a trench, to feel one had a right of way on the surface; good to let the eye roam away over the flat to the distant Pusht-i-Kuh. Snow-clad, pure and white, calm and majestic in the still, clean air, the Persian hills reminded one of the Safaid Koh, north of the Khyber, or of the mighty peaks of Kashmir, or of the long white walls of the Himalayas as you see them from the Indian hills. We wondered what was going on behind that barrier. Was the unrest in Persia increasing? Had the Germanised Mussulman got a firm footing there, or was he a fugitive? The object of our walk was to attend an auction of deceased officers' effects. These auctions, arranged by brother officers, and of which we had many as the siege wore on, were always, to my mind, very sad affairs, though necessary. Prices were always high, but in the later days the simplest articles or stores fetched fabulous prices. This particular auction was held aboveground behind a clump of trees. There was a goodly crowd of fellows there, many of whom we hadn't seen since the siege began, so little opportunity had we had for visiting.

About the 1st of the month the heavy battery bullocks began to be sacrificed, and British troops got half a pound of fresh beef every other day, alternating with a pound of horse-flesh. This arrangement lasted for a little over a fortnight, after which horse-flesh alone was available. Very few of the Indians, unfortunately, would eat either of these kinds of flesh at first, and so handicapped themselves very considerably. There were no fresh vegetables, no sugar and no bacon—a little butter, a little jam—our bread was half-wheaten, half *atta* or barley, oil was about finished, and wood was scarce. Roofs, doors, and verandahs were being pulled down to supplement the stock. There was a certain amount of ships' coal, mostly dust, and this we mixed with mud and crude oil and made into coal balls, which burnt indifferently well in improvised tin braziers.

We had a ration of dried potato-meal for some weeks and were able to buy a few quarts of dried beans and peas from the natives. Also, in one of the streets the Arabs were allowed to sell such produce as they possessed, and for some time they kept up small supplies of coffee, beans, peas, salt, and of "*kabaabs.*" "*Kabaabs*" are a sort of small, thick, sweet pancake, made of flour, *ghee*, and sugar. Eaten hot, with jam, they are not so bad, and we took to having them for tea as long as the supply lasted. They gave us the extra "bread stuff" which our diminishing cereal ration made a real want; we were not yet hungry and were all pretty fit, but we missed the sugar badly.

On the 2nd an aeroplane dropped some papers in which we read the Turkish account of Ctesiphon and after, which was of great interest to those who were there. They were pleased to remark that the British commander "fled" to Busra!

A picture paper of some date in January said it had just heard that Townshend had retired to a position at Kut, a "coaling station on the Tigris!" but no one seemed to know that we were very much besieged and had been for weeks, and we felt hurt.

The same day we lost a colleague. A popular doctor was shot through the head by a chance bullet. Fortunately, unconscious, he lingered for some days, but died within a week, much regretted by us all. We laid him to rest amongst the palms, and our hearts went out to the little woman we knew he had left behind him.

On the 4th we had a brisk evening bombardment which did very little damage, and some rather disturbing Reuters. Zeppelin raids at home seemed to be becoming serious, and one wondered where one's people were.

However, we of the saw-bones profession were kept too busy to brood over the depressing wires, and our days passed quickly. The usual evening hate took place on the 5th, and a sniper succeeded in hitting one of my patients. The poor wretch was basking in a square yard of sunshine, and picking innumerable lice off his blanket, when a bullet came round some corner and hit him in the leg. He was very depressed over it; said he had no luck in this war. He had lost two brothers in France, and this was the third time he had himself been hit. He had yet to become a prisoner, and God knows what has become of him now. Could he have foreseen this also, he would have turned his face to the wall and, silently acquiescing in his foreordained fate, would have joined his brethren.

I watched that evening "hate" from the Rajput roof with Gasbard. Coming home, as the sun went down, I came upon a crowd and a commotion at the *serai* end of the Bazar. Inquiry elicited the fact that something had collapsed in the first storey of the house they were staring at and looking up I perceived that the gunners' eyrie above the old coffee-shop had disappeared, and there was dust and confusion.

It seemed likely that there was work for a "*medico*," so I clambered up the gimcrack stairs and groped my way in. Passing through one room I found myself up against a mound of sandbags in the next. From the midst of this came mutterings and gaspings, laughs and curses, mingled with occasional short sharp orders of some invisible officer, and through the dust and semi-darkness I could make out straining figures pulling and hauling at something underneath. With a heave and a chuckle, a something was hauled out, and proved to be a dishevelled and dusty Tommy. The roof had collapsed under the weight of a mass of sandbags which went to form the gunner's directing post and had buried several Tommies underneath it—and now their pals were pulling them out from amidst the wreck of poles, matting, and sandbags.

Now a sandbag, when dropped on to your back from a roof, eight feet above you, is no light weight, and I quite expected to find some broken arms or legs; but one by one they were hauled out, and save for bruises and sprains and scratches, they were none the worse, and looked upon it all as a huge joke.

February 6 was distinguished by the reduction of the wood ration to half a pound per man—not much to cook with—and much advice as to how to make use of the crude oil that was about to be issued as fuel.

The 8th was rather a red-letter day, for by some happy chance we secured a small piece of bacon, which made breakfast a possibility for a day or two. Also, we were lucky enough to get hold of a few more tins of jam, thanks to the generosity of "Harold" next door, whose mess by an accident possessed a double supply. These we husbanded with the greatest care. No longer was a tin of jam common property, but each had his own tin, and labelled it in no uncertain way. Jealously he guarded it and was ever on the watch against unlawful depredations on the part of others.

Dashwood's Mess of four or five unequal appetites was comic in this respect. If one dropped in at feeding-time, one would find their small table covered with a forest of small tins and things. Each kept separate his own jam, his bit of butter, his box of sugar and tin of milk, at an early stage in the siege, and rigidly adhered to the plan they had adopted.

Our bread now suffered another change for the worse, and was made in thirds of flour, "atta," and barley meal, and it was diminishing in quantity, but was still good "wholemeal" stuff.

The early experiments in the use of the crude ship-oil were amusing enough for those not actually engaged in the trials. The experimenters became "sweeps" in a very short time, so thick was the smoke, and the hospital kitchen soon resembled a stokehold. But with experience came wisdom. Tall tin or zinc chimneys, supplied by the R.E., were soon erected to carry the fumes outside or above the verandah roofs, where they became more or less innocuous.

The liquid fuel was burned in inclined tin troughs, which were covered in by thin sheets wherein holes were cut at intervals for cooking pots to be placed over; the chimney took off from the lower end of the trough. This crude oil saved the situation as far as fuel was concerned, for, despite the utmost efforts of the S. and T., the supply of wood was hopelessly inadequate. One mess, I remember, found a few old Turkish biscuits. These, made of coarse brown meal and as hard as bricks, burned merrily enough in a homemade brazier, and lasted for a few days. Possibly, two months later, they regretted the destruction of so little of even such "food"; but the time was cold, and the brazier a godsend to those who were privileged to huddle around it.

That day, too, the general issued a *communiqué*, in which he gave us the news that a division was to commence embarking in Egypt for "Messypot" on February 10th. We calculated. How much exactly of all arms comprised a division? How many guns? How many transports will it take to bring it? How many days should we allow for embarkation and the voyage to Busra—for the transhipment to river craft and for the journey up? It would take them a good month, we said. Ye gods! must we wait another month? Heigh-ho! Anyhow they would, we were sure, make certain of it, if we were not relieved before!

The next two days it poured with rain. Half one of our mess walls came down with a crash, and I slept beneath the roof that night in some expectation of a further collapse.

The roads again became rivers of mud, which nobody enjoyed save the little semi-nude Arab *gamins*, who, with their one and only garment held high up round the chest, disported their chubby baby limbs with impish glee in the luscious quagmire. Fat as butter, they showed no sign of shortage of food or of fear of the cold. Although we had to feed some hundreds of the inhabitants—many of them gratuitously— few ever showed signs of starvation, even up to the end. This feeding of the people took place at a sort of soup-kitchen across the way, and daily in the early morning our own particular road was blocked up by a hungry multitude.

The rain meant extra work for the R.E. Night after night did their working parties go tramping by us on their way to the open ground, where they were constructing a new long "*bund*" to keep Kut dry when the worst floods should come. Night after night they were sniped at, and the early morning almost invariably found an extra case or two in hospital. Hospital life was made miserable by it. Roofs leaked, rafters broke, and walls here and there collapsed, and it was difficult to keep anything clean; but the patients bore it all with most extraordinary patience, and never groused.

A new sport arose about this time—shooting starlings and sparrows for the "pot." Of both these species there seemed to be unlimited numbers. Every evening at sunset they came home to roost in clumps of palms, making the while a terrible clatter. Someone discovered how good "starling pie" was, and it soon became a popular dish so long as *atta* or potato meal could be obtained. It was at any rate a notable addition to our menu, and a very welcome change from the eternal horse-meat. But one evening a pellet or two happened to hit a famous general, with the result that bird-shooting was limited, by order, to certain restricted areas.

The 11th gave us a "late at night" strafe, but also bequeathed us a dainty "Kirschner," which Trixie found in an old 'Sketch.' "*Petite*" and redolent of Home and Beauty, she was framed with loving care, and hung in the best light, whence she presided over our scanty board and chased away depression.

We had a hard and fatiguing day on the 12th, for the shelling was more than usually destructive. It cost us, amongst others, the loss of a valuable medical subordinate and some good gunners. The next day we got our first taste of the enemy's bombs. Three times "Fritz" flew over us and dropped four or five bombs each time. He didn't do very much damage but gave us a little extra work.

The bombing coincided with a recrudescence of enemy activity in other ways, so that instead of our "confident expectation" of relief in the first half of February being fulfilled, conditions rather grew worse. The "hates" became more intense, and night bombardments became a regular and annoying feature. We supposed they were trying to wear out our nervous systems. One shell fell in the "bakery," and laid out six members of a most important unit. Sniping increased until you couldn't put a nose beyond a protecting wall. Many casualties occurred in the streets, and a bullet even managed to burst through our one and only mess window, although our little courtyard was surrounded on all sides by quite high walls. It was a cold or "*thandi*" bullet, as the Indians say.

There were rumours that the Turks were bringing down H.E., and all those who hadn't done so were enjoined to prepare dug outs; so, we started to dig one in our own place. What H.E. would do to us in that wretched little mud town we didn't like to imagine; common shell and shrapnel and bombs were steadily wrecking it; holes and ruins were all over the place; but H.E.! we should be blown to bits!

The health of the garrison was very good so far, but now scurvy began to show itself, and, as we had no vegetables, was bound to increase amongst the Indians, who wouldn't eat the fresh meat. Of dates we still had a few, and of *dhal* and rice a little, but not enough to keep the disease at bay. We began a garden, but things take time to grow, and we had to look on, as the cases grew more numerous, and to deplore our impotence.

For a day or two we were very busy making Red Cross flags for the guidance of "Fritz." The flat roofs of the East form excellent sites for pegging them down on, and each hospital laid down several in the hope of diverting bombs from the sick and wounded.

About the 17th good news from the outside world reached us, headed by a gracious message from the King-Emperor, telling us of the efforts being made to relieve us, and of his concern in our welfare. It showed we were after all not forgotten and bucked us all up. Aylmer let us know that he was not quite ready but meant to do the job well when he did move.

We heard, too, that he was getting up an extra brigade of artillery. Reuters told us of the fall of Erzerum at the hands of the Russian Bear. We could imagine the gallant Cossacks swarming in on the east as the discomfited Turks streamed out along the roads leading west and south to Erzinjan and Mush. Those Turks had a bad time in Erzerum. We learnt a little about it later on in Baghdad.

But as a set off against all this good fortune, the Turks gave us h—ll that night, and we had a man killed in hospital. Our new dug out was several times in urgent demand. What a damp hole it was!—it radiated dampness. Beetles and slugs and scorpions made it their playground. I often preferred to risk the shells, and Trixie loathed it. One of that night's shells tried hard to deprive us of our medical chief by sailing through his room. Wood and mud and broken glass came tumbling down, but he had retired below, and fortunately missed it all.

The bombing continued, generally in the afternoons. Our own aeroplanes came up in the mornings and often dropped something or other—anything but a "mail." Occasionally they dropped things into the river, much to our chagrin. Whenever "Fritz" came to bomb us, their snipers always got busy. They had discovered that people were inclined to frequent the roofs, out of curiosity or for safety, for, short of a direct hit, you were safest there, and they sent a hurricane of lead skimming over the house-tops in the hope of hitting a head. One day they managed in this way to wound one of our generals.

Our gunners did their best to hit the flying man. Much ingenuity was expended on improvised gun mountings. One machine gun near to us was mounted on the rim of a weighted barrel, which served its purpose admirably, but they never appeared to trouble the aeroplane, nor were the enemy gunners any more successful in their efforts to damage ours.

Our own flying men in Kut watched the evolutions of both friend and foe in impotent impatience, for they had no chance of using their own two pets that rested cold and disconsolate under a tarpaulin without the town.

They spent their time and their mechanical genius in helping the R.E., and in producing inventions to help us along. One of them served us to good purpose by erecting acetylene lights for our operating theatre, which were invaluable.

Late at night on the 21st we were suddenly brought up to concert pitch of expectation once more by getting secret orders for the morrow. We slept in our boots. By five o'clock next morning we were out, and getting all our convalescents together, and armed for "town duty" if necessary. All night the booming of the guns of the R.F. came floating up the river, and as day broke they were still hammering away. Expectant, we stood to and waited. Our men easied, we stood about in groups in the cold still dawn, conversing in low voices, listening to the distant guns, hoping hard. Hour by hour went by and found us still waiting and tense with excitement.

Was it relief? Would a few hours, or a day or two, see the end of it, and a chance of fresh air and a rest and—our letters? At nine the guns ceased their *"grondement"*—all was still. At eleven o'clock an aeroplane sailed over us and flew away again. At three another appeared and dropped a message. At five the word was passed along to "fall out," and the tension relaxed. At seven the camp fires of the enemy could be seen near Sinn, apparently undisturbed. At eight a furious rifle fire broke out, and lasted for an hour, and we loosed off a few rounds of the 4.7's.

Night came, and with it a *communiqué* to let us know that Aylmer's operations were successful—and left it at that. So, ended a nerve-straining day, finishing up with glorious uncertainty. The general gave it as his opinion that we should be relieved in a few days, and with that we had to be content, and turned in dog-tired.

February 23rd to March 10th, 1916

All this left us restless and expectant. It was difficult to settle down again to the daily round, and my evening visits to Gasbard and his gramophone became more frequent. It was good to listen to the stirring strains of the "*Marseillaise*" or to the old songs of the Homeland. They made one forget the hates and took me over the seas to the wee "but-an'-ben" and the wee wifie waitin' there—waiting, waiting. How much longer were we to keep her in suspense? No wonder we asked for more needles!

One day I walked out with Trixie to the fort for the first time since the siege began. By the zigzag and tortuous communication trench, with its frequent traverses, it must have been a matter of two and a half miles before we reached it. We smelt it long before we saw it, and the malodour got stronger as we approached. We knew what it was. . .
. . . We picked up the machine-gun officer on the way and got him to show us round. Except for the open space in the middle, the place was a maze of trenches and dug-outs, sandbags and loopholes, beams and corrugated iron. Its walls were battered and torn, its bastion a wreck. The M.G.O. explained the fight of Christmas Eve, and pointed out the evidences of the desperate struggle.

The bastion was a veritable ruin. The walls and shelters behind them were no longer separable into their component parts, but were a jumbled up mass. Barbed wire was straggling about, sheets of corrugated iron here and there were twisted and torn and riddled with holes like a sieve, and the present line of defence spoke eloquently of the haste in which it had been strengthened. Looking through periscopes and taking hasty peeps through loopholes, we could picture to ourselves the furious assault of two months ago. We could see that which we had smelt before. They were hanging in all sorts of grotesque attitudes on the barbed wire—grim and horrible scarecrows—or lying as they fell on the scarp or in the ditch amongst the new green shoots of the grass of early spring. A few yards away were the Turkish trenches, now often empty. Between theirs and ours the dead men's land looked pathetic and desolate, for none might walk therein.

The middle of the fort was open and deserted; it always attracted, fortunately, a goodly number of the shells during a bombardment. But the fort had not been worried much of late. The garrison lay out in

The Mess at Kut, 1916

the sun, and looked fit and well, contrasting most favourably with our etiolated selves from the dens of Kut.

The long walk in the fresh air made us feel life was worth living, and, getting back, we found the R.F. planes had dropped more papers. These, however, contained the casualty lists of Sheikh Sa'ad, and so one had to bid farewell to yet some more of the "Old Brigade" whose names we read there.

Day after day went by, but we heard no more of the R.F. optimism still reigned supreme, but the prolonged uncertainty was very trying. The river was higher than ever, and the R.E. went on making things to cross it with. Our diminutive courtyard was becoming a little club, into which most of our medical chums and others would crawl as the sun went down. Alas! there was no bar, and the vermouth had nearly run dry. That meeting for a pre-prandial hour became a sort of institution. There was O'Grady with his monocle, who had kissed the Blarney Stone, accompanied always by pessimistic Horace, who carried the lamp; Swingfeld-Myth, our mechanical genius, and his stable companion the observer; Mac with his yarns, and Harold with his conscience; Canning, the photographer, and Martel, the big man with the appetite.

All would stroll in to exchange the latest rumour or freshest anecdote and kept us from getting dull.

Dashwood would "blow in" energetically, invariably followed by his satellite the Appendicoot. Dashwood had always discovered some terrifying piece of news about H.E. or new Turkish army corps, and "I'm just on my way," he'd say, "to tell little Penguin. I love to pull his leg." And having unburdened himself thus far, he would rush off, trailing Appendicoot behind him. Hepaton would look in on his way to the Officers' Hospital hard by and smoke a pipe of what passed for tobacco. The "baccy" problem was becoming acute. It was still possible to buy small quantities of half-baked green tobacco leaves from the natives, and the "wet bob" would spend hours damping it with rum and binding it up into a sailor's "perique." But the baccy soon gave out, and lime leaves, dried and broken up and flavoured with a suspicion of real Navy Cut and a lot of imagination, held the field.

Melliss, the lion-hearted, generally passed by, followed by his two rough terriers. Led by "Betty," these two always dashed in and chivvied the cats. Of cats we had a large collection that lived in and about the mess—black cats and tortoiseshell, tabby and grey Persian in infinite variety. They were fine cats, but it was pathetic to watch them gradually losing their "silk." As time wore on they became a nuisance. Hunger made them bold, and it was all the cook could do to preserve our own scanty rations from their depredations. They sat round and watched him as he prepared our dinner and made a dash for dainty morsels whenever he turned his head, but there was always a terrible scuttering on Betty's volcanic approach.

Those evening meetings will linger long in my memory—often they took place during a hate, and on those occasions, we huddled the chairs together and sought slight protection under the lee of our cookhouse wall. We talked of the menu, of the chance of leave when it was all over, and of what we would do if we got it, and always of the Relief—the Relief!

We also did our crawls and paid our visits, generally including a few minutes with one or all of the invalids, Lancelot, Lambert, and others—and now Gasbard had joined the band of crocks, but fortunately only temporarily.

Lancelot was so much better that he began to fear he'd be too well to be invalided when the relief did come; but he needn't have worried.

The end of the month found us still in suspense. One evening there were several bursts of cheering in the Turkish lines—why, we never knew, and we thought nothing of it. The most likely explanation seemed to be that they had had a "pay day."

Somebody got up some sweepstakes—three of them—on the date of relief, and we all took tickets—dates up to the 30th of April. The favourite date was about March 10 or 12, and the "draw" took place on the 1st March.

March came in in the traditional manner, like a lion. Its roar was due to a heavy evening strafe from guns and planes and caused a good many casualties. One bomb dropped into an Arab house where eight people were sitting. It killed or maimed most of these, and as those who were left and their neighbours were trying to succour them, another bomb dropped in the same spot and reaped another harvest. We had several bad cases in, and were operating throughout the turmoil, but escaped particular molestation by the *obuses*.

Rations continued to diminish. Dates 1½ oz., jam 1 oz., no sugar, milk, eggs, butter, or vegetables. Eggs and milk had for long been set aside for the hospitals, and the supply for them was woefully insufficient. Of horse-meat, or camel or mule, we had 1¼ lb., and of bread 12 oz.; a little tea and as much coffee.

Scurvy was rapidly increasing amongst the Indians, saving the

Gurkhas, and there was a good deal of pneumonia and consumption. Through these and the casualties there were many deaths daily—a dozen or more, and they mounted up. The worst of the scurvy was that it upset the healing of wounds, and we most anxiously watched the growth of the radishes in Cotton's garden wherewith we might fight it. Very few of the Indians were eating the fresh meat that would have helped them, in spite of a comprehensive routine order issued near the end of February, which explained to them that the holy books of the Hindu religion do not forbid the eating of horseflesh, and that their spiritual heads had wired to say so.

For a day or two following this breezy advent of March there was comparative peace. We got no news from below, but we could hear their guns from time to time. We lost another good officer at the hands of the snipers: poor Baillie of the Dorsets, who had come through the whole campaign without a scratch, now met his sudden death as he was walking along a communication trench. These "accidental" losses are so sad. There's no glory, no excitement; just sheer bad luck! The same day, I remember, occurred another instance of persistent ill-luck that seems to dog some unfortunates. A bright lad in the Binkshires, who had already been wounded on three separate occasions, was sitting on the bottom step of the entrance to a dug-out, chatting to his pals, when a stray bullet found its way down and shot him through the chest. He was "fed up." "It's no bloomin' use," he grumbled, "they're set on 'aving me, and they've got me all right this time"—and they had.

The weather was still very cold and we had some more rain. The pioneers and the sanitary squads did their best with the awful roads. One day they would scrape the mud off one side of the street and pile it up on the other. Another day they would dig a deep drain a foot wide and two deep on one side of the lane, use the drier subsoil for the road, and then fill up the ditch with liquid mud. This was all very well so long as you didn't happen to step in it. If you did, you went in over your knees at once. Often at night in the pitchy darkness a transport cart would get one wheel in, and it would take the struggling mules a good half-hour to get out again.

A lot of horses over and above those required for food had to be slaughtered about this time to save the barley they would otherwise consume. And so, the population of the horse lines got sparser and sparser, and the shadow of their doom seemed to hang over the poor beasts that were left. What a shame it seemed to have to "put them away"!

But now we got wind of another impending attempt of the R.F. to relieve us. Fresh schemes for the part the garrison should play as soon as Aylmer got going were constantly being prepared, and by the 6th we were again on tenterhooks of anticipation and suspense.

We were persuaded now that a few more days would set us free. The roof of G.H.Q. became a frequent resort of mine. From it one got the most tantalising sight of huge flocks of sheep grazing contentedly behind the enemy army they were so unsuspectingly rationing. They made one's mouth water and caused one to realise how caged in we were.

Once more, on the 7th, we got our secret orders for the morrow—more breathless expectancy—and to be up at 4.30. So, we arose in the chilly darkness and turned out and armed our convalescents. The guns of the R.F. began before dawn and we hoped for great things.

Having posted my convalescents and orderlies, I walked away briskly to Dashwood's ambulance to get warm. I found them all booted and spurred and gulping down a "*chota hazri.*" Dashwood and Appendicoot, it appeared, were off to take station just outside the town with the mobile portion of their ambulance, whilst Martel looked after the immovable patients. They were in high spirits at the thought of getting a move on at last, and our blood raced through our veins with the anticipation of exciting events. From the roof we could see nothing, but a violent explosion not far away made us all jump.

The cause of this we discovered later: our engineers had tried to float mines down to the Turks' bridge on the Hai, but they refused to turn in at the mouth, and one of them blew up just off the entrance. At half-past six, as there seemed to be nothing doing, I turned in again to get an hour's sleep. I was becoming a little sceptical about these alarums and excursions and thought an extra hour would be a useful asset. The long hours of waiting dragged by slowly, and nothing happened until teatime, when a continuous gun fire started, which we could see as well as hear. For an hour we watched the distant bursts beyond Ess Sinn, but then the Osmanli gave us a very considerable "hate," the results of which kept us busy until nine o'clock.

Next day at dawn the guns began again and seemed much nearer. We "bucked up" and went about with a spring in our walk, but their grumbling ceased at midday, and soon afterwards another disappointment was crystallised in the form of a message: "Aylmer has not succeeded in his great effort!" This was a great shock, and we were not a little depressed.

Hard on the heels of the message followed the visit of a Turkish officer under the white flag. We heard that he had brought a message to our chief, politely demanding surrender, and intimating that we had done all that could be expected of us.

He was courteous to our interpreters and offered them cigarettes, and the cut of his riding-breeches was beyond reproach.

But the general, of course, as politely refused, and cut down our rations instead.

Bread was reduced by yet another two ounces, a lot more horses were shot, and Townshend squared his jaw and hung on.

On the 10th March he issued the following *communiqué*:—

As on a former occasion, I take the troops of all ranks into my confidence again.

We have now stood a three-months' siege in a manner which has called upon you the praise of our beloved King and our fellow-countrymen in England, Scotland, Ireland, and India, and all this after your brilliant battles of Kut-el-Amara and Ctesiphon and your retirement to Kut, all of which feats of arms are now famous. Since 5th December 1915 you have spent three months of cruel uncertainty, and to all men and all people uncertainty is intolerable. As I say, on the top of all this comes the second failure to relieve us. And I ask you also to give a little sympathy to me who have commanded you in these battles referred to, and who, having come to you as a stranger, now love my command with a depth of feeling I have never known in my life before. When I mention myself, I would also mention the names of the generals under me, whose names are distinguished in the army as leaders of men.

I am speaking to you as I did before, straight from the heart, and, as I say, I ask your sympathy for my feelings, having promised you relief on certain dates on the promise of those ordered to relieve us. Not their fault, no doubt. Do not think that I blame them; they are giving their lives freely and deserve our gratitude and admiration. But I want you to help me again, as before. I have asked General Aylmer for the next attempt to bring such numbers as will break down all resistance and leave no doubt as to the issue.

In order then to hold out, I am killing a large number of horses so as to reduce the quantity of grain eaten every day, and I have had to reduce your ration. It is necessary to do this in order to keep our flag flying. I am determined to hold out, and I know you are with me heart and soul.

Next day the army commander sent us a message of sympathy in our disappointment and tried to cheer us up, he wired:

Rest assured that we shall not abandon the effort, and that for the next attempt the maximum force will be employed.

So, we rested assured, but we were bitterly disappointed.

CHAPTER 12

March 11th to 25th

The reaction from high hope to bitter disappointment left one rather battered. We, who had seen the river a year ago, were fearful of the effects of more floods, and began to entertain a doubt that Aylmer would be ready to do much more before the snow-water came down and swamped everything. Even now there were rumours that the floods were coming, and, to make matters worse, it rained again heavily. The river had risen to within a few inches of the record, and hundreds of acres of country were inundated. Beyond our front line was a huge lake, which stretched from the river on the west almost right across the peninsula to the fort.

The fort, in fact, was for a short time quite cut off. But this lake served the most useful purpose of keeping the Turks at a distance, and so lightened the work of our men. They had, however, to do a lot of digging, and the engineers were incessantly on the alert to keep the water out of the trenches. The men's digging powers, too, were very sensibly decreasing. They found by practical experience that the less potential energy you put into the human machine, the less power you'll get out of it. They "tired" quickly and had to work in short shifts. The slow starvation was beginning to tell on the body, but the "morale" was not affected.

The possibility of becoming prisoners obtruded itself upon us at times, but very few ever thought it would come to that. There were a few bets made on the subject, and an odd pessimist or two gave odds against the Relief—one of these gentlemen got hauled over the coals for his prophetic insight, and for acting in a manner "calculated to cause despondency and alarm amongst troops" (how does the regulation run?) Knowing this, we could not miss the opportunity of pulling Major Boswell's leg over an inoffensive level bet made long weeks ago. When assured that the general was on his track, his apprehension was pathetic, and he lost no time in cancelling his bet and impressing us with the innocence of the transaction.

On the 13th the 100 went up! a hundred days! Strange how used to things the human becomes! We were used to being besieged and began to take a pride in the number of days we were piling up. It looked as if we might vie with Ladysmith, and as the days went on we grew keen to beat her total of 120. There were three or four fellows amongst us who had been there. They said they infinitely preferred their first siege to this one. There they had plenty of room to move about in—could even ride about; there were not many guns against them, and there were no aeroplanes, whilst the climate was good. They had no use for Kut besieged.

There was now no getting over the fact that Aylmer had failed badly, and that it must take time to get ready for another shot. We knew, too, they must be having a pretty bad time in the wet down below. We felt listless and mentally bruised. To work for a bit became an effort. Thanks to the scurvy and the vanishing ration, the surgeon's hand had often to be held when in normal circumstances it could have healed with certainty. One of the hardest things the doctor had to bear was the sight sometimes of battered humanity beyond the reach of his art, because he could no longer expect Dame Nature to do her part. Large wounds would sometimes begin by showing promise of healing for a few days but would then stop and progress no further; would bleed when touched, and by their presence react on the enfeebled body that had no energy to deal with them.

At times one wanted to get away from it all and dreaded the morning round. One longed for nurses and unlimited invalid foods. Fortunately, and thanks to the prescience of the medical storekeeper, we had at first abundant medical and surgical supplies, and we were only now having to start economising.

But the sun was getting more powerful, and the grass began to grow on the plain outside, between the town and the trenches. As often as possible we walked out to the front line to get away from the stale town, from the noise of the snipers and the shells. It was good to sit on the fire-step out there with one's back to the parapet and bask in the spring sunshine; to feast one's eyes on the fresh green carpet of young grass, and to watch the drop of the bullets as they whizzed overhead and landed a hundred yards behind; still better to see the bursts of the "windy Lizzies" in the town, and know one's self well out of reach of their eternal *éclatement*, and free to act the part of distant spectator.

Behind your back you could hear the gentle *lip-lap* of tiny wavelets, and a peep through a loophole disclosed the great expanse of flood stretching from a foot or two below the parapet to the group of sand-hills a thousand yards away....

As soon as the herbs of the field grew long enough, parties were sent out at night to cut them. The Indians revelled in it, and many "grass-cuts" went out on their own account day and night. It was touching to see the many friends of the wounded and sick bring to their comrades in hospital presents of green stuff—grass and weeds of all sorts! All were eagerly roped in, and they sat with pathetic contentment preparing for the pot the nourishment their bodies craved.

Our A.D.M.S., indefatigable as ever, convened a committee of those most likely to know to examine every green thing that grew, so that things that were poisonous might be readily spotted and avoided. But very few had to be picked out, and the vast majority were boiled up and served as a spinach! It was exceedingly nasty, for we all ate it, but it saved the situation. In a very few days the number of scurvy cases began sensibly to decline, and in a few more its defeat was assured. The vegetable garden, so carefully tended by poor Cotton of the Nth Punjabis, began to justify its existence, and considerable supplies of radish and other "tops" found their way to the hospitals and helped on the good work. To ensure the regular watering of the tender young plants, our gardener-in-chief had a well dug behind the wall which protected his garden from the snipers on the other side of the river, and so he was able to produce a decent crop.

On the 17th the airmen dropped us some saccharine, which was a great boon to those who had a sweet tooth. For a week or two also, hereabouts, we got an issue of 1½ oz. of bacon and ½ oz. of butter. It was just a flash in the pan. The S. and T. had taken stock of their last reserves and given us a treat. But on the 19th our barley-bread was down to half a pound, and the jam gave out.

The Turks gave us no rest from their hates, and on the 18th there occurred a shocking accident. After a bad "shelling" their aeroplanes came over, and a bomb dropped plumb in the middle of the British Hospital in the upper part of the Bazar.

Owing to lack of ward room, the fairway of the Bazar road itself was used as a large ward, and there were two rows of beds down the middle. At the time of the accident there were several men in visiting their chums in hospital, so that there were a good many present in a small area. As ill-luck would have it, the bomb came through the roof and landed on the side wall of the Bazar, with the result that it burst before reaching the ground and sent a shower of wicked metal over the devoted sick beneath. Three or four poor fellows were killed on the spot and thirty others injured; of these, a dozen died within the next two days. The place was a shambles.

The wretched victims lay about in all directions amongst the bricks and dust and blood. A couple of doctors were in the hospital at the time, and within five or ten minutes half the rest of us were on the spot.

It was a sad party that staggered home in the small hours of the next morning and sat down to a cold dinner—Trixie and I and the "wet bob." We hated all war and turned in cursing the Kaiser.

The next night we had another and most unpleasant surprise. Through the haze of a troubled sleep I became conscious of a distant buzzing. It sounded like an engine; but thinking I had dreamt it, I turned over to woo the fickle goddess once more. But No! the buzzing grew louder and I more wakeful. A quarter after midnight! Surely it can't . . . but, by God! it is that infernal Fritz taking a moonlight ride. After yesterday's experience I knew what that meant, so went up on our little roof to see the terror that flew by night. Louder and louder, nearer and nearer, straight for us came that abominable machine.

With field-glasses I sought to catch sight of it, but, despite the bright moonlight, I could not pick it up.

Nearer still, it seemed as though it must hit us, so low did it appear to be flying. The calm night air vibrated with the throbbing menace, and then . . . *Swish!* we were for it. Unconsciously I crouched against the little mud wall,—a mighty bang, and a flash of yellow flame— missed me by fifty yards! *Sw-i-s-h, bang!* another behind us. Thank God it's gone by! *Bang! bang! bang!* through the sleeping town. Plague take it! what next? . . . Now he was turning, and the throb of the engine grew louder again as he passed by on his return journey. Would he pay us another visit, or leave us to sleep? It was plucky of him, we admitted, to fly by night, but a poor game to bomb a sleeping town. The object, of course, was to wear us out. A little judicious bombing at night would, they doubtless argued, add considerably to the effects of starvation and frequent bombardments on the morale of the garrison, for "*qui dort dine.*" But we consigned him to h—ll and turned in again.

The 21st was worse than ever. The planes bombed us in the small hours, and the guns began at dawn. They sent along over 1000 shells that day; but casualties were not numerous, and only a few fell in the hospitals. The next night was again bad and forced us to bed down in our "black hole."

In the middle of it all an excited voice shouted down into the dug-out, "Is a doctor there?"

"Why, yes," we say.

"What's wrong?"

"Morton's hit by a shell."

Good Lord! it is but an hour since we walked home together after "taking food" with Dashwood's lot. Trixie hurried out, and we others followed, prepared for more work. The Turks had got their own back at last, and landed a shell straight in Morton's den; for he was a gunner of no mean parts, and had given them many a bad five minutes. Now it was their turn, and they got him in the foot. His room was full of bricks and dust and fumes, but Trixie soon fixed him up and moved him to hospital.

The following days were equally vile. Abdul seemed determined to frighten us into submission, but I think he was finding it a costly method.

As for me, I got a cable from Home: all was well, so the world was looking rosier. There was firing, too, down below, and a report went round that the R.F. had taken Hanna. This was a bit premature, but it kept us on the *qui vive* and showed us they were trying again.

CHAPTER 13

March 26th to April 11th

The river went on rising during the last days of March, until it reached and passed the record. It came over the banks and washed against the outer walls of the lower Bazar. Looking round the corner of the barricade of earth-filled oil-tins near the old coffee shop, which was by this time a hopeless ruin, one gazed on a swirling, muddy torrent. Over on the other side, "Woolpress" village just kept its head above water. It seemed to be standing up to its neck in a great lake, so that the inhabitants looked quite marooned and liable to be washed away at any moment. But they had a much better time than we and were scarcely ever shelled. Their only link with us was our little warship, the quondam tug *Shutan*, which on most nights steamed across to them with provisions, discharged patients, and so forth, running the gauntlet of snipers, and returning with sick men.

By day she was moored to the bank below the Rajputs—a perpetual target for the Turkish guns. Now and then they hit her, smashing her bridge or holing her funnel; but she was ever undaunted, and continued to do her job cheerily and efficiently to the bitter end.

As the waters rose, our hopes declined. We pictured to ourselves the state of the country down below, and knew it must seriously, if not fatally, delay matters. A few more inches and the whole country would be inundated; nothing would be seen above the surface save the little group of sand-hills. Surely the legend of the Flood had its origin in this country of the great rivers, and a sand mound was its Ararat!

For many days after the bomb dropped in the hospital we were busily engaged in building partition walls of mud and brick at intervals in the fairway of the Bazar, so as to split it up into very small areas, which would serve to limit the damage should another plane make a mistake and hit us again. Of course, it didn't, as a natural consequence, and the sort of maze that was thus constructed increased the cheerlessness of the place.

One day we were startled to hear that "salt" had given out, and we doctors of a physiological turn of mind were very uneasy. It wasn't quite true, most fortunately, but there was nothing left except horribly dirty stuff that had been obtained from the Arabs, and we had to be content with a few grains each. Some, too, of the remaining stock of barley was found to be unfit for food—it had to be very very bad to be condemned—so the Indian ration was cut down to 10 oz., little enough to keep body and soul together if you have nothing else!

A good deal of amusement was caused about this time by the practice of "swopping" comestibles that came into vogue. The sweet tooth, for instance, who was the happy possessor of a few ounces of alcohol, would advertise the fact with a view to bargaining with him who was willing to give up his last tin of jam, small packet of macaroni, or bit of butter. Relative values changed enormously. Nothing could be bought for cash. The only basis was physiological need. The bargaining was often excruciatingly comic and revealed business instincts in the most unsuspected quarters. I made desperate efforts to "swop" a last bottle of whisky for jam or marmalade, but it was not to be had, and the "craythur" finally went in exchange for tinned milk, two or three tins of which somebody still hung on to.

We were getting very hungry, and belts had to be taken in; the fat kine developed graceful figures, and the lean ones looked more finely-drawn. News came through the general's letters that people at Home were getting interested in us, but we'd got beyond caring much whether they did or not; our thoughts were all on Gorringe and his fight with the floods.

Just before the end of the month we lost poor Lambert, and also another good man who died very suddenly of intestinal trouble. The former had had three long months of illness, and until a few days before his death we hoped he would pull through, but he did not, and joined the great majority. He'd had no fun out of the siege, though his spirit was ever keen and full of hope for the future. The loss of a good friend at such a time touches one up, and I wanted to speak to none that day. As the curtain came down on March, the flying men dropped a bag of letters into the river! It was maddening! Each thought that there might have been one for him, and groused accordingly, though probably there were but a few for the staff only.

The next day, conscious of its designation, brought with it a violent thunderstorm and unlimited rain. The very elements seemed to have conspired against us, and to wish to destroy all chance of our relief. The place was soaking. But the Turks managed to move about a bit, and there was more firing below. How they got their camels to keep going on the slippery road was more than astonishing, but long strings of them were often seen moving slowly "over the face of the waters," so to speak. In the morning there was another sad auction, and prices were high. A box of cigarettes fetched 100 *rupees*, and many other things went for large sums.

In the afternoon the doctors held a Scientific Medical Meeting. They thought it a pity not to make a collective clinical study of the diseases which the peculiar conditions of the siege had brought about. Although it rained, most of us turned up, and our interest in the "exhibits" caused us to forget for a time our surroundings and did us all a lot of good. We moved from hospital to hospital and engaged in impromptu discussions on the features of interest that were pointed out by those in charge of the cases.

April 3rd.—"Felt seedy and slack," so the diary relates, but we had an idea that things were moving down below. "Turks seen dragging two big guns down to Ess Sinn." They mean to do their damnedest to stop Gorringe! Also, a deluge of hail, with lots of stones an inch in diameter. It was well to get under shelter, for they hurt! Today the score is 121, so we have beaten Ladysmith.

Yesterday the three heroes of that siege met together and had a dinner to commemorate their relief on that occasion. Their menu, set in a suitable design, ran something like this—

POTAGE AUX OS DE CHEVAL.

SAUTERELLES SAUTÉS.

STARLINGS EN CANAPÉ.

FILET DE MULE.

ENTRECOTE DE CHAMEAU.

ROGNONS DE CHEVAL À LA DIABLE.

PAIN.

On the 4th, starting at daybreak, they shelled us a good deal, and two officers were knocked out. They probably did it to induce us to keep quiet whilst the rest of them went off to meet the R.F.

The morrow was a great day. We awoke to the sound of a terrific "*grondement*" of the guns down below—the most intense we had yet heard—a continuous roar, that sounded as if they meant business this time. It was still dark, and from the roofs we could see hundreds of "flashes" vivid and quivering in the dark grey of the early morning. As day broke one saw heads on all the roofs, eagerly watching the signs of struggle fifteen miles away. "Harold," whilst doing so, was nearly blown off by a "*whizz-bang*," but fortunately just escaped.

At 8.30 Gorringe sent up to say he had taken five lines of trenches at Hanna! "Good enough," we thought, and all was merry and bright. As evening came on there was more firing, and we rested our arms on the housetop walls and gazed and gazed through our glasses till our eyes ached. The "flashes" seemed no nearer, worse luck! We worried the enemy over against Megasis Fort with our 5-inchers and waited for the morrow. We talked again of getting some leave, of getting out of this godless country for a bit to India's coral strand, and of having a holiday in some nice safe place!

But as if to try our nerves and tempers to the utmost, no news came along for nearly two days, and we began to dread another disappointment, for the sound of the guns grew no nearer. We walked about restless and irritable, unable to sit still, and feverish with the intolerable suspense.

Kut was quiet, save for desultory sniping, and wore an air of desolation and ruin. The gaunt spectre of famine was making itself felt. I walked, to see Gasbard, by the A short cut through the lower Bazar, where they were pulling down the gabled roof for the sake of its wood, past the Engineers' shops, where nothing was doing, and then I came upon the flour-mill. It was still. The wheels that had so faithfully revolved, the belts that had flapped round them for weeks without a rest, had ceased to move for want of food. I peeped in, but all was silent and deserted. I almost feared to disturb its sleep. But the mill was dead. The darkening shed was chill and uncanny, like a sepulchre. Like everything else, it had the air of having finished. It had done its job, and now its heart had stopped!

Nearby, in the little mud yard, grew two tall palms. They were holy palms. Tin labels fixed to the trunks testified to the fact. They were sacred and spoke of an eternity. Rearing their feathered heads in silence high above the squalor of the deserted hovels beneath, they seemed to point the way to better things and to pity the sadness and brevity of human life. I pursued my way in a chastened mood, and soon gained the roof to do more gazing.

The afternoon of the second day we heard that Gorringe had taken Abu Roman, and had wired that all was well—"advance continues." But two more days of sickening uncertainty followed, and the General let us know that he thought it best to reduce the Indian ration to 7 oz. of meal until he got good news! The news was not long in coming, but it was not good; for on the 10th Townshend issued another *communiqué*, and our suspense at least was ended. Here it is:—

The result of the attack of the Relief Force on the Turks entrenched in the Sanaaiyat position is that the Relief Force has not yet won its way through, but is entrenched close up to the Turks; in places, some 200 to 300 yards distant. General Gorringe wired me last night he was consolidating his position as close to the enemy's trenches as he can get, with the intention of attacking again. He had had some difficulty with the floods, which he had remedied. I have no other details.

However, you will see that I must not run any risk over the date calculated to which our rations would last, namely, 15th April, as you all understand well that digging means delay, though General Gorringe does not say so. I am compelled, therefore, to appeal to you all to make a determined effort to eke out our scanty means, so that I can hold out for certain till our comrades arrive, and I know I shall not appeal to you in vain. I have

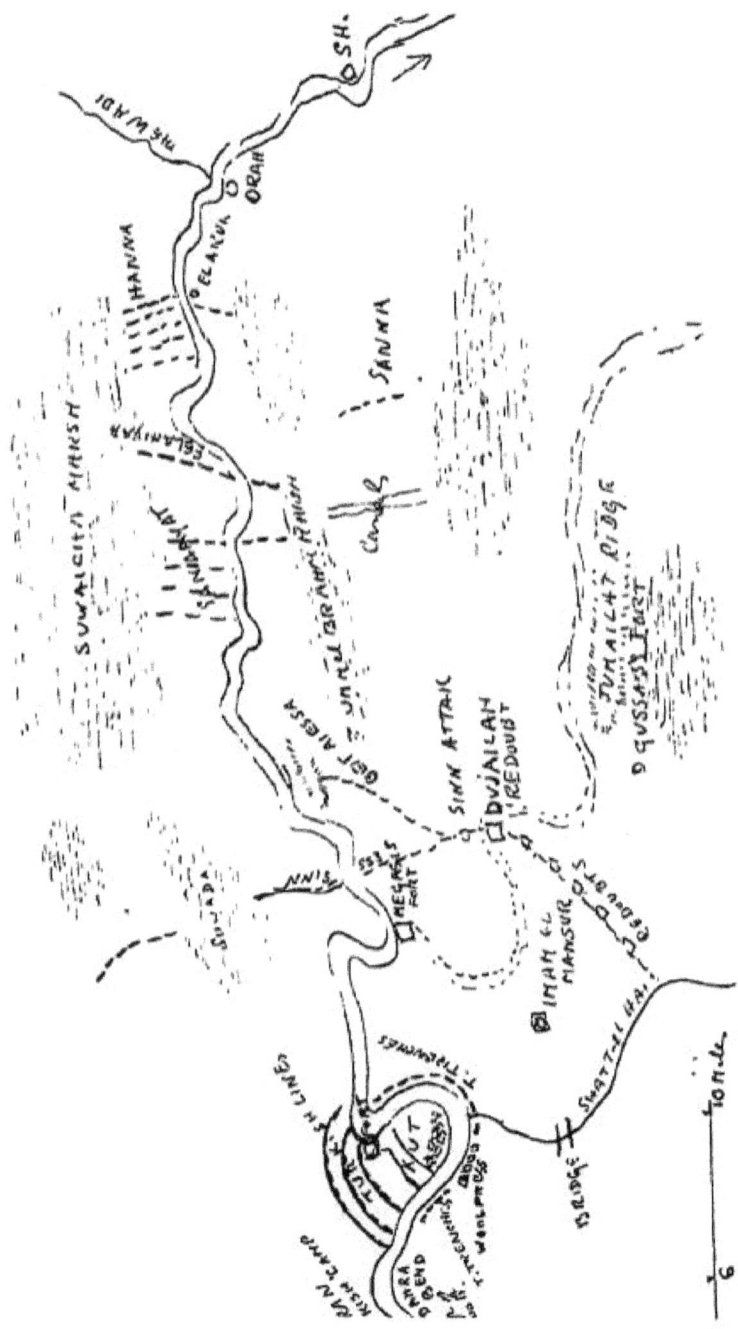

THE TIGRIS NEAR KUT, SHOWING THE POSITIONS OF THE TURKS AND THE RELIEVING FORCE

then to reduce your rations to 5 ounces of meal for all ranks, British and Indian.

In this way I can hold out till the 21st of April if it become necessary. I do not think it will become necessary, but it is my duty to take all the precautions in my power. I am very sorry I can no longer favour the Indian soldiers in the matter of meal, but there is no possibility of doing so now. It must be remembered that there is plenty of horse-flesh, which they have been authorised by their religious leaders to eat, and I have to recall with sorrow that by not having taken advantage of this wise and just dispensation, they have weakened my power of resistance. . . .

In my *communiqué* to you of 26th January I told you that our duty stood out plain and simple: it was to stand here and hold up the Turkish advance on the Tigris, working heart and soul together, and I expressed the hope that we would make this defence to be remembered in history as a glorious one, and I asked you in this connection to remember the defence of Plevna, which was longer even than that of Ladysmith. Well, you have nobly carried out your mission; you have nobly answered the trust and appeal I put to you. The whole British Empire, let me tell you, is ringing now with our defence of Kut. You will all be proud to say one day, 'I was one of the garrison at Kut' And as for Plevna and Ladysmith, we have outlasted them also. Whatever happens now we have all done our duty. As I said in my report of the defence of this place, which has now been telegraphed to Headquarters, it was not possible in despatches to mention everyone, but I could safely say that every individual in this Force has done his duty to his King and country. I was absolutely calm and confident, as I told you on the 26th January, of the ultimate result, and I am confident now. I ask you all, comrades of all ranks, British and Indian, to help me now in this food question, as I ask you above.

The next day we were given another *communiqué*—a short one:

The army commander wired to me yesterday evening to say 'there can be no doubt that Gorringe can in time force his way through to Kut; in consequence of yesterday's failure, however, it is certainly doubtful if he can reach you by April 15.' . . .

So, we tightened our belts again with a grin, and sat down to go on with it, for the idea of giving in to the Turk was unthinkable.

CHAPTER 14
The Fall of Kut

The last phase! It couldn't be a long one, we knew, but we still had great faith in our comrades down below and had no thought of giving in before every ounce of our stuff had been consumed.

The idea of having to open our gates to the enemy made one furious, and one resolutely put aside the possibility of becoming prisoner for yet another week or more. Nobody grumbled, save at unkind Fate, and large numbers of the Indians at last took to eating the meat. Poor devils! they were desperately hungry and were glad of anything they could get. Though we jested and joked and made light of each other's vanishing figure, yet it was a time of misery—a long-drawn-out agony of suspense and disappointment, and of not a little suffering. There was no lack of incident: the slaughter down below, the herculean efforts our people were making to relieve us, and their attempts to feed us; the effects of starvation on the garrison, the unrest amongst the Arabs—all combined to make it a time to be remembered and deplored.

General Hoghton lay dying. He could not eat the horse meat and became a shadow of his former robust self. He was one of the first victims of an acute intestinal trouble that was fatal to so many in those last three weeks. He died on the 13th and was buried the same day. All who could do so attended his funeral to bid farewell to a good man and to mourn his loss. A military funeral is always impressive, but under those conditions it was doubly so. Silent and sorrowful we stood around and listened to the well-known service recited in the *padre's* solemn tones. They ceased—a brief pause, and then the bugles took up the refrain, and clear and mournful rang out those wonderful notes of the "Last Post." Were they prophetic, we wondered, of the fate of Kut? . . .

The weather grew cold again; the wind blew from the north east and brought with it a perfect hurricane and yet more rain, but the R.F. stuck to it in a wonderful way, and we constantly heard their guns at work and saw their flashes at night, though the 15th came and they seemed no nearer. They wired to say they were going to feed us by aeroplane and to drop us 5000 lb. a day. It was about time; we were down to 4 oz. of bread now: coarse, damp stuff, made of half-ground barley meal with a plentiful flavouring of sand; and we had issued to us the last two days' emergency rations, which were to be kept until further orders. It was said that our people down below wired up suggesting that we should search the town for food! It was a brilliant idea but was a few weeks behind the times.

On the 16th April they made several trips and dropped us a good many sacks—two at a time. We felt as Elijah must have done when he had to depend on the ravens. But it takes a lot of aeroplanes to feed 15,000 to 20,000 people. Had they started a month before it would have made some appreciable difference. As it was, it only enabled us to hang on for another couple of days or so. Watching food dropping became a popular amusement, especially amongst our Indian patients. A plane would be heard approaching; spectators would rush out and stand gaping, laughing, and chattering about it like children. "*Dekko! Dekko! abhi girega! Nahin, Nahin! itna nazdik nahin hai. Abhi dekko! Aah! giradya*" ("he's made it fall"). A wee speck could be seen leaving the "bus"; over and over it turned, larger and larger—generally two of them—faster and faster, till it whizzed down behind a house, and one imagined the "*wump!*" with which it landed.

They always put one sack inside another and larger one, so that when the inside one burst the outer one prevented the scattering of the precious flour. Now and then they dropped a load into the river or into the Turkish lines, where they were doubtless thankful for some extra rations. It generally seemed to be the sailor-men who did this. Perhaps with the larger vision one acquires at sea, it was difficult to see so small a bit of land as Kut. These "boss shots" gave occasion, at any rate—so it was said—for the sending of facetious messages over the wireless to them down below:

"Would H.M. Navy mind dropping *us* something now and then instead of to the Turks?" "Was the R.F. quite sure it was on the right river?" and so forth.

On the 17th we heard a great battle going on. Machine-gun and rifle fire was distinctly audible and we were mightily cheered. It was the fighting at Beit Aiessa, only six or seven miles away! In the middle of it all our men in the trenches started cheering, with the result that there was a wild stampede of Arabs "down our street." They thought the Turks were coming, but there was nothing to be seen, and goodness only knows what it was all about, unless our men thought they saw a body of Turks retreating. Our hopes that such was the case were soon dissipated, for they started shelling us again, so they were evidently not upset very much.

That same night there was more furious fighting over against Beit

Aiessa, where the Turks were counter attacking and losing so heavily. We heard afterwards that our people counted 1500 dead next morning.

In the morning of the 19th there was more heavy cannonading, but we didn't learn the result. The 20th came, and the army commander sent in a message, saying:

Stick to it, Gorringe will relieve you in a few days.

We stuck to it. The next day we heard that the Turks had lost very heavily and that the R.F. were consolidating their position! But our rations were almost at an end; the emergency ration had to be used on the morrow. We began to grow despondent. We were hungry and thin, and getting weaker. The steps up to the roof seemed to get larger, and one was often "blown" on reaching the top. Sapper Tomlin came in and said they were bored to tears. "There's nothing to do," he grumbled; "the men are too weak to work, so we're out of a job."

We ourselves had plenty to do, but the work was heart-breaking. The small stock of rice that had been set apart for the hospitals, with which we had been feeding those who couldn't eat solid food, was used up, and the milk was reduced to a bottle or two. Some of the patients were woefully thin; and when an Indian gets thin he is an appalling object. Many died, chiefly from intestinal troubles; but we were helpless; it is useless to oil or stimulate a machine if you can't give it coal for its engines!

It made us long for the end——any end almost, for the sake of the miserable sick. In any event another week would settle it.

We talked of "menus" often, in the manner peculiar to starving people, and of what we would first have to eat when we were free again; where we would go for leave, and how luxuriously lazy we would be for the first few days. Our bread came to us in 8-oz. loaves for two people. So fearful were we of not getting our full half that it became an invariable rule that one cut the loaf and the other chose his half. This method ensures the maximum amount of care and accuracy on the part of the cutter.

On the night of the 21st a party of Arabs deserted the town and got away across the river. The rats were beginning to leave the sinking ship! The Turks let us know that they would not receive any more but would shoot them if they tried it. But, although the Arabs were told that if they left the town they wouldn't be allowed in again, they persisted in their attempts. The next day a large group of them was very busy for hours in the open street making a large raft out of wooden settees and inflated skins wherewith to cross the stream. But they didn't succeed, for the Turks were as good as their word, with the result that there were several in hospital next morning.

On the 22nd there was a heavy cannonade in the morning, and we could see the bursts of H.E. over a long line of a mile or more; but the result was another disappointment, for the next day we got a *communiqué* to say that the R.F. had not taken Sanaaiyat but had advanced a little on the right bank. As a set-off the aeroplanes made fourteen or fifteen trips and dropped food.

It was Easter Sunday, and Trixie and I went to church in the morning. The two little rooms, still intact, were crowded with officers. Why had so many come that day? Was it to share in the joyous festival of Easter, of the resurrection of the God-man, or was it the growing fear in our hearts that the service would be the last of its kind in Kut, and that the future was so full of uncertainty?

Be that as it may, there was a very good attendance, and after the morning service the Communion was held. One by one, in a silence that could be felt, the gaunt and war-worn defenders, with the thoughtful eyes of those who had seen much, went up each in his turn and knelt before the *padre*. A deep hush fell over us all, and in those few moments men got near to their God. . . .

On the 24th a quiver of excitement went through us when we got wind of the impending attempt of the R.F. to run the blockade that night by a boat full of food. We could hardly sleep for thinking about it and were up on the H.Q. roof as the sun rose. There she was, the gallant *Julnar*, over against Megasis Fort, stuck in the mud just within range of our longest guns, with her splendid captain on her bridge lying dead in a pool of his own blood. So pleased were the Turks—so one of their officers who was there told me afterwards—with the gallant bravery of poor Cowley and the other man with him on the *Julnar*, that they, then and there, gave them a special military funeral in recognition of their magnificent effort, which so nearly succeeded. But the enemy had her, and her capture sealed our fate.

Deep down within us we knew we were now done for, that our people couldn't get through, and that for us it meant Baghdad, or Mosul, or God only knew where! We did not acknowledge it yet, however, and that day another auction was held, at which prices ruled higher than ever: a box of cheroots fetched 206 *rupees*, and a tin of fifty Wills' cigarettes were sold for over £3—surely the biggest money ever paid for "Three Castles"!

That night, after leaving us almost alone for a day or two, the Turks gave us a bad "*strafeing*," and followed it up by an evening hate next day and another night bombardment, much to the discomfort of a Turkish envoy who stayed the night in the town. They also accounted for at least one of the aeroplanes of the R.F. that had been working very hard at our food supply, but now got interfered with by the Fokkers, that had the wings of them.

On the 23rd and 24th we had eaten our first day's emergency ration split into two; on the 25th and 26th we fed on the aeroplane supply, and on the 27th we broached half of our last day's reserve ration.

On the 26th we heard that negotiations were in progress, that all was about to be over, and the next morning the general went to interview the Turk. It was unthinkable that the old flag would have to come down, and we were heartbroken about it. After the many disappointments and the awful suspense, we had passed through, the final blow seemed almost too much. One had thought during those last few days that almost any ending would be preferable to the intolerable uncertainty, that any settlement would be a relief to the mental tension, but it was not so; when the end came the disappointment was too great—it overshadowed everything else.

The town was quiet, the guns and the sniping ceased; the silence was uncanny! The Arabs came out of their houses in large numbers and hung about, talking in groups. There was no disturbance: guards of British Tommies had been placed at different points to prevent it. We wandered about listlessly or sat in our courtyard and guessed at the terms we should get.

Would they take us all prisoners, or would they let us go on parole? Would the Geneva Convention hold, and the doctors go down with the sick, or would they be exchanged? These and a hundred other questions remained unanswered whilst the hours dragged slowly by, I met the general with his staff returning from the interview. He looked fairly well and carried his head high. He had done all that man could do and had no cause to be ashamed—but what a disappointment after five months of gallant resistance! General Melliss, too, felt it most acutely: he had been ill for some days, and I shall not easily forget the signs of suffering I read on his weather-beaten face; the surrender seared his very soul.

The next day, the 28th, we destroyed things. Guns were blown up, and bits of them were flying about in a most dangerous way; rifles were smashed up, waggons were burnt; ammunition was dumped into the river at night; field-glasses, swords, and pistols were broken and thrown away. Some day in the future, when those Arabs dig up their cess-pits or clean out their wells, they'll find many a bit of rusty old iron of suggestive shape; maybe their drinking-water will develop tonic properties and improve the village health—who knows?

Finally, Townshend issued his last characteristically optimistic *communiqué*, and prepared us for the morrow's surrender. It was all over; the unbelievable had happened: Kut had fallen! Thus Townshend, on the 28th:—

It became clear, after General Gorringe's second repulse on 22nd April at Sanaaiyat, of which I was informed by the army commander by wire, that the Relief Force could not win its way through in anything like time to relieve us, our limit of resistance as regards food being the 29th April....

I was then ordered to open negotiations for the surrender of Kut; in the words of the army commander's telegram, 'the onus not lying on yourself. You are in a position of having conducted a gallant and successful defence, and you will be in a position to get better terms than any emissary of ours.... The admiral, who has been in consultation with the army commander, considers that you, with your prestige, are likely to get the best terms; we can, of course, supply food as you may arrange.'

These considerations alone, namely, that I can help my comrades of all ranks to the end, have decided me to overcome my bodily illness and the anguish of mind which I am suffering now, and I have interviewed the Turkish general-in-chief yesterday, who is full of admiration at 'an heroic defence of five months,' as he puts it.

Negotiations are still in progress, but I hope to be able to announce your departure for India, on parole not to serve against the Turks, since the Turkish commander says he thinks it will be allowed, and has wired to Constantinople to ask for this, and that the *Julnar*, which is lying with food for us at Megasis, now may be permitted to come to us. Whatever has happened, my comrades, you can only be proud of yourselves. We have done our duty to King and Empire; the whole world knows we have done our duty.

I ask you to stand by me with your ready and splendid discipline, shown throughout, in the next few days for the expedition of all service I demand of you. We may possibly go into camp, I hope, between the fort and town along the shore, whence we can easily embark.

The following message has been received from the army commander: 'The C.-in-C. has desired me to convey to you and your brave and devoted troops his appreciation of the manner in which you together have undergone the suffering and hardships of the siege, which he knows has been due to the high spirit of devotion to duty in which you have met the call of your Sovereign and Empire. The C.-in-C.'s sentiments are shared by myself, General Gorringe, and all the troops of the Tigris Column. We can only express extreme disappointment and regret our effort to relieve you should not have been crowned with success.'

Copy of a telegram from Captain Nunn, C.M.G., R.N.

We, the officers and men of the Royal Navy who have been associated with the Tigris Corps, and many of us so often worked with you and your gallant troops, desire to express our heartfelt regret at our inability to join hands with you and your comrades in Kut.

And so, with a farewell from our friends below, we went into captivity.

CHAPTER 15

In Kut After the Surrender

The 29th of April 1916—the surrender was an accomplished fact. Going to hospital early that morning, I saw nothing of the "taking over" or of the Division marching out, but I walked on to the river bank for a few minutes, where there were signs of the new state of things. A motor-launch flying a white flag was spudding across to Woolpress; a Turkish barge was working its way down by the bank, and the few Turks aboard her were throwing service biscuits to the very few Arab *gamins* and loafers whose curiosity had brought them forth. For five solid months that bank had been a no man's land, and it was strange now to be walking about it without being shot at—one felt naked and unsafe. I couldn't trust myself to go towards the *serai* to see what had happened to the "flag," and I never knew when it came down—imagining it was more than enough. My first intimation of the change of ownership of the town was when, returning to my quarters, I found Turkish soldiers patrolling the streets. They had just come in, and I was astonished to find things quiet and orderly.

On the threshold of the mess I was met by an excited servant. "Master, come quickly, there are enemy soldiers in your room stealing your things!" I ran up to an upper room, where the day before I had been looking through my kit, and found there three ragged, bronzed, and hefty Turks disporting themselves amongst my wardrobe, and bashing open my boxes with the butt-end of their muskets. I proceeded to expostulate in every language I knew other than English, but they merely stared. Doing so they noticed my revolver, which I was unfortunately still wearing. One fellow promptly seized it and pulled. My protests only irritated him, and he pulled and wrenched the more, whilst his nearest comrade closed up with an ugly-looking bayonet, so I came to the conclusion that the Geneva Convention was just then a broken reed and withdrew my objections and went outside to see if I could find someone in authority.

This I did by chance at the gate and explained the matter with some heat to a Turkish officer who was passing by. He said that all arms had to be given up, doctors' and all, but took my name and the pistol, and promised to have it returned to me if it could be allowed. Of course, I heard no more about it. However, he moved on my "looters," and we proceeded to put what remained to us in as safe a place as possible; but more things disappeared. All day long and at night the Turks wandered in to see what they could pick up. They were not offensive in any way, but just walked in and turned over anything they came across, and if they fancied it, took it. As we had to stay behind alone amongst the new masters of Kut, this sort of thing became a nuisance; but after two or three efforts, we got them to put a sentry at the door of the "*hakims*'" dwelling, and we had no more trouble.

Returning to hospital, I found very considerable looting going on. The Osmanlis were sauntering through the Bazar looting blankets, boots, *puttees*, and anything else of a useful nature, from the miserable patients. Looking at them, one didn't wonder. Their uniforms were ragged and patched in all directions, their boots were worn beyond hope of repair, and they were generally most disreputable-looking specimens of a modern army. But they were good-natured-looking fellows—broad, strong as oxen, with plenty of bone, ruddy complexions, and in many cases blue eyes and ginger whiskers. They looked what they were, I suppose, just easy-going, illiterate Anatolian peasantry; but get them really annoyed, and they are very rough customers, and would, I should say, stick at nothing.

After a good deal of trouble and of worrying a *jeune* Turk who was in charge of our "quarter," we got them to place sentries at most of the openings into the hospitals, and matters improved considerably. The difficulty thereafter was to prevent our men fraternising with the enemy and selling to him for any sort of pittance such things as they still possessed.

The next thing was a meeting of the respective medical chiefs of the two forces to decide upon rations and the treatment of the sick and wounded. I had the good fortune to be present at this interesting conference. We were taken on board a big river steamer of theirs which had just come down from Shamran, one of those we had so often espied from the roof. With great show of politeness our chief and the rest of us were led on to the upper deck and introduced to the *médecin-en-chef* and his entourage. Coffee was brought and cigarettes were handed round. Then they got to business. "Strengths" were noted, questions asked regarding numbers of sick and kinds of diseases, and arrangements were made for Turkish medical officers to visit our hospitals, and, together with our own officers, to examine and pick out all the most seriously sick and wounded. These it had been arranged were to be sent down the river in exchange for Turkish prisoners.

Before leaving, we chatted with the Turks for a few minutes: they deplored the war and the suffering it entailed and spoke of the humanitarian nature of our profession which enabled us to meet on common ground. They referred to the gallant effort of the *Julnar* to get through to us and expressed the greatest admiration for the officers and crew who manned her.

By this time the aspect of Kut had changed—the town appeared to be *en fête*, Every other Arab house flaunted a red or red-and-white flag, even as some months before they had put up their white one for us to show their respect and friendliness for the conqueror. The streets were thronged with Arabs and Turks, apart from those on duty, wandering about inspecting the village and doubtless noting the ruin their shells had caused. Mounted patrols of Arab cavalry, looking as though cut out of a picture story, covered with pistols and extraordinary trappings, rode through from time to time and added to the picturesqueness of the scene and to the disorganisation of hospital life. The sight of these cut-throats seemed to rub in the indignity of being a prisoner, and one cursed one's fate.

The next morning the promised rations did not turn up; it was not until late in the afternoon that we got hold of them and were able to feed our famishing patients. After that we got them regularly. During the day the *Firefly* came down and moored alongside the bank. Painted up by the Turks and as clean as a new pin, she looked very smart and English, though she no longer flew the white ensign. The Turkish sailors looked very natty in their white duck trimmed with red and blue, and they moved about nimbly enough.

As I stood there looking on, all eyes turned shoreward, and following their gaze I saw the Turkish *generalissimo* approaching with his staff, and with him General Delamain and two or three staff officers. With set face and self-conscious mien Khalil Pasha walked aboard followed by Delamain, and up the little companion to the bridge deck, where they seated themselves in chairs placed for the purpose. He gave a short, curt order, and the sailors immediately cast off and headed upstream. So, with honour, a British general passed into captivity, but it was not good to see him go. Khalil Pasha is young and handsome, well made, of average height—an open face with fresh complexion and deep-set brown eyes, and a well chiselled chin—he did not look more than thirty-three years of age, and his movements were quick and purposeful.

The next few days we were busy showing our cases to the Turkish M.O.'s, explaining briefly their trouble and condition, whereupon the Turk would examine them and decide their fate. It was pathetic to watch the anxiety of some of the lads, as they watched the deliberations and awaited the verdict that should decide their fate.

The work was strenuous, for the weather was hot, and we were glad to get out on the river bank in the evenings. Kut from the river presented a sorry sight; the *serai* was half down, the S. and T. *go-down* beyond it a wreck. The old coffee-shop was a ruined mass of brick, and the lower Bazar and the rest of the Front showed numerous holes. Within a couple of days, the Turks were pulling down what was left of the portion nearest the river. Further signs of the Turkish occupation, of a more gruesome character, were also very soon in evidence. Three rough wooden tripods about eight feet high were erected on the most open portion of the bank, and on these they hanged various delinquents whom they suspected of helping their enemies.

The wretched Sassoon, who had been of such great assistance to our S. and T. Corps, was one of these. Just before the fall of Kut he had gone into hiding, but his hiding-place was betrayed to the Turks, who chased him from it and finally caught him on a roof. Here they beat him unmercifully, and then took him out and hanged him. Their method is a simple one—they just string them up and let them dangle with their toes an inch or two above the ground. Several batches of other poor wretches were also shot with their backs to the wall. I came across five in a row one morning, lying in all sorts of positions, and saw another batch of a dozen being led off to a place of execution. They had gambled and lost!

On the 1st of May a river hospital ship came up from the R.F. with a medical staff on board. The presence of the staff dashed our own hopes of taking the sick down, but otherwise we were more than pleased to see them, and to shout a message or two for them to send home. They brought up with them a barge full of food stores, which were taken up to Shamran, a few miles up the river, where our troops were encamped, the barge returning in the evening. We in Kut had been left out of the calculation and got nothing, but Trixie and I managed to get as much as we could carry from our friends on the boat.

We were strolling along having a look at the hospital ship, from approaching which we were debarred by sentries, when a *medico* on the barge hailed us with the words, "Could you do with some jam? Do you want any baccy?" *Could we do with some jam?*—they didn't seem to realise that we'd had none of either for weeks! Anyhow, a good-natured sentry saw what was toward, and allowed us to get near enough to catch the precious tins, and even to take a half-filled case of "bubbly." He summoned also an orderly to help us carry the swag, so we sent him a present of a bottle and all was well. We were popular members of the mess that night—and how good that champagne was!

Our little mess had swollen to double its size, for the colonel and B. M. and Hepaton had joined the chummery for company's sake, and Booth of the R.E. also became an Honorary Member. He was staying behind with a burying party to perform a necessary though gruesome task, and he made himself very useful as a foraging officer. To the tinned milk, jam, and champagne he added a leg of mutton, so "all merrie."

In the afternoons, on two or three occasions, Turkish officers paid us visits of ceremony. We took tea and smoked cigarettes together. One of them, an Arab, had escaped from Amara after our occupation of that town, and laughed with great enjoyment as he recounted his method of fooling, in the disguise of a native, the political officer of the moment. Another was one Haider Ali, who, brought up in America, seemed to like to "buk" with us in English. He was, of course, much in demand as an envoy between the two armies and as an interpreter. He also censored the few letters that came through from below, and also took some of ours and promised to have them sent down the river to our people.

Emin Bey, the *commandant*—a thoughtful, capable-looking man of forty or thereabouts—was courteous and reasonable enough in his treatment of us. From time to time, if he thought we wanted too much, he would tell us a long story of his unfortunate experiences amongst the Russians; how that, on the outbreak of war, he was with a military mission in the Caucasus, and a guest of the *Czar*, but thereafter was treated with very scant ceremony and put to much inconvenience before he got home again.

"I," he would say, "treat you much better than that, and you are prisoners of war!"

The sifting of the sick and wounded went on steadily and kept us busy getting them ready to embark. Each evening the hospital ship went down with a load; each morning she returned for another. Every man, before he was allowed on board, was searched; and everything of value save his money, if he had any, was taken away from him. None of us was allowed to speak to the British doctors on the ship, nor to board her. It was a galling thing to be standing on shore within a yard or two of one's friends of the R.F., and not to be able to talk to them; for there were a thousand things we were dying to ask and to learn from them. Abdul Kadir, the Turkish medical factotum, however, assured us that the M.O.'s still left in Kut—fourteen of us—would be exchanged and go down with the last boat-load. The negotiations, he said, were not quite complete; but it would be all right; and we believed him. We exulted in our luck, stifled our qualms, and counted the hours to our release.

One day we were informed that all our kit of any military value, which we as medicals had been allowed to keep and which we expected to take down with us, was to be given up "in exchange for a receipt by the Turkish Government." Tents, saddlery, pistols, field-glasses, surgical instruments, and our swords were piled together and handed over, but we got no receipt. How we wished we had smashed everything up, especially our swords! But it was too late, and they wolfed the lot. However, our eyes were on the "last boat," and on the evening of about the eighth day we were told to be ready to embark the next morning, and to have our kits ready on the bank by nine.

Needless to say, we were there in time, sitting on our boxes, eager to catch sight of the boat as she came round the bend. But an hour passed and no boat appeared.

The factotum got anxious and said he would send us down on a barge and proceeded to get one. Another hour passed, but just as our spirits had sunk about down to our boots the hospital ship appeared. No yacht ever looked so fair or liner so desirable; on she came, and our spirits rose to par again. She came in to the shore and tied up, and we prepared to go aboard, but, alas! we had not done with disappointment. Someone handed a note to Abdul Kadir, who turned to us with a white face:

> Our general at the front line has not received an answer about you from the British Headquarters. I am very sorry, but you will not be able to be exchanged at present but will have to go to Baghdad!

This was really a bolt from the blue, and it left us stunned. Life held no further bitterness for us; we had touched bed-rock of disappointment. Wearily we gathered our men together, once more shouldered our baggage, and, disconsolate, returned to our lodging.

CHAPTER 16

Voyage to Baghdad, May 1916

On May 9th we sailed for Baghdad on a finely-built river steamer called the *Khalifa*. Whilst I was strolling about waiting to embark, a good looking German sailor accosted me in very good English. He belonged to the *Goeben*, and was, he informed me, a petty officer, and in civil life an electrician in Hamburg.

"I'm sorry," he said, "to see your fellows going away into captivity. I don't suppose ten *per cent* of them will ever see their homes again." I asked him what he meant, and he answered with a shrug of his shoulders that they would have a bad time. "Our Germans who go to England as prisoners will, we know, be well cared for and will get back again, and so will your English who go to Germany, but those who go to the Turks—no, perhaps not so many as ten in a hundred will ever get back!"

This was not in any way cheering, but I thought he was exaggerating. Still, I wondered how much truth there was in his remarks; he had travelled down from Gallipoli and knew what the route was like and the Turkish manner of doing it. Many a time since I have thought of what he said, apparently in all sincerity, and I fear for the truth of his prophecy!

Only four or five of us, including pessimistic Horace and Lancelot, with certain of our hospital personnel, travelled by the *Khalifa*; the rest of the disappointed fourteen, with their men and all the sick and wounded who remained unexchanged in Kut, were put on board another ship. I believe it was the old *Julnar*, the upper deck of which was devoid of awning. This was a serious matter for them, for the sun was now fiercely hot after 10 a.m. So, we of the *Khalifa* scored heavily, for we had no sick on board, and took only four days to reach Baghdad, whereas the others on the *Julnar* had a bad time and took ten.

Moreover, our ship's doctor, Hassan Bey, made himself agreeable; and presently, as we were sitting about on our kit on the lower deck, the *commandant*, Emin, came along and inquired if accommodation had been provided for us. On our replying in the negative, he said he would clear the upper deck at once and make room. Within an hour or two this was done. A round dozen or so of German officers were removed to one end inside a railing, and the rest of the large roomy deck cleared of Arabs and other *impedimenta*.

Soon we were invited to come up and doss down where we liked. As we were doing so one of the Germans came across and politely suggested that we had chosen a bad place, and that we should be more comfortable on the other side, since we were likely to be crowded out by Arabs where we were. We thanked him and moved and were glad later on that we had done so. We spoke a few words with the Germans from time to time, though our relations were always marked by more reserve than cordiality, whereas with the Turks we were friendly enough. One of the Germans had been a business man in Baghdad for the past two or three years, and spoke appreciatively of the many Englishmen he had known, and mixed with there, during that time.

The Turkish *commandant* and his staff came on board and took up their quarters well forward on the same deck, and we then cast off and said goodbye to Kut. We hoped we should soon see it again on a return journey, for we had been given to understand that we should be exchanged before long.

At Shamran we stopped to take on board practically all the officers of the old VIth Division, or those that were left of them, and every square yard of deck was soon occupied.

There had been a big camp here, but the men had been marched on, save the sick, and those whom even the Turks considered unfit for the journey. They had revised the "unfit" list of our M.O.'s, and reduced them to a minimum, with the result that they had to carry hundreds up by boat from the first stage at Baghela. Going ashore at Shamran I came across the colonel, and "Mac" and Canning, and one or two more who were in charge of the sick there. They said a good many of our fellows had died, but that things were now improving. Living in the open, with plenty of food, had done wonders for them, and they were looking nearly well again. We got a few of their surplus stores and resumed our voyage. The journey to Baghdad was got through without incident, and comfortably enough, save that we were packed like sardines.

Each morning and evening, however, the C.O. agreed to tie up at the bank for half an hour or so, to give us an opportunity of stretching our legs, and of washing and bathing, which was a great boon. The country was as flat as ever, mostly desert, and desperately uninteresting. Here and there we passed an Arab village, the *denizens* of which would come out and gape at us, and cheer and extol the Turks with their haul of prisoners. Linked arm-in-arm, all the males of the place would run or dance in line, keeping pace with the ship, yelling or chanting a song of triumph, and blazing off any old muskets or pistols they happened to possess. But the Turks only smiled, called them "*canaille*," and shrugged their shoulders.

At Baghela we passed the other boat with the sick on board. She was tying up there to take on several hundreds of sick men of ours who had fallen out on the march up from Kut. We heard afterwards that she couldn't take them all, but she filled herself up to her utmost capacity, and we thanked our stars that we were not travelling in her, for the discomfort on board her was extreme, and several deaths occurred. There were so many delays, due to sand-banks and lack of fuel, that the food gave out, and altogether they all passed through a horrible ten days. About half-way to Baghdad we passed Azizieh, on the left bank, and those who had spent many hot weeks in that miserable mud village the October before shuddered at the remembrance of them.

The third day we passed Laj, and soon afterwards came in sight of the wonderful old arch of Ctesiphon, and the scene of the battle of six months before. We could see the famous arch for miles before we got there; it looked like a big brown haystack or an airship-shed in the distance but assumed noble proportions as we neared it. Ctesiphon, as everyone knows, was a great and magnificent city at one time under the Parthian kings, who made it their winter residence.

Under the early Sassanian monarchs, it was a place of great importance, but of course it was plundered by the Arabs in the seventh century. It arose after the decay of Seleucia, the great Greek capital, which was situated opposite it on the right bank.

The arch—which comprises the *façade* and the huge vaulted hall of a palace—is an enormous thing and gives one some idea of what must have been the glory of the city that could produce it. It measures, they say, over 120 feet high, 160 odd wide, and 180 long. Apart from this wonderful arch, there is little to suggest that here once flourished a great city—nothing but a few low mounds and a long wall (the "high wall" of the Battle of Ctesiphon), and the tomb nearby of Suleiman Pak. What remains looks horribly lonely and desolate—"*dust thou art, and unto dust shalt thou return*"; how literally true that seems in this country!

Soon after leaving Ctesiphon we passed the mouth of the Diala River, which joins the Tigris eight or nine miles from Baghdad, and on the banks of which the Turks had prepared a position to retire on after Ctesiphon, but never needed it. Beyond this the banks were lined with date-groves and gardens—we were approaching the magic city.

Presently we came to isolated riverside houses, and then more, until finally they were almost continuous—now a row of mean dwellings, now a more pretentious mansion.

At last a *vista* of good-looking villas, with upper stories overhanging the river, nestling in their gardens of palms, orange, vine, and fig trees, lining both banks, with the broad smooth river between, opened out before us; minarets and domes we could see reflecting the morning sunshine. The prospect was a pleasing one, and, under the circumstances of our arrival, one to be remembered. Very many of the larger houses flew the red crescent flag, and on their balconies were groups of sick soldiers, dressed in their loose red or blue cotton gowns, with small caps of the same material—Baghdad seemed to be mostly hospital. At last, just as we came in sight of the bridge of boats, we slowed down opposite the largest and most imposing building we had yet seen, and which we recognised as the British Consulate, and there we stopped and prepared to disembark.

The glory of Baghdad has departed, but some of its wonderful reputation still lives on amongst us, and its history is a great one.

Essentially an Arab city, it was founded on an uninhabited site—so, at least, say the Arab writers—in 762 *A.D.* (145 H.) by the second of the Abbaside Caliphs, El Mansur, as the capital of the Empire of the

Arabs.

But although the site was bare at that time, remains of a former habitation have been discovered, notably those by Rawlinson, who found the remains of a riverside wall built of bricks stamped with the name and superscription of Nebuchadnezzar. All around it lay evidences of the existence of great cities of the past. Thirty miles to the south west are the mounds of that great city, Babylon; twenty to the east, the great arch of Parthian Ctesiphon stands sentinel over the surrounding waste, and hard by had flourished Seleucia of the Greeks, whilst farther away to the north proud Nineveh once held sway.

In the eighth century the country was still prosperous and watered by the extensive system of irrigation channels which once turned the fertile plain into a land flowing with milk and honey, so that the site of the new city was doubtless well chosen, both by reason of the wealth of the country and because of its situation amongst the supporters of the *Caliphate*.

Commencing as a comparatively small city on the right bank of the river, it was built around the *caliph's* palace as a centre and enclosed by three circular brick walls and a ditch. It was so arranged that the palace was separated from the innermost wall by a large open space, whilst the houses of the inhabitants were all erected between the in-ner and middle walls, a road separating the latter from the outermost rampart.

The city rapidly spread in extent and in population until, by the end of the eighth century, it covered some twenty-five square miles.

Enriched and adorned by Sultan Harun el Raschid, it gathered to itself all the wealth, art, and learning of the East. Its colleges became famous the world over; its bazars attracted merchants from the four corners of the earth, from China to Spain. Its mosques reared their lofty domes and graceful minarets in all quarters of the city and re-sounded with the vigorous polemics of religious contestants.

Its palaces were bathed in luxury and splendour, and its enormous revenue was spent with a royal prodigality.

Its merchants sailed far and wide in their quest of rare and costly goods, and the adventures of one of them, old Sindbad, have fascinated us all.

Medicine and mathematics, astronomy, alchemy, and algebra were all pursued with enthusiastic zeal, and we owe much to the labours of Avicenna, the great physician, and his contemporaries.

Baghdad, in a word, became the foremost and most renowned city in the world, and it remained the seat of the imperial power of the Arabs for close on 500 years.

But the seeds of decay were early sown in this Abbasid Caliphate which once held sway from India to the Atlantic, and Baghdad felt and shared in the various vicissitudes through which it passed. Early in the ninth century civil war broke out between the followers of rival viziers, and the city experienced its first siege and capture in 813 *A.D.* Disintegration of the Empire began to take place—North Africa was lost to it early in the same century, and the Emirate of Cordova, already independent, proclaimed itself a rival *Caliphate* a hundred years later. Syria and Egypt soon declared their independence, and Northern Mesopotamia fell under the dominion of the Arab Hamdanids.

In Baghdad itself the Creed, that great binding force which kept together the differing racial elements of the Empire, began to lose its cohesive power through heresy and schism, and heterodox doctrines of all sorts were taught and discussed in the schools and the mosques. The weakening of the Faith was inevitably followed by a steady increase in the vices and degeneracy of the *Caliphate*, though the city still flourished and remained for long the great emporium of the commerce of the East.

By the end of the tenth century the vast empire of the *caliphs*, weakened by internal dissensions, had become little better than a collection of scattered dynasties that paid but scant respect to the *caliph*, and it was about this time that a very numerous tribe of Turkish nomads from Central Asia, led by Seljûk, appeared in Bokhara. Early in the next century they crossed the Oxus and defeated and displaced the Ghaznavids, from whom they absorbed the tenets of orthodox Mohammedanism. Adopting the Faith with fervour, they brought new life to the dying *Caliphate*. Under Toghril, they overran Persia, Mesopotamia, and Syria, and made successful war on the Emperor of Byzantium, and in 1055 *A.D.* Toghril came to Baghdad to pay homage to the *caliph*, el Kaim, as successor of the Prophet, who invested him with the title of "representative of the *caliph* and protector of the Moslems."

Toghril Bey was succeeded by his nephew Alp-arslan, who overran Asia Minor and defeated the Byzantine emperor Diogenes Romanus, whilst under his successor, Melik Shah, the Turks extended their dominion to Egypt.

Under their protection the *Caliphate* of Baghdad obtained a new lease of life, but a century later, in 1180, an attempt was made to secure its independence of the Turks by the aid of the Shah of Kharezm. This was followed later by the deposition of Caliph el Nasir, at the hands of the Shah, against whom he had intrigued.

The *caliph* appealed for assistance to Chingiz Khan, the terrible Mongol, who defeated the *Shah* in 1219 and then proceeded to overrun Armenia, Georgia, and Mesopotamia.

Chingiz Khan was succeeded by his son Ogotay, who continued the congenial work of devastation and pillage. The Caucasus, Southern Russia, Hungary, and Poland were overrun, as well as Anatolia, where the Seljûk Sultan of Rûm was defeated about the year 1240. It was Hulagu, the brother of the next Mongol ruler, who was sent to destroy Baghdad, and to this end he besieged the city in 1258, took it, and put to death the *caliph*, Mustasim Billah. The city was sacked and given over to pillage for many weeks, for it was a city worth looting. A million of its inhabitants were put to death, and all its priceless works of art and its manuscripts were destroyed, so that "Moslem civilisation has never recovered from the deadly blow."

Hulagu ruined the whole system of irrigation canals which made Mesopotamia perhaps the richest country in the world, and thus "destroyed the work of 300 generations."

The Mongols ravaged, plundered, and killed wherever they went, but, curiously enough, treated Christians not unkindly, and Hulagu and others married Christian women.

Deprived of the *Caliphate*, which now found a new home in Cairo under the Mamlukes, and blasted by the devastation wrought by the Mongols, Baghdad survived as a second-rate city, but continued to take a share in the events of those turbulent times.

The Mongols could not hold the countries they had overrun, and their power was soon wrested from them by the Seljûks in Anatolia, and by others.

The Seljûk (Turk) empire of Rum was divided up into ten provinces, ruled by as many different chiefs. Of these the house of Osman and that of Karaman were the most important, and they indulged in a long struggle for supremacy during the fourteenth century. At last the Osmanlis, under Bayezid 1st, gained the upper hand and extended their rule at the expense of the Byzantine empire, but they were temporarily submerged by the wave of conquest of Timur (Tamerlane) of Samarcand.

Timur, like his great predecessor, Chingiz Khan, was a terrible destroyer. He carried out his campaigns with a ruthless disregard for life and property, and he instigated wholesale massacres of Christian communities. He conquered Transcaucasia and devastated Mesopotamia, so that Baghdad very wisely opened its gates to him in 1393. Unfortunately for herself, the city was ill-advised enough to revolt against the conqueror, with the result that he returned in 1401 and thoroughly sacked it. It is said that he put the inhabitants to the sword, save only the holy men, and "90,000 skulls were piled up in pyramids before the walls."

For the next hundred years Baghdad remained under the power of the Mongol dynasties, who had embraced the Shiah variety of the Moslem faith, but after the death of Timur the Osmanli Turks soon regained their supremacy in the West and rapidly extended their dominion in all directions. In 1517 the Osmanli chief Selim 1st took over the rights and insignia of the Caliphate from the Mamluk Sultan of Egypt, and it has remained an attribute of the Sultanate of Turkey ever since. His successor, Suleiman 1st, the great lawgiver, turned his attention to Persia, and on his return marched back by the Hamadan route and took Baghdad, without resistance, in 1544.

Suleiman interested himself in the city and in the neighbouring shrines, and rediscovered the bones of the Great *Imam*, the Sunni Abu Hanifah, and departed after a sojourn of four months. In 1602 the city was captured by the Persian, Shah Abbas the Great, but it was soon lost again to the Turks. In 1623 it once more fell into the hands of the Shah through the treachery of the son of the Turkish *commandant*. Shah Abbas, as a punishment to the people, gave them over to the torture for a week, and was only diverted from a general massacre by the deception of the guardian of the Shrine of Hussain, who intervened on behalf of the Shiahs (to which heresy the *Shah* belonged), and then reported large numbers of Sunnis as belonging to the Shiah sect.

But the ancient capital was given no peace, for two years later it was besieged unsuccessfully for nine months by the Turks under Hafiz Pasha, and again unsuccessfully by Khosru Pasha in 1630. In 1638, however, the bloodthirsty *Sultan* himself, Murad IV., marched against it with a large army, and after a siege that lasted forty days captured it on Christmas Day of that year. In the time-honoured way the garrison and many thousands of the inhabitants were butchered, and Murad, with an eye to spectacular effect, "had the gratification of seeing a thousand executioners strike off a thousand heads at once."

The city henceforth remained in Turkish hands, reduced to a comparatively unimportant place under a *pasha*; but it stood yet another siege in 1733 by the great warrior Nadir Shah, who failed to take it, and it finally passed into the hands of the British under Maude on March 11, 1917, who was welcomed by a large section of population only too glad to be released from the domination of the unscrupulous Turk.

Baghdad is still a holy place to Mussulmans the world over, and the centre of a district rich in sacred shrines and remains revered alike by Sunnis and Shiahs. Sixty miles away to the south west, not far from old Babylon, is the tomb of the martyred Hussein, son of Ali and third Imam, contained in the great golden-domed mosque at Kerbela. Nejef or Meshed Ali, away to the south, is another most holy place, where Ali, son-in-law of Muhammed and first Imam, murdered at Kufa, lies buried in a beautiful and famous mosque. It is to these sacred cities, which form the "Mecca" of the Shiah Mussulmans, that every Shiah comes on a pilgrimage once during his life if possible, and, if he can afford it, gets buried there. Kerbela and Nejef flourish on the gifts and fees of the faithful, and caravans of corpses from Persia and beyond are a common feature of the landscape on the mountain paths of Iran and in the plains of Mesopotamia.

Besides these two chief shrines there are those of four other *Imams* in the neighbourhood, and of many mystics and of Sunni doctors in the law, and the tombs of the prophets Esdras and Ezekiel, of Noah and of Adam himself, and many other relics of interest to Jews, Christians, and Moslems are pointed out in the plains of the two great rivers.

> Then there is the cave (or *serdab*, in the Mosque at Samara) into which the twelfth and last *Imam* has vanished, and whence he will emerge before the Day of Judgment to preach in the pulpit that awaits him in the mosque of Gaur Shad at Meshed. There is also near ancient Babylon the well in which the fallen angels, Harut and Marut, hang head downwards until the Last Day, in punishment for trying to seduce the fair Anahid.

Thanks to the ravages of Hulagu and Timur, there is very little in the Baghdad of the present day to indicate its splendour of former days. There are no remains of the palace of the *caliphs*. The principal buildings are mosques, *khans* or *caravanserais*, and the *serai* or palace of the *pasha*. There are over a hundred mosques, but only thirty or so with minarets. The oldest is that of Caliph Mustansir, of which only the minaret remains (1235); that of Murjaneeya dates from the fourteenth century and has some remains of old and very rich Arabesque work on its surface.

The Mosque of the *vizier* near the Tigris and the bridge of boats has a fine dome and a lofty minaret. The domes and the tops of minarets are mostly covered with green or turquoise-blue tiles and stand out brilliantly against the dust-coloured brick of the surrounding buildings.

At the suburb of Kazimin, three miles away, is a fine mosque containing the tombs of the two Imams, Musa el Kazim, who was poisoned by Harun, and Hassan el Askari; it is an object of deep veneration to all Shiahs.

On the right bank in the old city is the tomb of Zobeide, the wife of Harun el Raschid. It is an octagonal brick structure surmounted by a lofty conical dome, and built in 827, but since often restored.

Of the old brick walls of the city small portions remain, and the great fosse still exists. There still stands also the Babel-Tilsin, or Talismanic Gate, which was walled up after the surrender to Murad IV. It bears a fine Arabic inscription in relief on a scroll border around the tower, which bears the date 1220 *A.D.*

For the rest, Baghdad is a commonplace and somewhat dirty city, but there is every reason to think that, under a strong and settled government, that will encourage the Arabs once more to arise from their sloth and help in the reconstruction of their country, and that will rebuild its ancient irrigation channels, and harness the great rivers to the service of man, the city of the *caliphs* will emerge from its decrepitude, and as the centre of a rich and flourishing district, capable of producing unlimited quantities of fruit and corn, take an honourable place once more amongst the great cities of the world.

Already one barrage has been built on the Euphrates, and Sir W. Willcox's plans for the development of a huge irrigation scheme await but the necessary capital to bring it into being. Canal colonies from Iraq or India would follow the water and reap rich harvests from the generous alluvial soil, which can produce anything from grain of all sorts and dates to peaches and pomegranates.

The Baghdad Railway lacks but a few hundred furlongs to make complete an iron road from Basra to Konia. Add branch lines from Baghdad towards Kermanshah, Kerbela, and Hit, and from Kut to Nasryah, and Baghdad will become once more an extremely important centre of commerce between India and Persia and the North and will regain much of the trade of those parts which it formerly held before it was diverted to Northern Persia and Erzerum. Though it can never repay us for the loss of the thousands of good lives that have been spent in winning it, yet it is to be hoped that so potentially rich a country will be made to yield a goodly return to the sons of those who laid down their lives in its acquisition.

CHAPTER 17

Prisoners in Baghdad

It was an unkind fate that landed us at the British Consulate—now no longer a Consulate, but a hospital. It is a fine new building, and we felt that for once the dignity of Britain had been upheld by a structure fitting her prestige.

The order came for all officers to disembark—officers only, none of other ranks, and no baggage. This was soon done, and we stepped ashore, wondering if we should ever see our kit again. We stood about in groups for a few minutes, or competed for a place in the shade of the very few young trees that lined the walk up to the main steps leading to a handsome terrace in front of the building, the while we watched, with a very natural interest, the confabulations of the Turkish officers, who seemed to be arranging our future movements.

Soon we were lined up in order of seniority, and, a few minutes later, to our surprise and not a little amusement, were marched off, very slowly, at a most funereal pace, into the town, headed by the senior colonel and tailed by the junior *jemadar*. We lacked but reversed muskets to complete the illusion that we were following our own funeral. Passing through the garden at the back of the Consulate, we debouched into one of the outer streets of the city, and so into the midst of an interested throng of eager sightseers, who had evidently been warned of the advent of the captured British. So, we found ourselves the cynosure of all eyes, and realised that we were to be shown to the multitude as the tit-bit of the Turkish Triumph.

As we slowly wound along a bend in the road, I looked back at the caterpillarlike column of British and Indian officers, and it was indeed no small "bag" that the Turks had secured; they could be pardoned for showing us off to their none too affectionate subjects in the ancient city of Baghdad.

What an interminable march that was! At two miles an hour or less we slowly wound our way along the streets, which were lined with a gaping populace and kept clear by the attendant military.

From the first-floor windows many a fair face studied with interest

110

the captured *Anglais*, and some of them were pretty enough with their fair skins and plaits of glossy black hair. But the people said never a word, and their silence in the sunshine intensified the solemn nature of the proceeding. We saw it had to be got through, so we smoked a cigarette and took stock of the town and its storks.

It was very hot, and no one was sorry when we at length reached the cool shade of the vaulted bazars in the middle of the city. These, like the rest of the route, had been swept clear of traffic, and their open-fronted shops were piled high with the merchants and their friends, amongst the generous jumble of their miscellaneous wares. Half a mile of these, and we emerged once more into the fierce sunlight, passed the Infantry Barracks, and marched out of the city by the north gate; down a slope on the Meidan, past a lake of flood water, and so at long-last to the Cavalry Barracks and our destination, some 2½ miles from our starting-point.

Hungry and thirsty, we were told there would be breakfast at noon, but it was nearer three o'clock when we got it—a mess of thin soup, vegetables, and some eggs—and then it was a scramble.

Another meal was prepared for us at about seven o'clock in the evening, by the contractor to whom the job of feeding us had been handed over, and we ate it at small tables set in the open in the barrack square. We paid a "*mejidieh*" a day (about 3s. 8d.) for our "board."

The accommodation in the barracks was limited, and we lay on the floor in rows, cheek by jowl with each other; but some of us were wise enough to sleep on the roof at night, and so escape the sand-flies that came out in thousands down below.

The next day a few of us got out for a walk accompanied by a guard. Some went to see the American Consul; we of the medical persuasion went to the Central Military Hospital to look up friend Abdul Kadir. Him we found in his bacteriological laboratory looking lovingly down a microscope, which was part of a very complete and workmanlike field-service Bacteriological outfit of Austrian make. He introduced us to the *commandant* and to another physician, gave us coffee and cigarettes, and then he showed us over the place. He took us in to see some British officers and men who had been captured from Aylmer's Force.

The officers were in a small ward which was clean and bright, and which they shared with some Turks. There were Tranquil with a broken thigh, Watson, and Gasson the flying man; they all looked pretty bad. They said the Turks treated them well, but they were full of gratitude to some French Sisters of Mercy who frequently visited them, bringing them fruit and jam and other delicacies from their convent. The men were in a larger general ward and seemed to be treated in the same way as the Turkish soldiers, and to be more or less contented. The hospital appeared to be clean and well kept; it is a large building arranged around an extensive quadrangle or garden, full of orange trees, vines, figs, and the like, amongst which are cut paths in all directions. Convalescents were wandering about amongst the trees and flowers enjoying the fresh air and gentle exercise.

Abdul Kadir informed us that four out of the five of our own particular party were to remain in Baghdad to look after the sick and wounded; the fifth would accompany the rest of the officers going north.

For four days we remained in the Cavalry Barracks. One evening somebody got up an impromptu concert which went on unmolested for some time, until in the middle of "Glorious Devon" or "Widdicombe Fair"—I forget which—the little Turkish officer who had been left in charge of us for the night suddenly conceived the idea that we were singing Russian Turcophobe songs and ordered a cessation of the proceedings. This annoyed our senior, Colonel D——, who strongly objected to doing any such thing and ordered the artists of the moment to continue.

There ensued, therefore, a most lively altercation for twenty minutes, conducted in a mixture of French and English by the colonel and an interpreting staff officer on the one hand, and by the Turk and his assistant on the other. Things began to look awkward, and it seemed there would be a row, but explanations finally prevailed and the concert continued.

At the end of four days we were suddenly ordered to pack up and move off to the station, with not more than 60 kilos of stuff for a field officer and not more than 30 for one below that rank. The result was a hasty scrapping of kit, and a crowd of Jewish and Arab scallywag merchants who swarmed among us reaped a rich harvest. The *commandant* of the "Place" had received no orders about the medicals, but in the nick of time we got hold of Abdul Kadir, who arranged matters, and four of us—for Lancelot had tossed with Horace for a place and lost—stayed behind with three or four other officers who were too ill to move. The rest of them lined up and started on their journey into the unknown.

With a lump in our throat we watched them move off to the station and wondered how many of them we should ever see again. The same evening, we who were left, and the sick officers, were taken off by our friend Abdul,—the sick to be installed in Turkish hospitals, ourselves to be shown new quarters. Our kit and servants followed in carts. Two of these carts were full of stuff belonging to officers who had gone north. The American Consul had promised to look after any superfluous kit they could send him. A Turkish guard was told off to go with it, and we did our best to keep an eye on it, but it never rolled up, and our inquiries the next day only elicited shrugs of the shoulders. To our surprise, we ourselves, instead of being deposited at once in our new abode, were taken along to a restaurant, where on a balcony overlooking the Tigris we were presented to the *médecin-en-chef* and other M.O.'s, and then dined by them as their guests.

Fifty or sixty other officers were dining there—Germans, Turks, Arabs, Austrians, and a Swede or two.

The Turks were attentive hosts, and the scene under such novel conditions was an interesting one. At its conclusion the *médicin-en-chef* of the group of hospitals to which we were to belong, conducted us through what appeared to be a maze of mediaeval alleys by the light of a candle-lamp to our lodging, where we were glad to find our orderlies already installed.

The next morning, we endeavoured to go out to the restaurant for breakfast, as we had been informed we might do, but to our chagrin we found that we were in the hands of a jailor who by no means agreed to our going. Persuasion and argument were equally useless with the stupid old Arab "dug-out" who was now our "director," and all we could get out of him was permission for a servant to go out and purchase food, since he offered us none himself. For two days we couldn't get out of the place, and then the restriction was as suddenly removed as it had been imposed.

The house we were in was fitted up as a hospital, filled with rough wooden beds covered with mattresses, and ready for our sick when they should arrive, but it boasted no drugs or instruments, which we had to indent for in the smallest quantities when required. It belonged to the *École des Soeurs*—the French Dominican Sisters, whose convent was close by, and whose headquarters establishment is at Tours. Our house was a two-storeyed building with a flat roof, and a central courtyard about 25 feet square, out of which opened the rooms of the basement and a staircase up to the verandahed first floor.

The lower rooms or "*serdabs*" were below the level of the courtyard—three steps down; they are to be found in all Baghdad houses, and are used in the hot weather for living in. Fresh air is conducted down to them by long chimneys, the tops of which project above the roof in the form of a cowl facing the direction of the prevailing north wind, and they are very much cooler than the upper rooms.

The housetop slightly overhangs the rest of the building, with the result that it nearly touches those of other houses. These, when we went up in the evening to take the air, we found occupied by a crowd of Baghdadis—Jews, Chaldeans, Syrians—all Christians, and all smiling all over at us, offering us fruit and cigarettes, and eager to greet us with a "Good morning, howwaryou?"

We found ourselves, in effect, living in the middle of the Christian quarter, the inhabitants of which spared no pains, when the Turks were not looking, to impress on us their whole-hearted sympathy with the Allied cause. Most of the men spoke French; a good many of them who had been employed in the offices of the English firms, also English; the women, with one or two exceptions, only Arabic.

The Christian quarter is of very considerable extent and contains a large number of well-built and commodious houses belonging to well to do people, who, I should think, monopolise the commercial business of the city.

There are practically no streets worth the name through it, but only narrow alleys which wind about in all directions. As the upper storeys generally overhang the lower, the tops of the houses approximate to each other, so that but little sunlight finds its way into the lanes.

They reminded one of prints of Old London before the great fire. Each house boasts a heavy wooden door with a large brass knocker thereon, and as there are no external windows on the ground floor, each forms a sort of self-contained stronghold. The necessary air space is got in the courtyard inside and, of course, on the roof, which takes the place of a garden. This type of house is doubtless a very necessary one, where not only is space limited but where a citizen holding fast to one faith is liable at short notice to be butchered by those holding another.

The important part religion plays in the daily life of the people in this part of the world was often brought home to one in the most casual of remarks. One would ask a man who he was, and would inevitably get the answer, "I'm a Christian," or "I'm a Mussulman," as the case might be. "Who is he?" "Oh, he's a Mussulman!" Never would the man's name or occupation be given, but always the central fact of his existence—so it seemed—his religion! The vital importance, to the individual, of a man's creed was impressed upon us again and again, and one came to realise how much a matter of life and death one's choice of a method of going to heaven might become at any moment.

They are well off for churches, and there are a couple of bishops—a Syrian and a Chaldean—one of whom we had the pleasure of meeting. There is also a large French Convent with an establishment of thirty or forty Dominican Sisters. The Chaldean church is a large building surmounted by a dome like a miniature St Peter's, and was close to our hospital of the *École des Soeurs*. We were allowed to attend service there if we wished, and our "director" himself took some of us there to attend Mass soon after our arrival. At the service, which was similar to a Mass in Europe, all the women sat together in the fore-part of the church and the men behind.

The women dress in semi-European fashion without the hat, but each wears a sort of flowing silk robe or large cape, which is worn over the head rather like an Indian "*sari*." Their shoes are of the high-heeled variety but have "uppers" over the fore-part of the foot only, and they are well made.

The men wear ordinary European clothing topped by the Turkish *tarboosh*. Very few of them were taken for military service by the Turks save as assistants in hospitals and offices, but they had to pay a heavy annual fee for their exemption, and as practically all their trade was at a standstill they were feeling the war acutely.

There are many thousands of Christians in Baghdad, including a good many Arabs, and during the whole of our stay in Baghdad these people lost no opportunity of talking to us when they could do so unobserved; they expressed their sorrow at our failure to reach Baghdad six months before, and hoped that it would not be long before the tables were turned.

"We are sorry to see you as prisoners. You were so close to us at Ctesiphon; we could hear the guns and were delighted to think the English were coming. But they *will* come, won't they? When will it be? in a week or two, a month, two months? They are good and kind, the English; they ought to take Baghdad," and so on. We assured them the English *would* come, perhaps in a month or two, perhaps longer, but they certainly would drive the Turk back and capture the city!

This friendliness of the Christian community was so pronounced at times as to be almost embarrassing, and we feared to get them into trouble by talking to them too much. Our old Arab "director" interfered at times and waved us apart, but he himself was a Christian and so was none too strict.

After a couple of days, we overcame his objections to our going out, and got away for a *petit déjeuner* at the Restaurant "Tigre." Horace and I revelled in the freshness of the early morning, sitting on the vine clad balcony overhanging the great river, and it seemed good to be alive again. Now and again small rowboats would pass up or down the stream carrying Turkish or German officers, sitting under a small awning, or a *"qufa"* or coracle would float down-stream full to the brim with green water melons. Three hundred yards above us lay the only boat-bridge connecting the two banks; the far bank was lined with balconied houses built on the wall at the river brink, and people could be seen in them taking their morning tea or coffee on the little verandahs. Just opposite, a gap in the row of houses was occupied by a palm garden, and to its left, above the trees, could be seen the high water tower belonging to the German railway terminus.

The restaurant proprietor was all for the *"Entente"*; though he had lived all his life in Baghdad, he looked more Italian than anything else. When no one was near he would come and talk to us freely, but when Germans were present he would be content with a few "asides." He would take any sort of money from us, he said, or none at all if we were short, and he appeared to tolerate with difficulty his German patrons. Later on, when all restrictions on our movements were removed, we got into the habit of dining there twice a week, besides an occasional breakfast.

Leaving the restaurant, we explored the bazars, and as we were walking therein we came across a large crowd, which we discovered was watching the marching into the city of our Indian troops, who had just arrived. They marched by, each carrying a small bundle of kit. Despite their fatigue, they came in well and at a good pace, and their faces were expressionless, or melancholic; doubtless it was *"Kismet."* But in a few moments, I turned away; it was too sad to see those splendid fellows in the hands of the Philistines!

The main bazars are two or three covered-in streets, with low vaulted roofs, running parallel to the river, in the middle of the city—they are more like tunnels than anything else, with cubicles on each side for shops. They are just wide enough for two *fiacres* to pass each other and are smelly and stuffy. At night, with dirty lamps placed at rare intervals on the walls, and deserted save for a watchman or two, they are weird and ghostly places, like a cathedral crypt.

The goldsmiths' and silversmiths' bazars form a series or rather maze of the tiniest little alleys, in which it is easy to get lost. In them we saw very little good work; nearly all of it was cheap and badly-made jewellery, such as one saw worn by the Arab women; but perhaps their best stuff was hidden away. In Baghdad as a city we were vastly disappointed; it has no imposing buildings save its various barracks, and the town is very commonplace.

Our freedom was short-lived, for we were soon shut up again for another day or two, after which the other boat with the sick and wounded arrived, and we soon had work to do.

The "*École des Soeurs*" house and another were filled up, and some hundreds more were dumped down on a bare piece of land near the station, with Trixie and others to look after them. It was a bad place. Save for a few bits of rush matting and a tent or two, there was no protection for the men from the sun, which by now was appallingly hot in the middle of the day; no sanitation, and insufficient water. Here they remained for two or three weeks, but every few days those thought fit enough were sifted out and sent up country in batches, sometimes accompanied by a medical officer, and sometimes without.

The American Consul, Mr Brissl, visited this camp almost daily, and worked hard to ameliorate the dreadful conditions our men were living in there. He supplied money; he bought sheep for them; had beds made for the sick and helped in a hundred ways. He looked after the cemetery and arranged for the Christian burial of those who died. He was indefatigable all through that hot summer, frequently visited us to talk things over with the colonel, lent us books, and did us all good by his cheery presence. He and Trixie became great friends and got through a lot of work in connection with the camp. We owed him much.

As beds became vacant in the hospitals the number of sick in the camp was gradually reduced, and the whole camp was later on removed to a much more satisfactory and shady site near the river, where the men could bathe and laze beneath the palms.

A few days later six of us were moved out of the "*École*" and quartered in the Artillery Barracks—sometimes called the Citadel—near the North Gate, and abutting on the old and ruined wall of the city, where we were soon joined by the colonel, who had at last arrived from Shamran. Here we had an upper room, which was desperately hot in the daytime and full of sand-flies at night. It overlooked the great barrack square, where the training of small bodies of men in gun drill, and of cadets in sword practice, was constantly going on. The barracks are built around three sides of this square, whilst on the fourth or river side are workshops and two or three magazines. We occupied rooms just to the left of the main gate as you go in, and between us and the nearest magazine at the corner, some fifty yards away, the barracks were used as a hospital, full of sick and wounded Turks. Soon after we got there the ground floor of this part was handed over to us for a hospital, which we filled up with men from the camp. From here two of us were told off to look after a lot of British and Indian men who were accommodated in a large hospital run by the Turkish Red Crescent Society. They were mostly men who belonged to the relief force and had been prisoners for various periods from three weeks to as many months.

They were very glad to see us and to be treated by their own doctors. Our coming, they told us presently, made a great difference to the attitude of the Turkish orderlies towards them; for whereas before our arrival some of the orderlies were inclined to knock our men about a good deal, and to be brutal on occasion, they now showed them much more consideration.

They had a fair amount of food: milk, and sour milk or "*lait caillé*," a popular morning dish in Baghdad, rice, bread, and a vegetable stew with a trace of meat in it. Most of them missed the meat, of which they got scarcely any, but a good many got to like the diet. The brown bread was coarse and a little sour, and several of the sick men couldn't digest it, so we always purchased some loaves of white bread on our way to hospital for them, and generally also some extra cigarettes. Both these little luxuries they appreciated very much, and they made them feel they were being looked after.

Our dealings with the bread-woman and the cigarette shop were usually watched by, a small crowd of interested natives, who followed us with curious glances as we turned away with our arms and pockets full of loaves and packets.

The chief surgeon of this hospital was one Kanin Bey, who before the war had been the "civil surgeon" of Baghdad, and still looked after the large municipal hospital on the other side of the river, which also took in many wounded.

He was thus acquainted with the members of the British colony in peace time. He was an intelligent Turk, had travelled a good deal, and had received his medical education in Paris; he was under no illusions regarding the position of Turkey, and saw that whichever way the war went she would gain nothing. He was a good surgeon, easily the best of the few I saw. Most of them seemed unsympathetic in their manner to their patients, and rough in their treatment and work generally. The hospital storekeeper was a horse-dealer, who spent much of his time in Bombay and was a constant visitor to the Poona races; but now his business had gone, and he divided his time between his store cupboards and his hubble-bubble!

The hospital boasted a Turkish bath, which we were invited to use whenever we liked, and we were able to order an occasional bath for our patients, who very much appreciated it. The attendant, Abdullah, was a friendly old Arab, whose ministrations were always most grateful and comforting. A most atrocious Turkish brass band played here about twice a week, but it cheered the men up a bit; it went round to most or all of the hospitals in town, played for a few minutes and then moved on. Its headquarters seemed to be the Infantry Barracks or the neighbouring "*serai*," where all the army offices were, and it was here that it played the gems of its limited repertoire.

We soon settled down to a sort of dull daily routine which tried our nerves and our patience, accompanied as it was for some time by irritating restrictions on our movements. Week after week we were promised "exchange soon," but as often were disappointed. The weather was terribly hot; we worked from an early hour till about midday as a rule, and then "existed" from one to five in our room in the scantiest of attire and prayed for sundown. Rumours of the tragic fate of large numbers of our men who were overcome by the heat on the marches up beyond the railhead at Samara reached us, and two of our number were despatched up the line to help.

General Melliss, who had remained in Baghdad sick for two or three weeks, recovered and departed north with his staff, and with Gaspard as medical attendant.

Of news we got little that we could trust. From the Christian side the most optimistic rumours reached us, whilst in the only paper that Baghdad boasted, printed in French and Arabic, we saw the description of events according to the German side. From the one we heard that Lord Kitchener had come out to Busra; from the other, a few days later, we heard that he had been drowned. For long, of course, we believed neither, till the very insistence of the latter forced itself into our minds and we feared it must be true. At the restaurant and elsewhere we often conversed with Turks.

The fall of Erzerum they would never acknowledge, but from a doctor who was there I heard something of the sufferings they went through. Typhus raged there apparently, and they must have lost thousands of men; for of doctors alone, according to my informant, they lost a hundred, he himself only just recovering. One interesting Turk was a most enthusiastic officer in the Turkish Mission to Persia. His eyes sparkled as he spoke of what they meant to do there. "Persia is ours," he would say, "and so is India by rights, for she is Mussulman and should be ruled by Constantinople, and one day we shall get her." He ignored the millions of Hindus, or knew little about them, and was quite persuaded that they would brush aside the British resistance. He departed for Persia a few days afterwards, and I have often wondered what has happened to him since and how he has taken the breaking of his dream.

Their views on the Armenian massacres were amusing. I asked one of them how he justified their appalling treatment of these people.

"Why do you butcher them?" I said.

Ingenuously he replied, "But of course we kill them; they are revolutionaries and anarchists and are always giving us trouble; the only way, naturally, is to exterminate them. Besides, what are *you* doing in Ireland?"

Of Germans there was a fair number in Baghdad—perhaps a hundred or so officers and half a battalion of pioneers, also half a dozen nursing sisters, and a few Austrians. Many of them and of the Turkish officers wore the Gallipoli campaign ribbon, and not a few had the Iron Cross. The Germans kept very much to themselves, and it was a rare thing to see Turks and Germans chatting together. The Turks themselves, strangely enough, did not hesitate to intimate to us their dislike of the Teuton. A short time before we left most of the Germans disappeared; they had, it was said, gone off to Persia.

One day, just as we had shut ourselves up to get through the heat of the day, a loud explosion was heard. It sounded like another midday gun, but we lost no time in going outside to investigate. Smoke was issuing from the magazine at the corner, and within a minute or so another bang, and another larger irruption of smoke and dust occurred. And now we heard the rattle of small-arms ammunition; explosion followed explosion in increasing violence until it sounded like a furious battle going on within a few yards of us.

We hastily dressed, told our men to pack up, and went outside and down the steps to the hospital to get the men clear. A Turk rushed in and told us all to clear out as fast as we could. Then came the biggest explosion of all, which nearly brought the place down, and the end of the barracks nearest the magazine began to burn merrily. There was a wild stampede of the Turkish sick and wounded from the upper rooms, down the steps and out by the gate. Bits of shell, shrapnel, twisted muskets, and debris of all sorts were raining down on to the roof and in the barrack square.

Hell seemed let loose, and shells and small-arm stuff continued to burst in every direction for another exciting half-hour. One shell landed in the hospital on the other side of the river, and there were several casualties in the town. A Turkish sergeant ran round to a mosque a quarter of a mile away, had it opened, and told us to take up our quarters therein for the time being; and a very hot afternoon we spent in moving all our patients and kit thither.

As was not surprising, a couple of poor fellows who were very ill succumbed to the exertion of moving, and for two days we camped out in the churchyard in a very uncomfortable condition. But on the third day they placed another house at our disposal for our personnel and sick, and ourselves they put once more into our old quarters in the Cavalry Barracks in the "*maidan*."

Here we were more comfortable, though it was extremely hot—the thermometer once or twice reached 114° in our room; but there was a good big flat roof, and the cool nights made up for a lot. There were a good many Turkish cavalry officers quartered there, and we soon got to know them, and even on occasion rode out with them. The *commandant*, a *bimbashi*, a swashbuckling soldier with fifteen years' campaigning to his credit, was a very good fellow, and treated us uncommonly well; "whilst we are actually fighting you," he would say, "it is à *l'outrance*, but the fight once decided and you in our hands, you are our guests; I treat you as my own officers."

From the roof of the barracks we had a very good view of the country round: two main roads passed by it—one along by the river to Kazimin and Mosul; the other, merely a track over the desert, led away north-eastwards to Khanikin and Kermanshah. Along the latter we constantly saw troops and munitions pass on their way to meet the Russians. One day, for instance, forty motor-lorries from Germany arrived in Baghdad from the North and passed by us on their way to Khanikin. The Turks were sending every available man to push the Bear back, for the Russians got very near at one time, within a few miles, and one felt the uneasiness and subdued excitement in the city.

Our chief consolation in life at this time was the abundance of fruit and vegetables that were obtainable in Baghdad. The oranges were over, but there was a profusion of every other kind of fruit: nectarines, grapes, apples, plums, figs, melons, and pears grew in plenty, and were to be had in the markets.

Otherwise life was none too pleasing, and we sometimes envied the fellows who had gone north into a cooler climate, for our exchange seemed to come no nearer, and we began to give it up as a bad job. Slowly the numbers of our men decreased; some died, and some were discharged fit for the journey to Mosul. We had great difficulty in fitting out the latter, for most of them had little or nothing in the way of clothes, or of such necessary equipment as water-bottles and canteens. Several of them had been stripped on the battlefield and had arrived in hospital in nothing but a shirt. But we got hold of the kits of deceased men after considerable argument, and by the addition of small purchases of shoes or cooking-pots managed to fix up most of them fairly satisfactorily, and to give them a few *piastres* to go on with.

The American Red Cross people cheered us mightily one day by sending T£3 to each British officer, and T£1 to each British soldier who was a prisoner in Baghdad. We appreciated this most highly (notwithstanding the fact that the Turks paid us in paper which was worth about three-fifths of its face value) and were touched by the kindly thought of the society which sent us help from their friendly country 10,000 miles away.

CHAPTER 18

Exchanged

But all things come to an end sooner or later, and our imprisonment was no exception to the rule. One day, when we had just about given up all hope of getting away, the news came that ten out of the eleven doctors in Baghdad were to be exchanged; the eleventh, the colonel, was to stay behind as a hostage against the return of an important Turkish doctor. But still better things were in store for us, for the colonel made further inquiries, and, thanks to Brissl and Khalil Pasha, the order was amended, with the result that eleven doctors (including three sick), eleven combatant officers who were in hospital, and three hundred odd sick men, were now told to go.

It was almost too good to be true, and we trembled lest something should go wrong and upset all arrangements; but nothing did, and on August 8th we embarked on the old *Khalifa* once more, had it all to ourselves, and weighed anchor for Kut. A goodly number of sick, together with three *medicos*, including Horace, Pearson, and Clifford, were also brought down from Samarah, and we thought they were to be released with us; but just before we started a Turkish deputation came on board, re-examined the men, and picked out fifty whom they considered too fit to be exchanged, so these poor devils were again disembarked and sent back to camp with the three M.O.'s. For those poor men this last act of cruel disappointment must have been almost too much to bear. We were very sick about it but could not prevent it.

A splendid bit of "eyewash" on the part of the Turks was perpetrated just before we left. To our surprise and amusement, they brought on board a lot of new boots, with which they fitted every man who had none or no good ones, just to show our people down below how well they looked after their prisoners! whilst during the whole time of our stay in Baghdad we could not get boots out of them for love or money for the men who had to march up country, and in several instances, men were despatched on their travels without. When we remonstrated with them, they would say that their own men often went without too, which was true enough, but they were doubtless used to it.

We started away at last and dropped down the stream, but we hadn't got clear of the suburbs before we stuck on a sandbank for some hours. We were in a fever of impatience to get off again, for we were desperately afraid that the Turks would change their minds and recall us before we got well away.

However, nothing happened, and we pursued our way. It took us seven days to do the two days' journey to Kut. The river was low, and we investigated the adhesive power of every submerged mud-flat in that hundred miles of tortuous waterway. The sense of approaching freedom and the fresh air of the desert put new life into us, and despite the meagre diet of rice and vegetables we put on weight. At length we reached Shamran and tied up at the left bank, close to a Turkish hospital camp and within sight of old Kut and its minaret once more.

Here we quite expected to wait a day or two whilst they arranged our transfer, but no one was prepared for another three weeks of suspense on board that beastly boat.

But there we stayed day after day, counting the hours, playing bridge, watching British aeroplanes sail over us once more as of old in Kut, wondering what the delay was about, and being unutterably bored. We never got off that boat for a solid month; we fed on rice and beans and lady's fingers, bread and soup, twice a day; soup and beans and rice—dates and eggs when we could get them—until we began to dread the sight of those piled-up plates of greasy rice.

Haider Bey came to see us every few days, and sometimes some doctors of our acquaintance or a flying man or two, Haider seemed invariably to tell us that the exchange was practically fixed up, but that he could not get the final answer—to something—from our people down below. What that something was we could only guess; they were, we felt sure, trying to drive too hard a bargain with General Maude.

Whatever it was, we were convinced we could never count ourselves safe until we actually set foot on British ship or soil; for by now we knew our Turk and knew that words are nothing to him save a vehicle for fooling or soothing the man he is dealing with. Truth in the abstract does not exist for him. One day Haider and his friends brought us an ice machine, with a great show of "doing us well," but the ice machine was a "frost"; it would not work, and I am quite convinced that they knew it would not before they took the trouble to have a couple of hundredweight of useless glass and iron carted along to our saloon!

But the negotiations did come to an end; steam was got up once more one night. We were given strict orders to arise next morning at three o'clock—we were all sleeping on deck—and to remain in our cabins thereafter; we were ordered to give up all gold we might possess, and all our kit was inspected and our papers and letters examined. All night long, it seemed, they were putting up canvas screens all around the decks, rendering opaque all cabin windows, and hermetically sealing them, so that the place became like an oven. Sure enough, at 4.30 a.m. we started on our last jaunt, and moved off down the stream. The plunging and cranking of those noisy ship's engines was the sweetest music I have ever heard. We were to meet a British Hospital ship near Megasis, so they said.

Soon we were slipping past Kut, and just got a peep at its ruined front as we went by, and shortly afterwards passed the point on the right bank to which our army had then advanced. Thence for miles we sailed through a no man's land between the British lines on the right bank and the enemy's lines on the left,—a most interesting lane to pass along. All was deadly still—hostilities were in abeyance for our journey through; here and there we saw a head or two on one or other side, till at length we passed Megasis and saw, with a joy that words will not describe, a little two-decked sternwheeler approaching us and flying the Red Cross flag.

That little ship, canvas-covered, hideous though it was, was symbolic of all that makes life possible—of Home, and Love, and Beauty; of the might and majesty of the British Raj; of liberty to come and go: it spelt "freedom" and the thought of "freedom." The knowledge that it was all over at last, that we were to be free men once more, was almost too great for words; it left us dumb.

In a remarkably short space of time we were anchored alongside each other. The exchanged Turks were the first to be passed over, and they were soon all aboard the *Khalifa*, whilst we lost no time in setting foot on the dear old *Sikkim*. We shook hands heartily with Haider and Dr Hassan, the same ship's doctor we had gone up with four months before, and from the bridge of the *Sikkim* waved them a cheery goodbye. As the good ships separated, and the Turks went "up" and we went "down," we turned with a sigh of contentment into the little saloon, looked at the white cloth and the marmalade, and smelt the bacon and eggs; whilst Trixie, voicing the sentiments of us all, sat himself down at the laden board, and with knife in one hand and fork in the other, exclaimed, "Gad! I've been waiting for this for a y-e-a-r!"

CHAPTER 19

Down the River

Downstream we paddled without further delay, but in a few minutes, we reached a spot at Sanaaiyat opposite the opposing lines on the left bank. Here we stopped to drop the Turkish officer who had accompanied the ship from this point upwards to see that no intelligence officer of ours took an undue amount of interest in the enemy's arrangements on the left bank. From the boat we enfiladed, so to speak, the advanced trenches of both Turk and Englishman, which were here only thirty yards or so apart.

In the one we could see a Turk or two peeping round the corner, whilst in the other we caught sight of a Tommy's cork helmet. On the foreshore of the no man's land between the two was a tangle of barbed wire down to and in the water. All was very still. No one spoke, and the silence was only broken by the sound of the oars in the rowlocks of the little boat that was working its way over to the bank.

As it reached the shelving shore the Turk stepped out just below the end of the British trench and proceeded in the direction of his own line. Walking along the foreshore amidst a silence that could be felt, he looked horribly lonely and unprotected. All knew that, hidden in the ground all around him were thousands of invisible armed men only waiting for the dropping of the little flag of truce which protected this lone man from all harm, to be at each other's throats again. Although one knew both sides were quiet by arrangement, yet one almost held one's breath as he neared his lines and the safety of mother earth, but safe beneath the truce he clambered leisurely up the steep bank, stepped over a barrier of sandbags, and disappeared in the trench on the other side.

So again, nothing was to be seen save the little cuts in the bank which marked the open ends of the two hostile trenches, and it remained but for us to get out of the way to allow hostilities to be resumed.

No time was lost in doing this, and we who had escaped from prison took no risks of offending a jealous God by glancing backwards towards the land we had left, but looked forward with the interest of those coming Home to see what changes had taken place in our absence.

Much had been done in a twelvemonth. Round every fresh bend of the river, so it seemed, we came upon a huge camp of white canvas glistening in the sun, or upon smaller rest camps or supply dumps, trim and tidy, and protected by a machine-gun or two against marauding Arabs. At Sheikh Sa'ad we found hospitals and old friends, from whom we got a first instalment of a year's arrears of "personal notes," and we simply devoured all the papers we could get hold of.

Amarah we scarcely recognised, so great were the changes and additions. Acres of new hutted hospitals peeped out from amongst the palm groves on the right bank, with, strangest of all, the white uniforms of nursing sisters dotted about here and there—the first we had seen in Mesopotamia—transforming the rough man's world with their civilising influence; monitors galore, it seemed, with their tall wireless masts and their polished guns; P. boats, numbered in three figures, where a year ago they had scarcely reached two; mountains of stores piled along the front on the left bank, and over all an air of settled activity which only Busra boasted in the old days. It looked as if the British army had come to stay!

But we spent only a night at Amarah, just long enough to despatch a cable Home, and were off again early next morning. The same signs of activity presented themselves on the way down: here a good view of the new road, there a glimpse of a bit of railway with, wonder of wonders, a small railway engine; past Ezra's tomb and on to Kurna. Only once did we hit a sandbank, so that we made a record voyage to Busra. Old Busra hadn't changed much; it was perhaps a little busier, and a few more hospital huts had sprung up, and there were nurses there, but otherwise it was just the same.

With great good luck we got in a few minutes before the arrival of a dainty Hospital ship, the old *Varsova*, which had taken on new functions since last we saw her as a B. I. transport, and on her, as we were all more or less seedy, we were all forthwith embarked, to our great content.

With a joy unspeakable, and a relief words could not express, we found ourselves slipping along that avenue of palms *en route* for Bombay. Despite their beauty, we felt that we never wanted to see those date groves again; rather did we say farewell—so we hoped—with an infinite satisfaction to the desert land where we had left only two good years of our life, measured by the standards of Time, but a good ten by those of our feelings.

A Kut Prisoner

KASTAMUNI

THE CASTLE ROCK (KASTAMUNI)

Contents

Introduction

The experiences related in the following pages are simply the individual fortunes of a subaltern of the Indian Army Reserve of Officers who had his first taste of fighting at the Battle of Ctesiphon and was afterwards taken prisoner by the Turks with the rest of the Kut Garrison, ultimately succeeding in escaping from Asia Minor. It is not intended to generalise in any way, since an individual, unless of exalted rank, sees as a rule only his own small environment and cannot pretend to speak for the majority of his comrades.

The book is published in the hope that it may prove of interest to the many relatives and friends of the Kut prisoners.

Acknowledgments are due to Messrs. Blackwood, the *Times of India*, and the *Pioneer* for their kind permission to republish those chapters which originally appeared in these papers.

CHAPTER 1

Ctesiphon

In India, in the early days of the war, a newly gazetted subaltern of the Indian Army Reserve of Officers was sent for a month's preliminary training to one of the few remaining British regular battalions. Afterwards he was attached to an Indian regiment, and, if fortunate, went on service with the same battalion. A great number, however, were sent off to join other units in the field. In this way I found myself arriving in Basra on October 2nd, 1915, with a draft for a regiment (66th Punjabis) of whom I had known nothing a few days before leaving India. However, the "Nobody's Child" feeling was very soon a thing of the past, and I was welcomed by a mess full of the best comrades any fellow could desire.

The Battle of Es-Sinn had just taken place, and the 6th Division under General Townshend were then following the Turks up the Tigris above Kut. Our own fortune appeared to be to remain in Basra as part of the garrison; but, much to every one's delight, different news came a week or two later and, on the 25th October, we set off upstream, hoping to get right through to the front but with some fear that we might be kept at Amara.

In those days travelling up the Tigris took a long time, and we spent a fortnight in reaching Azizie, a journey which can now be accomplished mostly by rail in two days.

The regiment was accommodated on two of the river steamers, each having two big barges lashed alongside. The current is considerable and the heavily weighted steamer could only advance very slowly. In many places the river becomes very narrow, especially between Kuma and Amara, and much time was spent in bumping into sandbanks and struggling to get clear.

We made short halts at Kurna, Amara, and Kut, the latter striking one as a horribly dusty and dirty little Arab town. Every night we used to tie up to the bank, as navigation by night was too risky with so little water in the river. On the last stretch to Azizie, we were warned to be on the alert for Arab snipers, and great preparations were made accordingly. A few shots were fired next morning, but nothing more than one Arab in the distance was seen. Other boats and convoys coming up had a much more lively time from raiding parties of the local tribes.

Azizie was reached in the afternoon and presented a scene of the greatest activity. The village itself consisted of only a few mud huts, but for some distance along the dusty bank of the river General Townshend's force was concentrated. Nothing could be a greater contrast to the deserted stretches of country through which we had passed than the bustle and life of a force about to advance.

A few days later—on Monday, November 15th—the whole of the 6th Division and attached troops were on the march for Bagdad, the first stage being El Kutunie, some seven miles only. Here three days were spent and the final preparations completed. There was a little sniping at night from the further bank of the river, but this was quickly dealt with by the *Firefly*, the first of the new monitors to come into commission on the river.

Great excitement prevailed on the night of the 18th when it was suddenly reported that the whole Turkish Force, which considerably outnumbered our own, was on the march to attack us and was expected to arrive and commence hostilities before morning. We spent a very industrious night, digging feverishly and wondering when the enemy would turn up.

Morning arrived, to find many trenches but no sign of the Turks, and we later found that the previous reports had been entirely misleading. However, fresh orders were soon received, and not long after daybreak the whole force was off again, split into various columns whose mission was to encompass and annihilate the Turkish advance troops at Zeur, about ten miles further on. However, the enemy eluded us, as he had done previously, and got away just in time. After doing several miles across country in attack formation, always expecting to hear firing beginning in front, we found we had arrived in the position the Turks had just vacated.

Next day a short march brought us to Lajj, a small hamlet on the river which was to be our jumping-off place for the forthcoming battle, and, as we believed, triumphal march on to Bagdad. All except the minimum of kit had been left at Azizie, whence it was to follow by steamer to Bagdad as soon as might be.

Before leaving Azizie, the general had given all senior officers some idea of the problem we had to tackle, and they realized it would be no walk-over. The rest of us, fortunately, thought only of a repetition of the former successes, and that we should enjoy a cheerful Christmas in Bagdad.

Detailed maps had been issued, not only of the Turks' position at Ctesiphon, but also of Bagdad and the methods to be adopted to push the enemy through and out of the city.

At Lajj we were about nine miles from the Arch of Ctesiphon, built by Chosroes I. in the 6th cent. B.C. and round which battles had been fought from time immemorial. From the top of a sand-dune near general headquarters, the magnificent ruin was clearly visible standing up gaunt and alone above the flat plain. The Turks' position surrounded the arch and stretched back on both banks of the river.

We bivouacked one night at Lajj and at nine o'clock the following evening—Sunday, November 21st—the final advance began.

Our plan was to surround and defeat the Turks on the left bank, where the greater part of their forces lay, and to drive them back on the Tigris or Diala River.

The force was split into four columns, which were to attack from different angles, the "Flying" column being deputed to complete the victory by dashing on to Bagdad and seizing the Bagdad end of the Samarra Railway.

At midnight we reached our station on some sand-hills about four to five miles due east of the arch, which we could see very clearly as soon as it became light. It was a bitterly cold night and after digging in we lay down to get what sleep we could before dawn broke.

The attack was to be begun by the columns further north, who had had a longer march and were further round the Turkish flank.

There appeared to be considerable delay on their part, and it was an hour after the advertised time when our advance began. In the meantime, a troop of Turkish cavalry had come out on a reconnaissance but had thought better of coming up as far as our sand-hills and, after hesitating, retired unmolested by us.

As we debouched from the high ground. we could see masses of Turks, apparently retiring in orderly formation towards their second line or still further, and the thought occurred that they were not going to wait even for us to attack. Actually, however, these were troops from the other side of the river being hastily brought across to strengthen the Turkish reserves opposite to us.

Our particular destination was a point marked V. P. on our map and understood to be the "Vital Point" of the Turkish line. It fell quickly to our attack, but was not carried at a light cost, and, still worse, was not so all-essential to the Turkish resistance as it should have been. Our advance was held up on the Turkish second line and, unfortunately, we were not powerful or numerous enough to break this also. The Turks had a fine position and their trenches were sighted with the greatest skill. Aided by the mirage effect, it was almost impossible to discern these trenches until right upon them; we, on the other hand, were out in the open plain, which was as flat as a billiard table and offered no cover of any sort. The Turkish front line was protected with barbed wire, and had they been provided with more machine-guns and been prepared to see things out a little longer, we should have fared very badly. As it was, we lost heavily in taking V. P. and the adjacent trench lines and were too crippled to do much more.

In the afternoon the Turks counterattacked; but our guns were too much for them, and they gained nothing.

Evening found a confused force bivouacked round V. P. There were dreadful gaps in all ranks. About midnight I found my way back to my own battalion, to discover the colonel and M. O., the only two officers still carrying on. One other subaltern besides myself had been posted away from the regiment during the day, but, of the rest, only two were left out of ten who had gone into action with the battalion that morning. Other regiments were in much the same state, and it was evident that we had suffered terribly and had not completely smashed the enemy. Later on, we heard that our casualties had reached a total of nearly 5,000, while the Turks were said to have lost twice this figure.

The next morning, we took up our position along the Turks' old front line, and no more fighting took place until the afternoon, when the Turks came back once more. Attacks followed during the night and prospects were considered anything but rosy for us by those in authority. However, the Turks had had enough, and by next morning were again out of range.

It was imperative for us now to get closer to the river for water, and accordingly the remnant of the force concentrated in the angle of the "High Wall," an ancient relic of the old wall of Ctesiphon, now a high bank, forming a right angle, each arm being about a quarter of a mile long. During the day the wounded were evacuated, being taken back to Lajj on A. T. carts. It was a pitiable sight, seeing these poor fellows go. These were the days before the Mesopotamian Commission—springless carts were all that were available and a number of wounded must have been literally bumped to death over those eight rough miles back to Lajj. The memory of those jolting carts with their grimy battered loads of tortured humanity is one not soon to be forgotten.

The night passed in peace, but the following afternoon the Turks were seen advancing in several columns, and we were given orders to pack up at once. Soon after dark we were ready, but it seemed an age until the head of the column got clear away and our own brigade, who were in rear, could move. Meanwhile the Turks were expected to arrive on the scene at any minute, and everything appeared gloomy in the extreme. Ammunition which could not be removed had been hastily buried. Large fires were lit to help our departure and endeavour to deceive the enemy. Cheerful prospects of rear-guard actions all night over unknown country seemed all that was in store for us. However, fortune was with us again; the Turks hesitated once more and we were not attacked at all during the night. After a weary march through thick dust and sand, we reached Lajj in the early hours of the morning, and were greeted by a heavy downpour, which, fortunately, stopped just before we were quite soaked through.

Digging was again the order as soon as it was light, and arrangements were made to give the Turks a very hot reception if they intended to come on at once.

The following day digging continued, but in the afternoon, we were again told to get under way, as the Turks apparently were close upon us.

A long all-night march, only varied by Arab sniping, brought us back to Azizie the following forenoon. Here digging began once more, and it was not at first known if we should remain here and see it out or go back further right down to Kut, some 58 miles. The latter course was decided on next day and, having collected what little of our old kit we could still find, we set off once again southwards, and bivouacked by the river near Umm El Tubul, eleven miles further on.

At eight in the evening, we were just congratulating ourselves on having at last a snug spot for a night's rest, when firing began and our pickets were soon driven in. However, the enemy did not make the expected attack during the night—which we spent in a *nullah* awaiting him.

As soon as it was light, we could see a large Turkish camp, not much more than a mile distant. The first orders were that we should go out and attack; so, we lined up for this purpose. Just as we were ready, fresh orders arrived, and we retired to the *nullah* while our guns opened with rapid fire on the Turkish camp. Meanwhile, there was great bustle in our rear, where the transport was being hurriedly got away for a further march towards Kut.

We were told later on that the Turks thought they had only come up against a weak rear-guard and were correspondingly dismayed by our gun-fire. They were said to have had 2,000 casualties on this day. However, they pushed on and we had to retire.

Previous to this, Turkish shells had been coming over, but not doing very much damage.

The old gun-boat, the *Comet*, and also the *Firefly*, were both put out of action while waiting to cover our retreat and had to be abandoned to the enemy.

By midday we had shaken off the advancing Turks, having done many miles across country which seemed to grow camel thorn in every direction. This shrub is most unpleasant to march through in shorts, and many were the torn knees in consequence.

A few hours on the ground late that night gave us a little rest; but it was too cold to sleep, and we were soon sitting up round fires of brushwood which the men had lighted. Many of us had had no food since daybreak and had to fall back on our emergency rations where these were still in existence.

Next morning, we were off once more, and after another long, wearisome day reached a camp only a very few miles from Kut itself, having done over 40 miles in the last 36 hours.

Kut was entered the following morning, December 3rd, but it was not decided till some hours later what position we should take up.

During the next two days we could walk about above ground without molestation, but snipers arrived all too soon, and by Monday, December 6th, Kut was entirely surrounded and the siege had begun.

CHAPTER 2

Kut

If the Turks had hurried up, they would have come upon us without properly dug trenches and we should have been taken at a great disadvantage. As it was, however, by the time they did arrive, we were dug in and had a good front line trench, although most of the support and communication trenches still had to be dug. After the first two or three days, all trench work had to be done at night, as conditions by daylight were not healthy.

Life was not particularly pleasant during any part of the siege, and for the first few days we who were outside Kut had no dugouts, all energy being spent on getting the front line firing trench ready. This would have been no hardship but for the fact that we had arrived back in Kut with a biting north wind, causing several degrees of frost at night, and an ice-covered bucket for one's ablutions in the morning.

Throughout the siege, the Tigris formed our only water supply, this being carried in at night in kerosene tins by the regimental *bheesties*. Drinking water was purified with alum, which got rid of most of the sediment. This is a poor drink at any time and seems particularly nasty when spoiling good whisky.

On Monday, December 6th, the cavalry brigade left at daybreak and were the last people to get away from Kut. Many wounded and sick had been sent down stream during the day or two previously, the lighter cases being left in the hospital at Kut to recover and rejoin.

In those early days, no one thought of a siege lasting more than a month, the general being reputed to be counting on relief by the New Year.

Meanwhile, the Turks had been very busy: not only had they been digging at a furious pace opposite to us and sapping up closer and closer, but they had also sent considerable forces further on down-stream, to near Shaik Saad, to oppose the Relieving Force which was there concentrating.

The night after the cavalry brigade had gone out, the boat bridge over which they had passed to the right bank was demolished under the noses of the enemy.

This gallant feat was performed by Lieut. Matthews, R.E., and Lieut. Sweet, who volunteered for the job. Both men, we hoped, would receive the V.C. By the greatest good fortune, the Turks were entirely surprised, and the bridge was blown up before they realised what was happening or could offer any resistance. Both officers received the D.S.O.

The story of the siege has been told in detail by others, and it is not intended here to attempt it. One saw only one's own small corner, and never knew what to believe of all the rumours and scandal in which a besieged town seems to be particularly prolific.

After the first fortnight, a regular routine was started. The 16th Brigade took alternate turns with the 30th along the main trench line, while the 17th garrisoned the fort, and the 18th looked after the town itself and Woolpress village.

Meanwhile the medical people had been busy moving from their hospital tents to the covered-in bazaar, which was now converted into wards.

For the first few days, the men were given extra rations to recuperate them after the wearying retreat and for the strenuous trench-digging in progress. It was not until January 10th that we were cut down to two-thirds full rations.

The first Turkish shells arrived on December 5th but did little harm. Throughout the siege, we had much cause to be thankful for the very large proportion of "duds" amongst all classes of Turkish shell. Fortunately, also, they had no high explosives, or Kut would have been a heap of ruins in no time.

The mud of Mesopotamia deserves mention in this connection. It is as disagreeable as but rather more glutinous than most other brands of the same substance, and when baked dry by the sun is singularly impenetrable to rifle bullets. All the rules found in military pocket-books were quite upset by it, some eight inches of the best variety being quite enough to stop any bullet. For the same reason, trench digging in some places was very slow and tedious work, as the ground at that time was dry and hard, seeming more like cast iron than anything else.

During the early part of the siege, regiments in the 16th and 30th Brigades, on being relieved in the front line, returned to a bivouac in Kut and did some hours' digging on the way, the operation being carried out at night. The following night was as a rule allowed us in peace, but for the next three or six nights, until again relieved, one was generally out digging or in "support" to some part of the line, so that "being relieved" did not mean much rest for anybody. The bivouac had a further disadvantage in that we had as many casualties here as in the front line. Dropping bullets would come in at odd moments from all directions, and it was impossible to keep clear of them. Some unfortunate was laid out nearly every day in this way.

The Turks never once tried to shell our front line but spent all their attentions on the town and the fort. A tremendous "hate" preceded their attack on the latter on Christmas Eve. They succeeded in blowing a breach in the mud wall of the fort in the north-east bastion, and afterwards assaulted with great dash. Fighting was extremely fierce and the Turks lost very heavily from our machine-guns. There was much hand bombing, this being the only occasion during the siege when fighting at close quarters took place.

After gaining a footing through the breach into our trenches, the Turks were dislodged, but came on again later, and at midnight, December 24th, were still in possession of the north-east bastion. However, they thought better of it, and by the morning of December 25th had all disappeared again. As a result of this fighting, we had about 400 casualties, while the Turks were said to have lost 2,000. Be that as it may, they never made another attack on our lines.

Khalil Pasha, the Turkish commander, was said afterwards to have told one of the British generals that he was just preparing another tremendous attack at the end of January, meaning to smash his way into Kut at any cost, when the floods intervened, and drove him back over half a mile, while we had also to return to the "middle" line—our second line trench some 300 yards behind the first. He stated that he was prepared to lose 10,000 in the attempt.

Christmas Day passed peacefully, much to our satisfaction, and from now onwards there was great speculation as to the day of relief. We knew that General Aylmer's force was to start during the first days of January, and it was predicted that by January 9th or 10th the siege would be over.

By the first week in January, all fresh meat was finished, but for a time we had "bully."

The Relieving Force suffered its first serious check at Shaik Saad and never arrived, as we had hoped. There was nothing to be done but to carry on and wait till next time. The weather now was cold and wet and the trenches often knee deep in mud and water. Kut itself was in a filthy state, the streets being a sea of mud after every downpour. The Tigris was steadily rising throughout January and by the 20th was near the top of the bund running along the bank. Heavy rain on this day and the next, together with the rise in the river, was responsible for flooding out the Turks' front line They managed, however, to turn the water over towards us, with the result that we, also, were drowned out of the corresponding part of our line, the effect of this being that there was now a good distance between the new front lines. For two days we could walk about in the open and were much interested in seeing the old Turkish trenches and taking all possible firewood in the shape of old ammunition boxes from their loopholes. We found that one of their saps was only forty yards from our trench, and many were the bombs they had thrown which just fell short.

The most interesting relics were numbers of pamphlets tied to sticks and bits of earth and thrown towards our line. These were ef-fusions printed in various languages by the Indian National Society, Chicago, (see Appendix B), and contained much startling information. The Sepoys were informed that no British were now left in several N.W. Frontier districts, and were recommended, as brave soldiers, to murder their British officers and join the Turks. The *Sultan* was repre-sented as being ready to give land to everyone who would respond to this invitation. As regards Gallipoli, it was stated that Sir Ian Hamilton had been wounded and that Lord Kitchener had run away in the night, taking the British troops with him and leaving the Indians, who thereupon murdered their offices and joined the Turks.

Very few, if any, of these leaflets reached the *sepoys*, and, as far as we could see, left them unmoved.

After two days' freedom above ground, a reconnaissance was sent out to locate the Turkish outposts. This had the immediate effect of starting great activity in the Turkish pickets some 1,200 yards from our line, and from that day onwards snipers were always busy. Even so, life was very much pleasanter than when the enemy was within 100 yards.

By January 13th we were down to half rations, and by January 23rd were still further reduced. On the 26th, the general issued a long *communiqué*, telling us of how the Relieving Force had been unsuc-cessful so far, having had heavy losses and very bad weather to contend against. He announced that there were 84 days' more ample rations without counting the 3,000 animals.

Actually, the siege went on for another 94 days, but the rations were scarcely ample, even including the horse meat. However, at the time, it seemed that there was nothing to worry about, especially as the general said he was confident of being relieved during the first half of February.

With the beginning of February, we started eating horse, mule and camel. There were very few camels, but they were said to be quite good eating. For the rest, mule is very much to be preferred to horse. There were also the heavy battery bullocks, but these were not numerous, and were very thin already.

All the eggs and milk obtainable from Arabs in the town were supposed to go to the hospitals, but it was always said they did not receive nearly as much as they should have done.

During January and February, one could buy several things from Arabs in the bazaar. *i.e.*, tea, dried beans, *atta* and "*kabobs*" or small hot *chapatties*, cooked in grease. The tea must all originally have come from the S. & T. All the Arabs in Kut wore army socks very early in the siege. In fact, it would be harder to find a race of more expert thieves anywhere on the globe.

Towards the middle of February, the Turks began sending over an aeroplane to bomb us. The pilot was a German and knew his business too well. After his first trip, machine guns were rigged up to welcome him the next time he came and the sappers mounted a 13-pounder to fire as an anti-aircraft gun.

Considering the difficulties involved and the absence of all special sighting arrangements this gun made some very fair shooting. But the only effect of all these efforts was to make Fritz, the pilot, fly higher and approach the town from a different direction. The first time he came very little damage was done; then one day a bomb demolished an Arab house, killing a number of women and children, and a second fell on the British hospital, where no less than 32 sick and wounded men were killed outright or horribly injured. The *padre*—the Rev. H. Spooner—told me afterwards that no sight he had witnessed at Ctesiphon could be compared to that hospital ward.

Presumably Fritz was aiming at the ordnance yard next door or some of the guns on the river bank only a little further on. Had there been more room and good buildings in Kut, it would no doubt have been possible to put the hospital in a safer spot, but, as it was, no other building was available. Fritz always succeeded in eluding our aeroplanes from the Relieving Force. He had so little distance to go home, whereas they had to come up 20 miles or more.

Two main observation posts were maintained, one above general headquarters in the town, and the other in the fort. There was great rivalry between the two, and on one occasion, a large flock of sheep was definitely reported in the town as a considerable force of the enemy moving to the rear. The fort maintained they were sheep and neither would give in.

We could see every day long strings of camels on the horizon, carrying rations for the Turks from their base at Shamrán above Kut down to their forces at Sanaiyat and Magassis.

The usual book of words about camels informs the reader that they are liable to slip and split themselves up if allowed to travel over wet or slippery ground. In Mesopotamia, however, the camel seems not to worry at all when going over land submerged by floods and carrying on generally under all conditions. He is a much wilder specimen than the usual Indian camel, and our experience before Ctesiphon was that he would only lie down if one of his forelegs was folded and bound up, and he was then hit on the head with a thick stick.

A feature of Kut which will not be forgotten was the little chapel which our *padre* rigged up in one of the few remaining upper rooms of the battled *serai*. This building was in an exposed position on the river bank and suffered more than any other from the Turkish shells. The *padre* himself was indefatigable, doing everything he possibly could in the hospitals in addition to his other duties.

Almost every day one or more of our aeroplanes came over Kut, and some things were dropped, but how we wished they would drop us some letters. We knew there must be a great accumulation of mails at Amara and it seemed so easy to arrange it. As it was, some bags of letters were dropped for the staff and even the S. & T. but, as usual, the regimental officers came off worst. We wanted news from home more than anything else, and, as it turned out, most of us never heard a word from our people till we had reached Anatolia the following July after an interval of eight months.

Fortunately, we could get messages sent out by the wireless, and once a month a telegram was despatched to the depots in India, saying that all were well, or something equally brief but satisfactory to our friends at home.

Another great blessing afforded by the wireless was the publication of a short summary of Reuter's telegrams, which gave us something else to talk of other than the everlasting questions of food and the date of relief. In particular, the taking of Erzerum by the Russians cheered us up and made us hope that the Russian force approaching Bagdad from Persia would be equally successful.

In fact, at one time the betting was said to be in favour of the Russian general, Baratoff, relieving us from the north, before our friends downstream.

With the arrival of March, everyone was full of excitement over the coming great effort of the relieving force, which was prophesied to take place on the 4th, but was actually the 8th.

Many schemes were prepared by which we were to co-operate, so that after the Turks had been started off rear-guards by General Aylmer, we might hasten their departure. In most of these plans one brigade would have to play the leading role, and probably come in for a pretty hot time unless the Turks had become quite demoralised; much speculation arose, therefore, as to which brigade would be given this post of honour.

March 8th came and went and we realised that another gallant attempt had failed. The bombardment could be clearly heard, and at night it was easy to see the shells bursting. During the attack on the Dujailah Redoubt our friends were only seven to eight miles from us, and we could hear their rifle and machine gun fire.

This failure was a great disappointment and we realised what it must have cost in casualties. There was only one thing for us to do, namely, carry on; so, the rations were reduced again and life went on in its, by this time, mechanical round. All were still confident of being relieved, and when it became known that General Gorringe had taken over command downstream we felt sure something decisive would happen and that he would get through, if anyone could.

After every unsuccessful attempt, a Turkish envoy promptly arrived with a white flag and requested us politely to surrender. He was as courteously and consistently refused.

Rations were now down to 10 oz. of bread, this being half *atta* and half barley. The dates were finished and the small stocks of mess stores which had been carefully eked out were nearly finished. Still we had jam and tea and the mule wasn't at all bad. Some saccharine dropped by aeroplane gave us something sweet and was a great blessing.

The efforts to get the Indians to eat meat at the end of February had failed. They declared that every village pundit would be against them on their return to India and that, in consequence, no one would give them their daughters to marry.

Everything possible to help religious scruples was done, and special permission obtained from the *Imám* at Delhi and other religious authorities; but it was no use, and not until the second week in April, when they were literally starving, did the Indian troops begin eating horse. No doubt, if they had done so earlier, we could have held out for some few days longer, but it is doubtful whether this would have sufficed for our relief.

After March 8th, all horses not wanted for food were shot to save their keep, and many a good animal was sacrificed in this way.

By the 19th, the bread ration was only ½ lb., while the Indians were getting 10 oz. meal. The small quantity of food began now to tell on the strength of all ranks, and cases of bad enteritis—so-called— were common, these resulting in many deaths during the last days of the siege.

It is really wonderful what an amount of satisfaction can be derived, under such conditions, from simply imagining a first-class meal, and I remember one day, in my dug-out, having a great time going through a long menu and choosing everything I should like best.

When the grass began to grow, towards the end of March, we gathered what the *sepoys* called *ság* or anything we could make a sort of spinach with. It was like eating wet hay, but, undoubtedly, kept scurvy down, and if well soaked in vinegar was not so bad.

In Woolpress they managed to get a little fish from the river, fishing by night.

Our activities after March 8th were directed to keeping out the floods. Two big bunds were made, one inside the other, round Kut. The Arabs in the town were forced to work on the inner one and thus saved the troops, who were weak enough as it was already with making the outer bund.

By the end of March, we had a splendid *bund* across the middle line capable of keeping out nearly three feet of water; this being 4 ft. 6 in. high and about 20 ft. thick at the base, all the soil having to be excavated from pits in front. The sappers had told us that our mess dug-out was just about the lowest spot round Kut and would be the first place to be flooded; however, when the floods really came, we found we were two feet higher up than the regiment a little further along the line. It was hard work making these *bunds*, and all the men not otherwise on duty were out every night. The *bund* also had to form the firing parapet, and with barbed wire entanglements in the "borrow" pits in front and again beyond we were well protected from any attack, not to mention the floods which would have made an advance by the enemy almost impossible.

All through April the water slowly percolated up and the dug-outs and trenches had to be continually raised, until by the end of the month we were nearly up to ground level. The river rose to its highest level during April, but fortunately news was received, by wireless, from a British officer with the Russians at Lake Urmia, of the various floods, so that we were more or less prepared. Actually, we had never much more than 2 ft. 6 in. outside our *bund*, which held well. Had we been driven back inside the inner *bund* the whole force would have been cooped up in a very small area and any shelling would have been bound to take a large toll.

For the last ten days there was no tobacco left. People were smoking used-up tea-leaves, orange leaves, liquorice, and even grass. Whatever smoking tea-leaves may be like for the smoker, it is exceedingly unpleasant for everybody else, especially in a dug-out.

Throughout the April fighting we followed each *communiqué* from General Gorringe with the greatest anxiety, watching his shells bursting over the Turkish lines by night and always hoping on until after the *Julnar* had failed to get through.

The men were not told anything about this attempt, but the 30th Brigade made ready to cover the unloading, in the event of the gallant ship winning through. She was to be beached by the fort the same night and unloaded before the Turks could bring their guns to bear on her next morning. I remember listening to the firing as she slowly made her way upstream; star-shells and flares went up and lit up the scene and she met with a terrible reception.

Then, after a time, all firing ceased and we realised that this splendid attempt had failed. According to one member of the crew, all went well until they reached Magassis, where they struck a cable which gave way, but a second one immediately afterwards stopped them. Commander Firman, the naval officer in charge, thought this was a sand-bank and left his protection on the bridge to shout to them to take a sounding. He was killed on the spot. Cowley, the well-known skipper of the ship, then took charge but they could not get past the obstruction, and he himself was soon very severely wounded by a shell, from which he died when taken ashore.

Eventually this magnificent attempt had to be given up. It was a most heroic effort and, had it been possible to steam faster, would probably have been successful. As it was, the ship was very heavily laden with a month's supplies for the garrison on board and could only do five or six knots against the very strong current. Even so, we still fondly hoped that General Gorringe might achieve the impossible at the last minute; but it was not to be.

The last few days we lived on the emergency and reserve rations which each regiment had in its keeping, and the food dropped by aeroplanes from the Relieving Force. These brought us white flour, some sugar and a little chocolate. The bread ration, however, was only 4 oz. or just one good slice a day each.

We were all very weak and there was a great deal of sickness. Enteritis, which seemed not very different from cholera, was prevalent and affected nearly everybody to some extent. Not infrequently a Tommy going into Kut from the front line would suddenly collapse, often not to recover. I remember feeling rather disappointed that I did not look thinner, and one felt one ought to be a dreadful scarecrow really to have done the siege justice.

CHAPTER 3

From Kut to Kastamuni

On April 29th, Kut surrendered, and it was with sad feelings that we watched two Turkish battalions marching in at midday. The bitter thought that they should have worsted us in the end, together with the knowledge of the useless sacrifice of life by our friends downstream, was present to all; but there was also a great feeling of relief that the siege was now over, and we had not realized until this moment how severe the strain had been.

We believed the Turks would treat all ranks well, as up to that moment they had always fought and behaved like gentlemen. Khalil Pasha, the Turkish general, had said we should be treated as his "honoured guests," and, since at that time we had not had much experience of Turkish promises, we were inclined to think all would be well, although we knew the Turks themselves were short of supplies and had great difficulty in feeding their troops downstream.

Orders came round telling us to destroy everything that could be of use to the enemy, only a few rifles being kept in case of trouble with Arabs in the town before the Turks arrived. Field-glasses, revolvers, maps, and diaries all had to be destroyed and saddlery burnt. It seemed a crime to be sacrificing so much that was valuable, but this was better than helping the enemy in any way. The last works of destruction had only just been completed when the Turkish troops arrived, and great was their disgust at finding all the guns destroyed, and nothing worth taking but a few rifles.

Some of us had kept our swords, thinking that they would be returned to us in traditional style, only to find them collected by the first Turkish subaltern or N.C.O. who set eyes on them. Those who were wiser had thrown theirs in the river or buried them, and we all wished we had done the same. Later on, we heard that the officers' swords from Kut had been displayed as an interesting exhibit in some museum at Constantinople.

The departure from Kut began that evening, one steamer taking a full load up to Shamrán, the Turkish base camp, some eight miles up-stream. We had still to depend on the remnants of our own rations for that day and the next, but fortunately they just sufficed.

Next day, as we moved up towards the old *serai*, near which the steamers were moored, we had to pass a palm grove which had been occupied by some Turkish soldiers. These men were systematically looting any kit which was being carried past, and to which they had taken a fancy. A good deal was lost in this way. The Turkish officers seemed powerless to stop it, the culprits merely walking away until the officer had departed.

The steamer made two or three more trips that day, but it was an-nounced at noon that all those left must march, their kit alone going on the steamer. How they managed that march in a starving condition they only know, who did it, but when the steamer reached Shamrán on its last trip at midnight they had all come in and been regaled with Turkish ration biscuits. An amusing incident occurred during this march. An Indian sweeper—the humblest of all regimental follow-ers—was trudging along behind his regiment carrying some of the articles of his trade, when they passed some Turkish gun-pits where there were several German officers standing. On seeing them the sweeper made obeisance with the deepest of *salaams*; whereupon the Germans promptly stood to attention, clicked their heels and saluted.

During the following days, we made ourselves as comfortable as possible at Shamrán, and, fortunately, got other food in addition to the Turkish biscuits. These biscuits need only be once seen or eaten nev-er to be forgotten. They are of a dark-brown colour; unless mouldy, about six inches in diameter and an inch thick in the centre, and made from a very coarse meal, which must contain anything except wheat. They are even harder than the hardest of our own army biscuits.

The Turks had allowed us to bring with us what tents we had in Kut, and, although we had to leave them behind at Shamrán, they were of the greatest comfort to us during the week which we spent there.

A launch arrived from the relieving force, bringing with it barges laden with food, including a number of mess stores and gifts. These we eventually got possession of, although the Turks would not allow them to be landed at our camp, but took them upstream some distance, where we expected they would take a systematic toll of everything. Turkish soldiers and Arabs brought in dates, a few oranges, and a syrup made from dates, which they sold at excessive prices.

Bathing was allowed in the river, and some enthusiasts who still had fishing tackle spent a considerable time on the bank, but without much success.

One day, General Townshend passed upstream in a launch accompanied by two or three of his staff *en route* to Bagdad. All ranks rushed to the bank to give him a parting cheer, which one felt meant that all knew he had done his best for us throughout.

With the end of the siege one had expected all the worst features of the last few weeks to disappear, but the heavy mortality from enteritis continued at Shamrán. It was especially heavy amongst the British ranks, in many cases being aggravated by a too suddenly increased diet, of which the Turkish biscuits formed a large part.

A few days after our arrival, it was announced that the men would all have to march up, while facers would be taken up in batches by the steamers. The first party to leave contained the generals and staff, and most of the officers from British units. The following day the men were to march. Our doctors insisted on a very thorough examination, as a large proportion of the men were unable to march. The Turks would not, however, accept the British doctors' decisions, and reduced the unfit to a much smaller number.

The result was that large numbers fell out after the first day, and had to be taken on board the *Julnar*, which was bringing up a number of men from the Kut hospitals whom the Turks considered not ill enough to be exchanged. We were all convinced that had it not been for German counsels at Constantinople some arrangement for our return on *parole* to India might have been made.

The men were told to take one blanket or greatcoat each, as well as their haversacks and water-bottles. They had no transport whatever, and our hearts misgave us as we watched them go. The column wound slowly out of the camp with many checks, and it was over an hour before they were clear; all seemed to be carrying big loads, and many things must have been thrown away or sold before they reached Bagdad. The Turks were only too anxious to buy, when they could not steal any clothing, boots, or equipment, their own clothing and equipment being at a very low ebb after months of service in Mesopotamia, to say nothing of the long march down from Asia Minor. Many had no boots, and were just wearing sandals of goat-skin, such as they are accustomed to use in the country districts of Anatolia.

When the men had departed, the camp seemed very forlorn; about 150 British and Indian officers were left, while the hospital tents contained many sick of all ranks.

Two days later, on May 10th, the second party of officers left on the steamer *Khalifa*, which had on board a few German gunners returning to Bagdad and a good number of Turkish officers. The journey took three days; on the second day we passed the *Julnar*. She was covered with bullet-marks, showing through what a severe fire, she had forced her way. Now she was loaded with sick from Kut. We waved to those on board but were not near enough to speak to them.

Our steamer used to tie up to the bank for a short while twice a day, in the morning and evening, enabling us to get a hurried bathe and a little change from the cramped space on the deck, where we spent the rest of the time.

The third day we passed the battlefield of Ctesiphon, full of memories of the victory which had proved so disastrous six months before. We halted for the night not far from the arch, and were greeted by the local Arabs, who danced and fired off ancient rifles and pistols in the air in derision at our captivity. The women also contributed their share by making a peculiar kind of trilling sound. How we hoped they might soon be singing in a very different fashion when our troops should advance again and take Bagdad.

We reached Bagdad the next morning. As we slowly paddled up the river, we could see the Red Crescent flag floating from almost every good house on the river sides; hospitals seemed to be everything here, and we realised what awful casualties the Relieving Force had inflicted on the Turks.

For some miles before Bagdad is reached, the river is fringed with palm groves, gardens, and cultivated land. When we left Kut the river was within a few feet of the highest ground, but here the banks were very much higher.

We were landed at the old British Residency, and, after a little delay, were framed up in order of seniority and marched off along what appeared to be the main road. It was evidently arranged as a triumphal procession to impress the inhabitants. At length, after a march of two miles, passing through the covered-in bazaar, where the shade was most welcome, we emerged on the north side of the town, and reached our destination at the Cavalry Barracks. We had been promised furnished quarters, but found bare floors and empty rooms; the building formed a large quadrangle, and was empty of all troops when we arrived. A little later our orderlies and servants appeared, bringing our kit from the steamer. On leaving Shamrán colonels were allowed to take two orderlies or Indian servants, other officers being allowed one each.

Fortunately, just before we left, some money in Turkish gold had been sent up by the Relieving Force by aeroplane, and thus all ranks had a little cash.

When the second party reached Bagdad, the first party had already departed for Mosul, and rumours arose about the journey, people saying at first that we should have carriages from the railhead at Samarra, then that only donkeys would be available, while others thought we should be lucky to get anything.

While at the barracks we were given a month's pay by the Turkish authorities, on what proved to be for senior officers a very generous scale, the greatest mercy being that half the amount was paid in gold. Had this not been done, we should have been in a truly sorry plight on the long journeys by road across the desert, since no Arab would look at Turkish notes, and insisted on being paid in hard cash.

At this time, the Russian force under General Baratoff had made a sudden advance through the Pusht-i-Kuh mountains and reached Khanikin, 90 miles north-east of Bagdad; the Turks were therefore very anxious to get us away, while some of the under-strappers, evidently thinking the Russians would reach Bagdad, began to talk in a very different strain, pretending that they had really been pro-British all the time.

Very few people succeeded in getting out of the barracks, but two or three officers, duly escorted, managed to get a *gharry*, and drove straight to the American consul, who arranged to give them money, and did everything he could for them. He said he expected to see many of us and went on to tell them exactly what he thought of the campaign up to date. He was very pessimistic over the future treatment of the British troops and declared that had we known what would happen to them we would have cut our way out of Kut at whatever cost. We hoped this was exaggeration, and that things would not turn out as badly as he expected; but events proved only too truly how entirely his fears were justified. Hopelessly inadequate rations, no transport, no medical arrangements for the sick who fell out, and utter incapability of all Turkish authorities, constitute one of the blackest crimes committed during any war.

It is only right to add that whenever we met German officers they did all they could to help us, more than one saying they considered that we and they were civilised people in a land of barbarians.

Two days after reaching Bagdad we were paraded in the hot sun in the afternoon and marched off to the station, passing over the bridge of boats and through the Shia quarter of the city, which lies on the right bank of the river. We were all only too glad to get away from the insanitary conditions which are inseparable from all Turkish buildings.

After a wait of two hours at the station, we were packed into a train which started about six o'clock. A few miles north of Bagdad we passed the Great Mosque at Kazmain, its golden domes and minarets shining in the setting sun. The train proceeded at a good rate; everything in connection with the railway was naturally German, and of a substantial description. The length of line then completed to the railhead at Samaria was 80 miles, passing through slightly undulating country the whole way. This had been finished by the Germans before the war broke out.

Most of us were weary, and many preferred lying on the floor of the corridors or vestibules at the end of the cars, to sitting straight up in the cramped compartments. We made several halts, and it was near midnight when we arrived. Our guards, a few *gendarmes*, seemed to have no idea where we were going, or what was to be done with us. Eventually we were told to leave our kit, which was to be brought along later, and were guided down towards the river. After walking a mile, we found ourselves in a small Arab village on the river bank and were conducted into a courtyard some 40 yards square, where we were told we were to stay.

There was a rough shelter round three sides, formed by brushwood supported on a rough wooden framework; this promised a certain amount of shade, and we were all glad to be in the open air rather than in another barrack building. There were no signs of any transport fetching our kit, so the most enterprising managed to procure two trollies, and trundled than up to the station along a narrow-gauge line. The Turks used this line for taking stores, ammunition, etc., to the railway, from the rafts on which they were floated down from Mosul. By dawn, nearly all the kit had been collected, and we had settled down as best we could.

There was a certain amount of food obtainable from Arab vendors, and as we had our Indian servants, and a few things left from stores received at Shamrán, we were fairly comfortable. As usual, no one seemed to know how long we were to be there, before our journey by road across the desert began. Fortunately, we were not guarded very strictly, and were allowed to go outside the courtyard, and down to the river to bathe; the current here was very strong, and only the most powerful swimmers could make any headway against it, and that only for a few yards.

The town of Samarra was on the other bank, and some little height above the land on our side. It stands back from the river, and contains a fine mosque, with a golden dome. The inhabitants cross the river in *gufahs*—the large round coracles which are used all down the Tigris. Owing to the current a start always has to be made very much higher upstream than the point where it is desired to land on the other side.

During the three or four days which we spent at Samarra, a large quantity of German gun-ammunition arrived by raft from upstream and was carried by Arabs up the bank to the trollies. These rafts carry big loads; they are formed by a skeleton frame of wood on which is placed brushwood, the frame being supported by inflated skins which are tied to it. On reaching the end of a journey, the skins are deflated and sent back up the river to be used again. As there are rapids between Samarra and Bagdad, it was not possible to float the rafts right down to Bagdad, and consequently everything had to be transhipped to the railway. One night some large motors arrived and went on at once by road towards Bagdad. Reports immediately circulated that Enver Pasha had arrived; but this cannot have been true.

We had now learnt who our *commandant* on the journey was to be. He was a *yuzbashi* or captain, by name Elmey Bey, a little man with an enormous moustache, which made him look very fierce. He knew a very little French and could therefore be approached without an interpreter. We did not really appreciate him until later. One morning he escorted a few of us over to the town; there was nothing to be seen except the mosque, and we were not allowed to look at this even from the gateway, much less to enter the courtyard.

After making a few purchases, we went into an Arab *café* and partook of coffee and tea flavoured with citron. Elmey Bey would not let

ELMEY BEY

us pay for anything, and we thought it most hospitable of him. He said
he would accept our hospitality another day. However, he eventually
left the *café* without paying anything, and apparently the proprietor
was really our unwilling host.

The town seemed very deserted, many of the inhabitants being
over on the other side, selling anything they could to the first batch of
troops, who had reached Samarra that morning by rail, and were now
camped in the open a little way above us. We were not allowed to go
to see them, but one or two managed to get messages through, and
an Indian clerk belonging to my regiment came to see us. He looked
thin and had evidently had a hard time. He said that on the way to
Bagdad the guards had flogged men who fell out, to see if they were
really ill, and that conditions as regards rations were pretty bad generally. None of our men, however, had succumbed so far, and, as many
of the regiment had been anything but fit to start with, we hoped they
would be able to stand it. We gave him a few little things in the way of
eatables before he went back.

The next day, we were told we were going to march; and the question of transport became all-important. At first the Turks said there
would be two animals—donkeys, mules, or ponies—to each officer;
this seemed much too good to be true, and when the time came
there was barely one animal to every officer. These had all been forc-

ibly commandeered from the villagers round, and a good many were taken back again on the sly by their owners before we could get hold of them. Others were taken by the *gendarmes* who formed our guard, while several were too small to be of use, or were hopelessly lame. By the time we had got our kit packed, we had left for riding one reasonably large donkey and a diminutive beast between the six officers and seven Indian servants in our mess.

We started at sunset in a dust-storm. Fortunately, it did not last long, and we got along without mishap till about eleven o'clock, when a heavy rainstorm came on. All through the night, and especially after every halt, we had been urged on by our Arab escort shouting "*Yallah, yallah!*" This really means "O God!" but is used by the Arabs for "Get on and hurry up." How we came to loathe that cry! About two in the morning, we reached some water; luckily, in the dark, we could not see what we were drinking. We must have done fifteen to twenty miles; and, as most of us bad not marched any distance for months, we were only too glad to fall asleep for a few hours. At dawn we were again on the move, having had some trouble in finding our own animals again; the wise had marked theirs with copying pencil, and this method was generally resorted to afterwards.

We went on with halts of a few minutes every hour and got down to the river again at midday. It was now pretty hot, and we were told we should arrive at Tekrit, a small Arab town, in one hour. Throughout Turkey and Mesopotamia distances are measured by hours; a good working plan is to add on 50 *per cent*, to the average of what one is told, as no two men will ever say the same; if journeying by night it is safer to double it.

That last hour to Tekrit was one of the worst we had; actually, it was nearer two hours. There was a blazing sun, and we were very tired. The road left the river and went up a hill, then down and up again. On each rise we expected to see the town, but it was dreadfully slow in appearing. From some distance off we were met by Arab boys and women selling eggs, raisins, sour curds, and *chapatties*. Finally, we were taken through the place down to the river edge, a sort of dirty, stony beach, where we were told to camp; we had covered 30 to 35 miles in the last nineteen hours, and most of us had marched almost the whole distance.

There was a small Arab *café* which we were allowed to use, but otherwise there was no shade. Arabs sauntered about our bivouac and were anything but friendly; the place was filthy, and we were far from feeling cheerful.

Some of the houses of the town stand up on a rocky crag above the river. Tekrit is a very old place, and at one time there was a bridge over the river here. It was laid waste by the Mongols and the people butchered. Before we left, we were all wishing that some such fate might be in store for the present inhabitants.

Some of us bathed, but the water was very shallow and dirty. Arabs could be seen swimming across the river supported on inflated skins, in exactly the same way as Xenophon has described their forefathers doing 2,000 years ago.

That afternoon we tried to arrange to hire extra animals, as we felt that we could never get along if the succeeding marches were so severe. A good many animals were forthcoming, mostly mules and large donkey. The usual terms were to be one pound in gold, paid in advance, and a second on arrival at Mosul. The following evening, just before starting, the owners demanded the whole two pounds in advance; there was nothing for it but to comply, the reason undoubtedly being that the *commandant* of the town and Elmey Bey both desired to have their share before starting, as otherwise they would not see any of it. A long delay ensued before we got off, and it was getting dark before we were clear of the town.

The march that night was uneventful, and we halted for a few hours before dawn near the river, continuing our way as soon as it got light. We passed a few Arab encampments, formed of dark tents, where the nomads come at certain seasons to cultivate the surrounding land, together with their flocks of sheep and goats. Not a single house, or even mud-hut, was to be seen. Our next halt, which we reached in the middle of the morning, was a *serai* standing by itself on a low ridge. It was built on the usual square pattern, and contained a well, which however, was not of very much use, as the water was unfit for drinking; drinking water had all to be carried from the river, over a mile away.

Elmey Bey, or "Phil May," as we christened him, had by this time shown how anxious he was to help us, by doing nothing at all to assist us either in buying provisions or keeping prices down. Our escort consisted of a few Arab *gendarmes*, and, on arrival at any village or encampment, they would make the people put up their prices, and insist on taking the difference as commission themselves; whenever they could manage it they prevented all country people from approaching us until their own demands had been satisfied.

Phil May rode the whole way and would hurry on and be comfortably asleep in his camp bed by the time we reached the end of the march. If worried sufficiently by the senior officers, he would occasionally go to the extent of abusing one or more of the *gendarmes*, and administer the usual punishment adopted by all officers in the Turkish army—slapping the face of the culprit. It says a good deal for the discipline of the Turkish soldier that a sergeant will stand up like a lamb and have his face smacked by the veriest nincompoop of an officer.

Leaving the *serai* again the following morning, we did a short march of some six or seven miles only, down to the river. This was to be a very strenuous day, for that evening we were to start on the long waterless march about which we had heard so much. It was said to be 40 miles, that we should halt during the next day, and not reach water till the morning after, thus doing two all-night marches. Most people had bought goatskins, tied up to hold water, from the local Arabs. Most of them leaked more or less rapidly the new skins being much the worst, and all gave the water a very strong flavour.

We got away about 5 p.m., and nothing special happened till about 11 o'clock, when suddenly the escort became wildly excited, and dashed up and down; we were halted and told there were hostile Arabs about; the *gendarmes* fired off a few shots into the air, but nothing more occurred. All we could find to account for the disturbance was that one officer had lost his donkey, which had got loose and gone careering off to the side of the road. As it was a dark night, this may very likely have alarmed one or two of the *gendarmes*, who did not strike us as being men of valour.

Two hours later we halted, and, after a sketchy supper, soon got to sleep. In the morning, instead of remaining where we were for the day, as we had expected, we had to move on once more to the tune of "*Yallah, yallah.*" After three hours or so we reached some low sand-hills, and amongst these found an unexpected stream, where we proceeded to camp. This stream, like so many more in this part of the world, was not pure water, but contained salts of various descriptions, said by the Turks to make the water bad for drinking. We drank steadily from this and other similar streams; and, luckily, for the most part, felt no ill effects.

That evening, we were again upon the road, our destination being Shilgat, a small Turkish post on the Tigris, which we were meeting once more. We arrived eventually about midnight, after a very wearisome march, and after a long wait were herded into the courtyard of the Turkish fort. When the kit had been sorted out, we were very soon asleep, the usual precautions being taken to see that boots were hidden under one's valise, or tied up in some way to prevent theft. As the Turkish troops were always badly off for footgear, boots were the articles most often stolen, and several pairs had disappeared in this way before we reached our journey's end. All were thoroughly tired out, and it had been decided that we would insist on a rest the following day. Great was our wrath, therefore, to find ourselves awakened again at dawn, and told we must move at once to another place. Phil May came in for more abuse and lost his temper promptly. We settled down, eventually, in another enclosure not far away, where we had more room. Later on, we succeeded in our efforts to get a whole day's rest.

In ancient times Shilgat was Assur, the first capital of the Assyrian Empire. Archaeologists had evidently been at work here; all the foundations of the old city had been laid bare; it had covered a considerable area and had been built largely of marble. Situated on a high promontory overlooking the Tigris and the flat plains beyond, the old town must have been an imposing sight from all the surrounding country. Now, only the foundations remain, and no carving or inscriptions are to be seen.

Next day, we were off once more across flat, uninteresting country, keeping close to the river. At the start, there was considerable delay owing to donkeys getting bogged in a creek which we had to cross. After a midday halt for a couple of hours, we continued our weary way, and finally bivouacked for the night on the bank of the river.

The following day's march proved one of the most unpleasant of the whole journey. After an early start, we soon reached a Turkish post, where a long delay occurred while our orderlies drew rations. At this place there were small bitumen works, these being the first signs of any modem industry which we had seen since leaving Bagdad. A little farther on, the track rose to higher ground, and we left the river away on our right. It began to get hot towards midday, and a warm wind got up, bringing clouds of dust to meet us. At length, in the afternoon, we reached a Turkish post, where after much altercation we were refused an entrance, and had to retrace our steps to a somewhat sulphurous stream a little way back, where we camped for the night.

The country all round at this time of year is covered with long thin grass, and in many places, there are quantities of wild flowers, scarlet poppies being very conspicuous.

In order to defeat the *gendarmes*, we had by now formed a kind of trade union for buying eggs from villagers. On approaching each place, it was decided how much should be paid for eggs, these being more in demand than any other kind of food. In the Bagdad district the Persian *kron* is the usual unit: a *kron* is equivalent to fourpence or two Turkish *piastres*; farther north the *piastre*, or *qrush*, is used. The cheapest rate we obtained for eggs was eight for a *piastre*, or four a penny, whereas when the *gendarmes* had their own way we had to pay a penny for each.

Our next march took us to Hamàmali, a place on the river, and containing an old bath, as its name implies. There are bitumen springs entering the river here, but they are not strong enough to render the water unfit for drinking. Supplies were very plentiful—eggs, raisins, bread, and dates being the most sought after. After a few hours' rest and a bathe in the river, we started off again in the evening, looking forward to a real rest on reaching Mosul the next day. We bivouacked beside the road and were moving at an early hour next morning.

The road wound up and down over low hills, and some attempt had been made to metal the surface and build good bridges, showing that we were getting near to an important place. As we reached the top of one ridge, a full view of the Tigris valley burst upon us, Mosul lying straight ahead of us, while farther to the right across the river lay the ruins of old Nineveh. In the immediate foreground, the course of the river was marked by green cultivated land and low woods, while away, in the distance, rose the dark mountains of Kurdistan.

On approaching the town more closely, one noticed a great difference in the mosques, as compared with Bagdad. Here the minarets were of plain stone-work and were not capped by gorgeous golden domes or brilliant blue tile-work.

We were marched into a large building, formed on the usual Turkish pattern of a hollow square. This seemed to be chiefly used as a prison. We were given three or four empty rooms on the upper story. Water was scarce and had to be brought in by hand. In other respects, the building had all the filthy characteristics inseparable from the Turk.

Soon after arriving, we were given Red Crescent postcards to send home, and these turned out to be the first news our friends in England received from us. For food we were allowed to go out to restaurants in the town. One of these, run by a Frenchman, was a great joy to us, after the scratch meals which we had been forced to be content with for so long. We had covered the 175 miles from Samarra to Mosul in just under tea days, and had it not been for the extra animals hired at

Tekrit we should scarcely have managed this. As it was. most people could ride for an hour and walk for an hour alternately, though some were not so fortunate.

We were promised many things in Mosul, amongst others that we should be allowed to go to bathe in the river. This was never allowed in the end, although we went in parties to the bazaar, where we laid in stocks of flour, rice, and raisins, for the journey on to Ras-el-Ain. We were told that very few supplies were obtainable on the road until we reached Nisibin, 120 miles away.

At Samarra, we had left behind a few officers who had not sufficiently recovered from the effects of the siege to proceed at once on the road journey. At Shilgat, we picked up one officer left by the first party and left one or two of our own servants behind. All these we hoped would recover enough to come on with the troops or subsequent parties of officers. At Mosul, we found one of our doctors left behind by the first party and attending to an officer who was down with enteric.

After a rest of two days at Mosul, we started off on June 1 for the 200 miles to the railhead at Ras-el-Ain. Our transport was now composed chiefly of carts, and a few extra carts were hired by paying in advance as before. There was the usual uncertainty as to how many marches it would take us, and how many hours we should be on the road the first day. We were now going almost due west, and would not see our old friend the Tigris, again.

In response to our complaints to the *commandant* at Mosul of the way in which our Arab escort had behaved, these men were changed for Turkish soldiers, who gave us less trouble. Our party was accompanied by three magnificent Arab horses, which were being taken to Constantinople for Enver Pasha. The Mosul district has been the finest horse-breeding country in Asia from the earliest times; indeed, it would be hard to imagine a country better suited for the purpose than the rolling grassy plains stretching away on both sides of the river.

After leaving the Tigris, we did not see a single tree for a hundred miles, and there was very little water of any description. The first night we spent by some dirty pools after a march of more than twenty miles. The carts were not as restful as might be imagined, since they had no spring, and every few minutes the *jehu* would urge his steeds into a canter to catch up distance lost on the cart in front, or merely to try to get ahead of it. The harness was largely composed of string and rope, which often gave way, thus occasioning a long rattle for all on

161

board before the former place in the procession was regained. Some of the horses had most appalling sores: they are evidently worked till they drop and receive the harshest treatment from the drivers. The boys driving our carts were Kurds, wild, quick-tempered, and reckless.

The second day brought us to a camp beside a stream of pure sweet water, a welcome change after all the dirty pools and salt-laden springs which we had experienced. The following day, after a halt near some dirty springs at noon, we started on another long waterless trek in the late afternoon. We went on steadily all night, passing a large prairie fire. These fires are started to burn up the old long grass and make way for the fresh growth. They extend for miles, and at night are a fine sight, with heavy clouds of smoke hanging above.

We halted for two hours about two in the morning, and then got under way once more. About nine o'clock we came to a good stream and towards midday reached our camp at Demir Kapo. Here, there was a small river which yielded a number of fish. We saw a few Germans, and a German wireless section was camped near. We bathed in the stream and were very glad to rest for the remainder of the day and the following morning.

Two more marches brought us to Nisibin. The country after leaving Mosul had been almost uninhabited, but here there were small villages dotted about. On getting nearer to them, we found that they were deserted; our guards told us they were Armenian village, and that the people had all been killed earlier in the war. We passed a great many of these awful testimonies to the barbarity of Turkish politics.

Away on our right, as we approached Nisibin, could be seen Mardin, a city built on a rock overlooking the plains, and forming, as it were, a lookout from the southern fringe of the Taurus Mountains. As to how far Mardin also was a city of the dead, it was impossible to tell. Before the war, the main Armenian population had extended from this district over a belt of land running north-eastwards up to Erzerum and Van.

At Nisibin, we camped near the river, and had a full day's rest. This place saw as much fighting as any spot in Mesopotamia in the old days, having been the frontier station between Rome and Parthia. There are not many relics of the past to be seen at the present day, but close to our bivouac stood four old pillars, bearing transverse stones which had formed part, of the Roman Forum. They stood out forlornly in a field on high ground, and. as might be expected, supported a stork's nest. These birds often build a new nest on the top of one or more old ones: they are very common in Mesopotamia, and several were seen in Bagdad.

The following evening saw us moving on again, and the day after we halted at midday at Tel Erman. At this point, there is a road branching away to the north of the route we had followed and leading up to Diarbekr. The Turks were moving a good many troops at this time up to the Caucasus front, through Diarbekr, to meet the Russian pressure. We found a large camel convoy just beyond the village; since leaving Mosul we had met no troops or convoys, destined for Bagdad or the Persian front; everything for Mesopotamia appeared to go down the Euphrates on rafts, this being the quickest way.

Tel Erman lived in our memories as being the first place where we had obtained any fruit since leaving Bagdad three weeks before. Some small cherries and apricots were to be had and were eagerly bought up.

During the evening's march, we passed a regiment of Turkish cavalry, who, for Turks, seemed to be wonderfully well equipped. The average Turk never looks happy on a horse, but these fellows made a better show than usual. As we approached the railhead at Ras-el-Ain, signs of activity increased, and there were more dead horses at the roadside, showing that the traffic was heavier.

The last day's march was one of the worst; during the morning stage the sun was hot, there was no breeze, and quantities of sand-flies assailed us. Towards midday, we reached a big Turkish camp, where there were a good many men and stores in course of transit eastwards. Here we rested until late in the afternoon, when our final march to Ras-el-Ain began. The last few miles were accomplished at a good pace to a sustained whistling accompaniment, ranging over most of the popular songs of the last few years.

Everyone thought that our troubles were over, as we were now on a railway, and whatever might happen would not have to walk any farther. These hopes were dispelled a few days later, when we heard of the two breaks in the line across the Taurus Mountains, which had not yet been completed, thus necessitating two more trips by road.

We bivouacked in the open by the station, and early in the morning wore told to get ready at once to go by the next train. An hour later, it appeared that we were not going till the following day. By this time, we had ceased to pay much attention to Turkish orders, unless we saw that actual preparations were being made to carry them out. In the afternoon, the Turks took away all Hindu orderlies and servants, and informed us that all the doctors in our party, except one, were to stay here to look after the Indian troops on their arrival, as the latter were going to be put to work on continuing the railway farther east towards Nisibin. We were very sorry for our medical friends, since their prospects looked anything but cheerful. Local food supplied from the country round seemed almost non-existent, and the shops in the village had very little.

By the time we reached Ras-el-Ain, we had. completed 200 miles from Mosul in ten days. Most of us had walked half the distance and bumped in carts over the other half. We had kept tolerably cheerful, apart from a few inveterate grousers; altogether we had survived wonderfully well and had fared infinitely better than the troops from Kut, who were marching along in our tracks a few days behind tis.

From Ras-el-Ain we started for Aleppo the next morning, the journey taking nearly twelve hours. The only interesting place through which we passed was Jerrablus, the ancient Carchemish, where the line crosses the Euphrates by a fine bridge. There was not much sign of activity on the river banks, but before we left the station a complete train loaded with German motor-lorries had arrived, and after a few minutes continued its way eastwards.

On reaching Aleppo, in the evening, the orderlies and servants were marched off by themselves, and after loading our kit on to carts we were driven away in parries from the station. This seemed to be almost the height of luxury, and we thought that at last we had reached a place where we should be really well treated. The *gharries* took us to various small hotels, but when once inside we were not allowed to go out again. The Turks said that our kit would be delivered at once; some people waited up hoping for the arrival of their valises, but the wiser seized what bedding there was obtainable in the hotel and laying it on a veranda made the best of a bad job and went to sleep.

In the morning, we were not allowed out to get any food. The hotel sharks refused to let boys come up with rolls but tried to sell to us themselves at double the prices. However, we eventually got hold of a boy who threw up rolls from the street below to our veranda, and thus outwitted our enemies.

All efforts to get out for breakfast, or to fetch our kit, proved unavailing, until about midday we were allowed to go a few yards down the street to where our kit had all been thrown inside a gateway the night before. Fortunately, although a good many valises had evidently been opened, very little had been stolen.

It was not until four o'clock in the afternoon that we were finally allowed out in parties to a restaurant not a hundred yards away. While we were shut in, we had seen Phil May in the road and shouted to him; but, although he could see very well what we wanted, he never took the trouble to come into the hotel, much less to help us.

The next day passed in much the same fashion, except that we were allowed out at midday, and no one was sorry when we were marched off back to the station early the following morning. Here we met the orderlies, who had fared much worse than we had. The first night they had been packed into a small room in some filthy barracks and had suffered severely from the verminous pests which flourish in every Turkish building.

A railway journey of a few hours brought us to Islahie, which was then the railhead for the journey over the Anti-Taurus range.

There were some Austrian troops in Aleppo, and we now began to meet many more Germans. Turkish training-camps were much in evidence at the stations we passed after leaving Aleppo, and a good deal of material was going south on the railway. Most of this was going to Egypt to assist in the attack which ended so disastrously for the Turks.

We spent the night at Islahie under some rough tent shelters. All our clothes had been fumigated in a steam waggon specially designed for the purpose.

The following morning, we noticed a crowd of men, women, and children moving off along the road and looking very wretched. Our guards said that these were Armenians who had been working on the line but were being taken away to make room for our troops, who would be set to work in their place; they also added that these Armenians would be marched off into a waterless spot in the hills and kept there till they died.

We left our camp in the evening, traveling the first part of the way in carts, over one of the most bumpy roads ever seen. After a halt at the foot of the pass, we marched up, starting at midnight. There was a fine moon, and the scenery as we climbed higher became very grand. The road appeared to be only lately completed and was probably due to German energy. As we neared the summit three or four bodies were seen lying in the ditch beside the road; these were evidently some of the Armenians we had seen starting off that morning. After descending the farther side, we bivouacked under trees in a pretty spot, and on the slope opposite saw the Armenians. Soon after they left and we did not see anything more of them.

That evening we continued our way downhill, meeting several batches of sturdy Turkish youths who had just been called up and were on their way to training-camps near Aleppo. We were descending rapidly, and our drivers maintained a headlong gallop, with the result that two carts were completely overturned, but fortunately with no ill effects to the passengers. We finally bivouacked not far from the railhead and reached the station of Mamouré early the following morning.

The railway journey across the plain, through Adana, took some six hours, bringing us to Kulek Boghaz, a station within five miles of Tarsus. From this point the road journey over the main Taurus range began. All supplies were being brought over by German motor-lorries, and everything was being run by a German *commandant*. During the night several helmets were stolen and probably found their way to German soldiers, who either had no sun helmets or very inferior ones. The *commandant* did his best to recover them, but without success.

He told us that we should leave the next morning at 9 o'clock. Punctually to the minute, a dozen motor-lorries rolled up, and we were soon speeding along the road towards the mountains. The road had been cut up dreadfully by the heavy traffic, so that we were jolted about almost as badly as we had been in the Turkish carts. The scenery grew finer as we ascended, until half-way we reached an open space amongst the hills, which the Germans had made the headquarters of their motor service and christened "Camp Taurus." Here were enormous repair tents, one for each make of car, with living quarters and offices all of a most complete and elaborate type. After a halt here, we continued our way, still rising slowly until we entered the Cilician Gates, where the road just finds room to pass through a narrow rocky gorge. On the farther side, the descent begins at once, and is very steep in places. The road here was being repaired by bands of forced labourers and had a much better surface.

As we neared the railway again, at Bozanti, we noticed a few British prisoners. These were naval men taken in the Dardanelles. They said they were being paid, and apparently had not much to complain about. We were not allowed to stop and speak to them and can only hope that they fared better than our own troops who were put to work shortly afterwards on the neighbouring sections of the line through the Taurus.

At Bozanti, we were able to buy a few stores, some of which were British and had been left behind at Gallipoli when we evacuated the peninsula. With only a short wait, we were packed like sardines into a train, and the next stage of the journey began.

The next morning, we reached Konia, and were told to leave the train, but not to take our kit out, as the train was stopping for some time. The local *commandant* arrived and proved to be the best Turkish officer we had met. Under his direction, we were taken to a hospital building, where there were two large rooms containing rough beds. These were a great delight after sleeping on the ground for weeks. The *commandant*, a little later, decided that we should be allowed to remain here until the next day, so that we might have a rest. If we had relied on Phil May, our kit would have all gone on in the afternoon to Constantinople, but luckily, we just managed to rescue it in time.

The greatest delight of Konia, from our point of view, was an hotel near the station, to which we were allowed to go for meals. This was run by a Frenchwoman, who was kindness itself, and could not do enough for us. Few of us will forget the delights of her omelets or the hot baths in a real long bath, the first we had seen since leaving India.

The journey next day was more comfortable, as we had more room. After spending another night in the train, we arrived in the mining at Afion Kara Hissar, where a good number of Gallipoli prisoners were interned. In the evening, we reached Eski Chehir, the junction for the Angora line. Here all our Mohammedan servants were taken from us. We were conducted a little way into the town to the houses where a number of Indian Mohammedan officers. who had come along with the first party, were living. They seemed to have fared pretty well, and certainly had very good quarters. They were very glad to see us, and we anxiously inquired after their experiences by the way.

Up to this point we had fondly imagined that Angora would be the end of our journey, but just before starting in the evening we were told that another ten days by road lay in front of us after reaching Angora. We were packed tight in the train, and rumbled on slowly through the night, arriving at Angora at eleven o'clock next day. Our kit was left to be brought in carts, while we were marched through the town to a big building over a mile beyond. This had been built as an Agricultural College, but latterly used as a Military School.

Here we found the first party of officers, whom we had last seen at Shamrán camp. They seemed to have had a much more unpleasant journey than we had; whether it was because they had most of the staff officers amongst them or had adopted the plan of telling every Turk and interpreter exactly what they thought of them, certain it is that they were not enjoying life, and when we arrived had not been allowed outside the building for two whole days.

We had bidden farewell to Phil May with great delight at Eski Chehir. and had since then been in charge of a much pleasanter officer. Thanks to his efforts, we succeeded in getting permission to stay out of doors to cook and to go down to a neighbouring stream to bathe in the evening. We felt that the first party really owed us a great debt of gratitude in thus providing them with an opportunity of washing and getting a little fresh air.

All our orderlies had been marched off from the station to some dirty Turkish barracks, so that we were entirely dependent on our own culinary efforts. Two days after our arrival, the first party left in carts for Yozgad, a distance of 100 miles due east on the road to Sivas and Erzerum. We remained for a week, being only allowed to go into the town once to make purchases. The journey to Kastamuni began under the best conditions. The weather was perfect, and as we were well over 2,000 feet above sea-level the sun was never too hot at midday. Also, we had a new *commandant*, who did what he could to help us. The distance in front of us was 140 miles, and we expected to take fully a week.

The road led through countless orchards for the first few miles, and then on into more open country. Cherries and small apricots abounded and supplies in general were plentiful; a very different state of affairs existed a year later, when prices had doubled and trebled, and in many cases advanced very much more. We reached a small village the first evening, and our *commandant* appeared much surprised that we should prefer to sleep in the open rather than in the very doubtful shelters attached to the local rest-house.

The following day we reached Kalejik, a picturesque little place with the ruins of an old castle perched on a rocky pinnacle in the centre of the town. Some such ruin seems to keep watch over all Turkish towns. We had already seen similar old forts perched on hills at Afion Kara Hissar and Angora.

Next morning, most of our carts wore taken away, and we were given donkeys instead. A small moke cannot keep pace with a cart, and it is an open question whether riding the animal with a loading saddle is less fatiguing than walking along and driving it in front of one. Provided all one's kit had been put on a cart, the easiest way was often to let the moke go where it liked and walk on oneself without it.

Two days from Kalejik brought us to Changri, a prettily situated little place, which came suddenly into view, as we rounded a bend in the road, after traversing a very desolate and uninteresting stretch of country all day. We bivouacked under some trees by a stream, which, however, was not fit to drink from. The local *commandant* and Town Council paid us a visit. We were allowed to visit the bazaar, and generally made ourselves comfortable.

In the morning, we were given more carts again, much to our delight, and continued our way northward. The road now began to cross some high ridges. On one of these we passed a police post, and a halt was made while our *commandant* stalked a few sitting pigeons with his shotgun, eventually securing one after a great deal of trouble. Beyond sand-grouse, between Bagdad and Mosul, we had seen very little game of any sort since we left Kut.

We camped by a stream, after a very steep and bumpy descent from a high ridge. It is extraordinary what treatment the light Turkish transport carts can stand without anything giving way.

Our next march led us up a very long ascent and proved the most enjoyable day of our whole journey. After ascending some distance, the road entered pine woods, and reminded us very strongly of roads near different hill stations in India. We halted at midday very near the top of the pass, which must be close on 4,000 feet, while the mountains on either side rise to another 2,000 feet. The views were glorious, and we wished it might have been possible to stay longer in such scenery. By evening, we had dropped down a long distance on the other side and were nearly out of the woods again when we halted for our last bivouac.

We were now within ten miles of Kastamuni, and by eleven o'clock next morning, July 5th, were in sight of the place. The old castle, standing on its rocky crest, was the first sight which greeted us as we looked down into the valley from the top of the ridge along which we had come. The town, spreading up and down the valley round the base of the castle rock, seemed very much larger than any Turkish town we had seen since leaving Aleppo. The valley was green with cultivated fields and trees, while the hillsides were bare and brown.

We were halted just outside the town, while a number of local *gendarmes* formed up on each side of the road. After a long wait. we thus progressed in state into the town and through the bazaar to our quarters, which proved to be houses from which the former Greek inhabitants had been ejected. In the end, although somewhat crowded, we found ourselves each with a bed, bedding, and a little other furniture. Most of us had not slept in a bed for eight months or more, apart perhaps from a few days in hospital, and all we desired at the moment was one long rest.

During the last week, which had been by far the pleasantest of the whole trek, we had averaged twenty miles a day. Our journey altogether had been nearly 1,700 miles, and was probably the longest distance across country any prisoners of war have had to travel to the place of their confinement.

CHAPTER 4

Life in Kastamuni

July 1916—August 1917

On arrival in Kastamuni, we were divided into two groups, one being accommodated in a large building, formerly a Greek school, with one or two adjacent houses, and the other in a number of houses in a street lower down the hill. Both places were on the edge of the town in the Greek quarter. The schoolhouse was perched high up and commanded a splendid view across the town in the valley towards the hills, beyond which lay the Black Sea, only some 40 miles away.

The houses were built up on a wooden frame-work, the bricks being thrown in to fill up the intervening spaces in a most casual manner. The best houses were covered with *stucco*; but, however good in appearance, each house in Turkey has its own numerous population of small inhabitants. An Austrian lady whom we met assured us that her house was the only one in the town free from these pests, and we could well believe it.

The town itself is shut in by the valley and presents a confused jumble of houses, with almost innumerable mosques, and in the centre one or two large government buildings. The mosques are not particularly beautiful, there being no golden domes or blue tile work. The most pretentious have plain grey stone minarets, while the smaller ones have to be content with little steeples of wood. During *Ramazan* a ring of lights is kept burning at night round each minaret, and gives the town a strange appearance, as these are the only lights showing, there being no such thing as street lamps, and very few lights in private houses—with kerosene at a prohibitive price.

After the weary march from Kut, we were only too delighted to get into our new quarters and sleeping in a bed again was a luxury not soon to be forgotten. A restaurant had been arranged, and we found a very good meal ready for us soon after arrival. Unfortunately, this was much the best repast we obtained from the contractor, and when it came to arranging a daily messing scheme we had to be content with a very moderate programme. However, everyone had got so tired of scraping along, cooking and foraging for themselves on the journey up, that any sort of plan by which someone else would do the work was not to be refused, even if we were to be done over it.

During the summer of 1916, food in the town was comparatively cheap, eggs being a halfpenny each or less, and good white flour about sixpence a pound. Fruit was to be had in prolific quantities, the cherries being especially good. But no one takes any trouble to cultivate fruit in this part of Turkey. There are grapes, melons, peaches, apples and pears in great profusion, but all of the commonest kind. Had the country any communications worth the name, no doubt it would be different, but, as it is, the Turk is content with what grows by itself and does not need any special attention. The local taste in over-ripe and bad pears was most surprising. For weeks one would see baskets of rotting pears in the bazaar on market days and the country people enjoying them.

The ruined castle on its rocky pinnacle must have dated back to very early times; it is now used as a "lookout" station and has three ancient guns, which are fired as an alarm in case of fire and at other moments of importance, such as the first sight of the new moon at the end of Ramazan. The greatest wonder to us was that the whole town had not been burnt down long ago, since all the bazaar houses were wooden and dry as tinder. The fire brigade consisted of one prehistoric manual pump which was carried about on the shoulders of five or six youths, with a scratch collection of hose and buckets. On one occasion a major of the S. & T. Corps was so overcome with laughter on seeing this apparition that the *commandant*, feeling much insulted, had him confined to the house for a fortnight.

This was our first *commandant*, a very ignorant specimen, who, so report said, had been a farmer in the Caucasus. He was a most depressing sight at all times. Most Turkish officers only shave on Thursdays, and he was no exception to the rule. His trousers invariably swept the ground; he always wore galoshes several sizes too large and an old overcoat. He would shuffle about with his hands in his pockets, his shoulders hunched up, looking the picture of misery. Yet, notwithstanding his apparent dejection, he was making quite a good thing out of us, as we found out later on. The restaurant contractor was paying him about £30 a month, and, between them, they were charging us

171

rent for our quarters, which was quite contrary to all rules. Another little source of income was making us each pay for a 5-*piastre* receipt stamp for our monthly pay instead of a 2½*d*.

This *commandant* knew no language except Turkish, and consequently an interpreter was needed on all occasions. At the start this was a Greek, who made great protestations of his friendliness to us; but we very soon found him to be a double-faced blackguard doing his best to make a good thing out of us by arranging for commissions with the shopkeepers with whom we dealt.

Fortunately for us, early in 1917, a Turkish colonel—Zeur Bey, from Constantinople—arrived unexpectedly on a visit of inspection, with the result that the *commandant* was promptly dismissed and matters regarding overcharges for house rent put right. The *commandant* was said to have been seen on his knees before the colonel imploring forgiveness. This at all events was the story of Sherif Bey, the second in command, who was by way of being very anxious to do all he could for us. On our march from Angora to Kastamuni he had certainly done his best for us. but later on, we were forced to distrust him.

Turkish officers, as a rule, have very good manners and promise one almost anything without the least idea of ever keeping their word. They speak French with a very good accent, which makes one give them credit for knowing a great deal more of that language than is usually the case. It is quite impossible to describe the uniforms worn by officers, as one so seldom sees two dressed alike. All material being so scarce and expensive, uniforms were made from almost anything, and there being no such person as a provost-marshal no one could interfere. Consequently, one saw some officers dressed in a highly picturesque style, looking as if they had just been taking a part in "The Chocolate Soldier" or "The Balkan Princess," and others whom one could only recognise from shopkeepers by their badges of rank.

The Greek interpreter was the first one of the original staff to depart. After him, two very much better fellows were sent us. One of these was a young Turk named Remzi, who had been a naval cadet in Constantinople when the war broke out—and still cherished the fond hope of one day being an officer in the British Navy, for which he had the most profound veneration. Unfortunately, in trying to help us, he wrote to Constantinople; got into trouble with his seniors and was sent away. We were thus left with the second man, an Armenian, who was always called "Napoleon" from his likeness to the Great Man. Napoleon was very cautious, but, considering the difficulty of his own position, he did us very well.

After our first *commandant* had disappeared, his successor arrived in the shape of a very small, but very stout and cheery little man, named Fattah Bey. He proved to be a very good fellow and things were soon running much more pleasantly. A great point in his favour was that he spoke German, and we were thus able to dispense with an interpreter. Capt. H., of the I.A.R.O., took charge of him on most occasions, and after we had had him a few weeks he was becoming quite pro-British.

The greatest events in our life were undoubtedly the arrival of a mail or parcels. The letters we received in July 1916, soon after our arrival, were the first news most of us had had from our friends at home since before the siege began in Kut nearly eight months earlier. On an average, letters came through every ten days or so, the quickest time taken from home, *via* Switzerland, Vienna and Constantinople, being 25 days. Parcels travelled by the same route but were very much longer in making their appearance.

At first, they arrived in three to four months, but gradually took longer and longer, until finally they were eight and nine months on the way. The reason for this delay was to be found in Vienna, where all parcels were transhipped, and apparently thrown into a depot until such time as the Austrian officials decided to send a few more on. Any big operations on the Italian front had the immediate effect of stopping all parcels and sometimes letters as well. There were exceedingly few cases of anything having been actually stolen and, up to a certain date, officers had received nearly all parcels sent from home.

Soon after our arrival, we received a number of gifts through the American Embassy in Constantinople, who were at that time looking after our interests. These consisted of thin cotton things for the summer, and, when wearable, were of considerable use. Unfortunately, they were much too small, and it was a very lucky man who could wear the trousers he was given. Later on, more clothes arrived, these being thick winter garments which, although not providing the same amount of amusement, fitted us better and were a great godsend, since it was not until the New Year that people began to receive the clothes they wanted from home.

The winter in Kastamuni and, in fact, over most of Asia Minor can be very severe; but it is a dry and healthy cold. In February 1917, we had well over 20 degrees of frost for days, and during the following winter the temperature at Changri went down to 6 degrees below zero. Indeed, it would have been hard to find a better climate than

Kastamuni, which was 2.500 feet above the sea. The rainfall there was very small and confined almost entirely to March and April. The summer temperature was very much the same as in England, but drier.

As one gets nearer to the Black Sea coast, the rainfall increases and the vegetation gets thicker. Between Angora and Changri there are wide stretches of almost desert land. At Kastamuni we had pine woods and shrubs on the hills, while all the valleys were extensively irrigated. On the Black Sea coast itself the climate is much milder in winter and there are thick woods of beech, oak and fir with heavy undergrowth.

Apart from the kitchen, which always has a huge open chimney, there were no fireplaces of the ordinary kind in the houses. All heating in winter is done by stoves of sheet iron with a chimney leading out through the nearest wall. These stoves, fed with wood, give out a tremendous heat for a short time, but it is very hard to maintain anything approaching an even temperature. Wood was plentiful during the winter of 1916-17, and we used to buy it in the form of whole logs. These we had sawn up by two Armenians into short lengths, which we then split with an axe.

This gave us a good deal of exercise during the cold winter mornings. Unfortunately, the next year, wood had become scarce and much more expensive and all prisoners suffered considerably in consequence. A good deal of charcoal is used for cooking, but we saw no coal being used in the district, even the railway up to Angora being largely dependent on wood.

After a few months at the restaurant, the contractor began to put up prices and most of us demurred. This finally led to the majority going on strike and deciding to mess themselves, as we were allowed to by the rules. The old *commandant*, however, and the contractor, had no idea of accepting the alternative if they could possibly help it. Consequently, we were first forbidden to cook in the kitchens of our own houses, for fear we should set the chimney and the houses on fire. To get over this, we made fireplaces in the back gardens or yards behind the houses. Other little pin-pricks of the same kind were tried, but we finally got our own way, and found that our mess bills were reduced to nearly a half what they had been before.

We had a number of British orderlies with us, who did our cooking and waited on us. To start with, there was some difficulty in getting a separate room as a dining-room for each mess, but eventually we settled down and furnished on an economical plan, our carpenters making benches, tables, etc.

The restaurant contractor was so disgusted at our strike that he closed down altogether for two or three days, thus throwing out into the cold the few who had remained faithful to him on any conditions rather than do their own catering. There was, somewhat naturally, a good deal of ill-feeling between the two parties in consequence, and it took time to die out. In the end, the restaurant supporters had to start a mess of their own and came into line with the rest of us.

We were allowed a fair amount of liberty, although at the start this did not look promising, the old *commandant* telling us we should be only able to go one short walk a week. Actually, we were allowed in the road for a hundred yards or so outside our houses and could go to the bazaar or Turkish bath any day by getting a sentry to go with us.

The *Hamáms*, or Turkish baths, of which there are a great many, are not the elaborately furnished places one sees at home, but consist of two vaulted chambers, supplied with vapour. Round the side are ledges on which one sits, and stone basins with a supply of hot and cold water. After being stewed in the hottest chamber for a quarter of an hour, one passes out to the outer room, where an aged attendant is generally ready to operate with buckets of cold water.

Next one proceeds to the dressing-rooms and reclines comfortably swathed in towels, while Turkish coffee is brought round. After the first few months, sugar became so expensive that it was no longer provided, and the coffee seemed very poor in consequence. Altogether, in a place where one had plenty of time to spare, the *Hamám* provided a very pleasant way of spending a morning.

The Turks used to put up numbers of rules for our benefit. These were written out in the best English the interpreter could achieve, which was never very clear. As a rule, we did not pay very much attention to them, and they, on the other hand, never seemed to care either. The rule was on the board, and, if any officious officer was to come round from Constantinople, he could always be shown it, and assured it was strictly obeyed.

On one occasion a notice was suddenly put up, informing us that all lights henceforth must be put out at 9.30 p.m. It was thought advisable to do so the first night; the second night, the time was about 9.45; and after that we continued to go to bed when we pleased and were never bothered any more about it.

Owing to the tremendously high price of kerosene, Daylight Saving soon came into force, and saved us a great deal.

The sentries, on the whole, were a very good-natured lot and would never have worried us with restrictions as far as they themselves were concerned. They were mostly old men who had served in previous wars and, until called up, were living on their own small farms. One of the best of them was "Johnnie Walker," a little man who had a most extraordinary stride and could walk any of us to a standstill. We always tried to get him when going for a long walk, knowing that from personal motives he would never stop us going a good distance. Another favourite was "Ginger," a very harmless old fellow with sandy whiskers. As one went past, he would lean over and whisper confidentially; "Ginger *fennah?*"—Is Ginger a bad fellow? Every now and then they went to their homes on leave and came back with a few pounds of butter or a bag of wheat-meal, which they sold to us without much difficulty.

On our arrival, the only weapons the guard possessed were ancient pinfire rifles, firing a huge lump of lead. Each man had exactly two rounds in his possession. Later on, some rather younger men came, armed with captured Russian rifles.

We soon managed to hire a field for football. It was very stony and by no means level, but, nevertheless, was a great acquisition. As a rule, each group of houses used it three days a week. To start with, we only had a Soccer case and no bladder. We stuffed the case with grass and played a very modified form of Rugger, where collaring was disallowed on account of the stones, and punting and place kicking forbidden in order to preserve the life of the ball. After some weeks we got some proper footballs from Constantinople, and others came eventually from home. We played matches against the other group of houses, Regulars *v.* Irregulars, and every other thing we could think of. Soccer Sixes caused much excitement and a local firm of bookmakers, who came into existence for the occasion, did a large business.

We could always rely on getting out somewhere every day. During the early summer we had splendid walks two days a week over the hills in the mornings. These long walks did not suit everybody, and a gentle form of meandering had to be organised for the "slugs." On one celebrated occasion, we walked out about five miles, taking our lunch, and had a very cheery picnic, but this was never allowed again, and in July 1917 all long walks were suddenly stopped, and we were barely allowed outside the boundaries of the town.

For news of the outer world, we were dependent upon the local telegrams, which the best Turkish scholars used to translate, and also upon the "*Hilal*," a German-run paper, printed in Constantinople. This paper, of which we used to receive the French edition, had been started for propaganda purposes at the beginning of the war. The news was, naturally, very one-sided, but, reading between the lines, one could tell fairly well what, was the position on the Western Front.

In addition, we had maps, and could follow the places mentioned, when, as during the Somme offensive, the Germans, "according to our preconceived plan," took up a position some miles in rear of their last. A serial story which ran for some time in this paper was called "L'évadé de Tsingtau," and gave the adventures of a German, who having escaped from Tsingtau after the Japanese had taken it, reached America, was caught while trying to cross to Germany, spent some time in Donnington Hall, but finally succeeded in escaping, and swam off from near Tilbury to a Dutch ship lying in the river, thus getting clear away. Whether true or not, it made a wonderful story. (This German was in fact Gunther Plüschow whose book *My Escape from Donnington Hall* is republished by Leonaur as *The Only One Who Got Away*.)

News carefully camouflaged in our letters from home invariably arrived safely; in fact, the Turks never troubled to censor anything in the letters we received. On the other hand, every now and then some officious creature in Constantinople would systematically cut up our long letters, which we were allowed to write twice a month, and only send on the first two and last two lines.

There were always plenty of rumours amongst the Greek shopkeepers in the bazaar. For instance, we were told the British had taken Bagdad long before they did, and our troops in Palestine were always said to be within three or four marches of Aleppo; the Russians were just outside Sivas, and Trieste had been taken by the Italians. The Turks themselves never believed these stories, and, in fact, even when the armistice was signed, many of them in country districts had not heard that Bagdad was in our possession. They received no letters from their friends at the front, no casualty lists were published, and the only news that seemed to reach them by post, was a few letters from Turks we had taken to Burma as prisoners, who seemed to be very happy and contented.

The country people never showed any "hate" against us, but the authorities used to make this an excuse for curtailing our walks, saying how fanatical the village people were in the neighbourhood.

Apart from football matches, we employed ourselves in various ways. There were soon two or three well-established firms of carpenters, who did a great deal of work and made a lot of furniture. Others took to cobbling and had plenty to do to keep our boots in order. A good many studied various languages, but Turkish was not very popular, as no one expected ever to want it again when once they had left the country.

We had quite a good library, and books came through without much trouble in parcels from home.

A long series of lectures were held during the winter, everyone who could do so lecturing to the rest of us. It is wonderful what a comprehensive programme can be formed when one is really put to it.

Another intellectual effort was a debating society; but this did not have a very long life.

Our greatest achievement was undoubtedly the band. This was started in the spring of 1917, under the auspices of our new *commandant*, who was very keen about it. At first there were only two or three violins which had been discovered in the bazaar, then others were found, also some clarinets; drums and banjos were soon made, and, finally—greatest triumph of all—two 'cellos and a double bass were manufactured by our most progressive firm of carpenters. Altogether, the band numbered about sixteen. At the start they had no music, and Lieut. Parsons, R.F.A., who conducted, had to score the parts for a number of pieces, most of which were wonderfully successful. Later on, music came from home, and concerts were given twice a week.

We even had a little dancing on one or two occasions, and one day the *commandant* brought two or three Greek and Armenian ladies. This was such a success that he became very excited and declared "Next veek plenty lady kom." life seemed to be improving all round, but it was too good to last, and suddenly everything was stopped. The *commandant* got into hot water with the other Turkish authorities in the town, who had probably reported him behind his back to Constantinople. Our walks were suddenly curtailed and no long walks allowed. Had the little man been able to stand up for himself, things would have been much better, but he was much too scared to take a strong line, and a few days later departed for Eski-Chehir to take the place of the *commandant* there, who, in turn, was to come to Kastamuni.

During the winter of 1916, prices began to rise rapidly in the bazaar and this went on all through 1917, until in 1918 all prisoners had great difficulty in getting food, even in the new camps, which were said to be better off in this respect than Kastamuni.

When we first arrived, there was a small amount of silver money in circulation, the smallest notes which were just being introduced being 20 and 5 *piastres*—3*s*. 4*d*. and 10*d*. in ordinary times. Not long afterwards, these were followed by 2½ and 1 *piastre* notes, which carried pictures of the Dardanelles and Kut on the back, Kut being quite unrecognisable. For smaller change recourse had to be taken to stamps and by midsummer of 1917 no coins of any sort were to be seen.

Money came through to us in various ways, but the best exchange we could get was by cashing undated cheques with the Greek shopkeepers in the town, who gave us 160 *piastres* to the pound, whereas through the Dutch Embassy we could only get 140, the exchange rate before the war being 112. The shopkeepers would not be able to cash these cheques till the end of the war, and it says something for the reputation of a British cheque that they would accept them on such conditions. They undoubtedly regarded such cheques as being a very much safer asset than the Turkish paper money, which was the only alternative, and, at the end of the war, would very likely be suddenly repudiated by a paternal Government.

We were paid by the Turks at the rate they pay their own officers, the equivalent of this being deducted from our accounts by the War Office.

On the way up from Kut we were given one month's pay in Bagdad, which for senior officers was on a comparatively generous scale. However, on reaching Kastamuni, these unfortunates were told that the Bagdad rates were quite wrong, and they were now to pay up the difference; this took several months in many cases.

Happily, for us, soon after our arrival, the Red Cross came to our assistance, working through the American Embassy in Constantinople. They gave us £T.3 a month, which, with a subaltern's allowance of £T.7 as pay from the Turks, made it just possible to carry on.

As food got more expensive, the Red Cross increased their allowance to £T.5 a month and had finally to increase this still further.

In May and June 1917, some additional orderlies arrived; these men had been in other camps up till then, and were not all Kut prisoners, some having been taken in the Dardanelles and others in Egypt. They brought dreadful stories of the treatment of the troops during the first few months, and it became clear that at least two-thirds of the Kut garrison were already dead. The last news they had heard was that all fit prisoners were being sent back to the North of Syria to work on the railway there. As conditions were very bad in that district when we came through in 1916, no one can say what those who returned a year later had to go through. This area was considered as one under military operations, and was, therefore, excluded from the agreement finally come to by which the Dutch Embassy in Constantinople was to inspect the various camps.

Unfortunately, some of these new orderlies contracted typhus on their way to Kastamuni, at one of the dirty halting-places, and three succumbed. They were buried beside three officers whom we had already laid to rest, in a little cemetery at the top of the hill overlooking the town, near the slope where the Greeks and Armenians are buried. Wooden crosses were at first put up over the graves, but these were at once torn up and stolen by the Turkish peasants. We then obtained heavy slabs of stone, on which a cross was carved and the names cut. A wall was built round the little spot, a number of officers going up every morning and working hard until it was completed. Now that no British prisoners are left in Kastamuni, one hopes that the little cemetery will be allowed to remain undisturbed on the bare hillside.

During the summer of 1917, a number of officers were in favour of getting the Turks to move the camp from Kastamuni to some place nearer to the railway, as it was thought that it would then be easier to obtain supplies of wood and fuel during the coming winter. It is doubtful if this would have been the case, but an official request was sent to Constantinople. Towards the end of July 1917, our liberties were considerably curtailed for no apparent reason, and after the escape of our party, on August 8th, very severe restrictions were imposed.

Nowhere in Turkey could life in 1917-18 be considered amenable, since food was so short in all districts. This, combined with the depreciation in the paper money, kept prices very high and made messing a great problem; if parcels could have got through more quickly from home it would have made a big difference. At the end of September, the first batch of officers was moved to Changri, and the remainder followed early in October. At Changri accommodation was provided in a dirty Turkish barrack, which, besides needing very extensive cleansing, required much glass in the windows. Shortly afterwards, two-thirds of the officers left for Gedos, a small place about a hundred miles east of Smyrna, where they were placed on parole, and given liberty to go where they pleased unguarded.

The remainder stayed for some months at Changri, where they had managed to make themselves fairly comfortable, although only allowed to go out to a neighbouring field for exercise. Later, however, they were sent to Yozgad, the camp to which the first half of the Kut officers had originally been sent.

CHAPTER 5
Escape from Kastamuni

Returning to events in Kastamuni, in November 1916 a little more housing accommodation had become available for us, and as a result I found myself sharing a good room with Keeling, a lieutenant in the I.A.R.O. One evening, soon afterwards, I asked him if he would make an effort with me to reach the Russians if, as we hoped, they should advance further west from their lines, which were then running due south to Erzinjan from a point a little way west of Trebizond. He replied that he had long been thinking of it, and had made a start towards preparing for such an effort by carefully preserving two 1 lb. tins of chocolate which he had received from home!

At that time such a journey meant a distance of 300 miles across country from Kastamuni, and we considered it quite hopeless in view of the mountainous country to be passed. It was also obvious that any attempt to get a long distance across country would stand a much better chance if made in the summer time. It would be impossible to carry enough food and we should have to fall back on such crops, fruit and vegetables as might be ripe and obtainable. We thought April or May would be the earliest possible month.

Another alternative was to get to the coast, only 38 miles as the crow flies, and then to steal a boat. This necessitated having one man in the party who knew how to sail a boat and added a big risk in the very fact of having to launch a boat secretly and get away from a coast which as far as we could hear was well guarded.

The general opinion was that it was quite hopeless to try to get away. This belief was shared by the senior officers and, under pressure from the Turkish *commandant*, most people gave their parole not to try to escape under present conditions. About ten of us refused: some because they believed such an act was definitely against army rules, and the others, like ourselves, because they hoped for a chance to get away and considered that they were justified in taking such a chance if it seemed to offer any possibility of success.

Pressure was brought to bear upon us by the Turks to change our views; but we remained firm. We were told our liberty would be curtailed; we would be put in a separate house by ourselves; while the others were to get additional liberty. What actually happened was ex-

181

actly nothing, and we all went on precisely as before. It appeared to be merely a dodge on the part of the Turks to save themselves trouble and responsibility. From time to time, owing to various good reasons, many others withdrew their parole, and by the date we departed—August 8th, 1917—nearly half the officers must have followed suit.

In the meanwhile, K. and I had been trying to collect information and had been sounding a few other officers. It was very hard to get anything which was at all trustworthy: some reports said there were no boats on the coast, others that a boat could probably be obtained. One Greek told us that it would be impossible to get through to the Russian lines, as the people east of Samsun were so wild and savage. This man was making plenty of money out of us in his professional capacity, and evidently did not wish any disturbances between us and the Turks to imperil his tranquillity and source of gain. We were not therefore much influenced by his fears.

Maps were a necessity, and the only one we had was on a scale of 32 miles to an inch. I made tracings of this, so as to have duplicate copies, but the scale was too small to be of much use beyond showing the general trend of the country. I also succeeded in making a compass of a rough description by fixing a dial to some magnetic needles and suspending it with a thread. Fortunately, however, a little later, we discovered a shop in the town where we could buy some cheap but tolerably serviceable compasses, and secured several of these, taking care that the sentry with us did not see what we were buying.

The best map we had seen was hanging up in our *commandant's* office. This was a German one and to a scale of about seven miles to an inch. No opportunity occurred, unfortunately, of being able to copy it. It showed us, however, a large number of farms and villages sprinkled over the countryside. The Russians had advanced no further, and the only plan at all feasible seemed to be to get a boat on the coast and make for Trebizond.

As the summer began our discussions took a more practical shape, and we got in touch with people who were in a position to know something trustworthy. One of those we approached was an interned ally. Under various pretexts I succeeded in getting a sentry to come with me to his house, which was strictly against the rules, saying I wanted to buy a guitar. On arrival he produced the guitar, and while pretending to try it we discussed the possibility of getting away. He considered that it would be possible to get a boat on the coast at Ineboli and suggested sending someone he could trust to find out how things stood and if possible to make arrangements. Conversation was not too easy, as his knowledge of English was very sketchy and I knew nothing of his language; also, the sentry was present, so that everything had to appear to be about the guitar and no names of places mentioned aloud. A little money and cigarettes to the sentry ensured his not talking later about where we had been, and I endeavoured to get the same man on the next occasion.

One day at this house I met a fellow countryman who as a civilian had been interned at Constantinople. For some reason the Turks had become more suspicious and he had been packed off to Kastamuni. He gave me some useful information about the state of the country further east but was not at all hopeful of our getting through. I did not see him again, as he was naturally very loth to be seen speaking to any of us, as that would mean his being sent out to live in one of the small villages away from every vestige of civilization. Meanwhile K. had been interviewing one or two people whom we thought might be trusted. For this purpose, an appointment was generally made at the *Hamám*, or Turkish bath. We were allowed to go to these baths, of which there were a large number in the town, whenever we liked, and, as the sentry always stayed in the entrance hall, one could speak freely to anyone inside.

On the whole these Allies recommended us not to make any attempt, one saying that had it been possible he himself would of course have gone long ago. Actually, they were afraid of trying anything of the sort or being in any way implicated by us.

We discussed the proposal of my friend with some of the others and decided to try his suggestion. Accordingly, ten of us collected about 50 *liras*—one *lira* equals 18s. 6d. nominally—which was handed to him. He in turn was to arrange with a Greek who was going to the coast and promised to bring back the information we needed. After some delay he finally departed, and, as we had feared, never turned up again.

Some of those who had subscribed considered any attempt without previously obtaining a boat to be hopeless and, when the Greek never returned, the number who were keen to go was reduced to half a dozen. Much discussion followed as to the size of the party, whether there should be two parties and who should go in which, and what routes should be followed. Eventually only four of us prepared to start, the others promising to give us all the support they could. Our party now consisted of Captains R. J. Tipton, R.F.C., R. T. Sweet, 2/7th

Ghurkas, Lieut. E. H. Keeling, and myself, both of the I.A.R.O. "Tip" had been taken in Egypt, while we three had all been in Kut.

There were two possible ways of getting out of the camp, or rather away from the street in which we lived, and either seemed fairly easy to arrange.

In order to get our provisions ready, we had to take one or two of the British orderlies into our confidence. We decided after much scheming that we would take 20 lb. of food each, consisting of 11 lb. of biscuits, 2½ lb. of cheese, 2½ lb. of smoked meat, 1¾ lb. of chocolate, 1½ lb. of Horlick's Malted Milk and the remainder of soup squares, cocoa and sugar, with a box of tea tabloids. The biscuits were made of good white flour, for which we had at that time to pay an exorbitant price as it was almost unobtainable; butter and sugar, which were also appallingly expensive, were added. Some were made with raisins, all being baked as hard as possible to save weight. These, with raisins, proved much the most popular subsequently.

Our mess cook, Gunner Prosser, R.F.A., made most of the biscuits and was very keen to do all he could to help us. In order to keep things dark, we told as few people as possible, but several people must have suspected us before we finally took our departure. The all-important question of the food to be carried caused much discussion before the final schedule was drawn up. Some were for taking one solid lump of duff instead of biscuits, but the latter won the day as containing less water and being therefore of more value weight for weight. K. had a profound belief in Horlick's Malted Milk, which was fully justified by our subsequent experience.

For some days prior to our departure a notice on the board, which was used by people who wished to exchange contents of parcels from home, informed all and sundry that Lt. K. could offer a very large variety of articles, ranging from honey to socks, in exchange for Malted Milk. This resulted in most of our supply being obtained. The question of meat was difficult, as tinned stuff received from home was too heavy and there was nothing to be got in the bazaar but smoked mutton, which was not very appetizing. Eventually, we decided on the mutton. We had a good many soup squares of different kinds, but on the journey, we wished we had had more cocoa instead. We decided to pack as much food as possible in small bags, for which some *puggaree* cloth came in handy, and an old pillow-case made a good receptacle for the biscuits. K. spent a long time sewing up small bags and in generally thinking out and preparing for all eventualities.

In the event of our being forced to buy food, we had decided that our only chance was to pretend we were Germans, since the country people, while seeing we were not Turks, would be too ignorant to know any difference between Briton and Hun. This also fell in well with our plan of going in uniform. To make things more secure we forged a passport. This was written out by Captain Rich, 120th Infantry, who knew Turkish fairly well, and purported to be a letter from the army commander at Angora to Hauptmann Hermann von Below, who, with three German orderlies, was said to be travelling on a surveying expedition. It was requested that the utmost facilities should be given him in his work. The name of the army commander we had managed to obtain correctly, and this was signed in a different hand and ink. A seal was also appended, as is usual in all Turkish documents, and suitably smudged so that the name which did not correspond with the signature might be illegible.

A volume dealing with woodcraft was perused by K., who discovered that the ordinary type of rock lichen was a highly nutritious food and, also, that nearly all forms of toadstool were equally useful. We hoped not to need such emergency rations and, fortunately, never got to that stage in our subsequent adventures. Over and above the 20 lb. of food we estimated that each one would need to carry 10 lb. more in kit and equipment, the former comprising a spare pair of socks, a "woolly" and vest or something similar, and the latter a haversack and water-bottle, matches, knife, spoon and soap. In addition, we carried a sail, about 40 feet of light rope, a light axe head, two canteens, a safety razor, housewife, nails and thread for repairing boots, maps, and compasses. These were divided up into equal weights between the four of us.

The sail was rather a work of art. It was made in two pieces from a bed sheet, the lining of two Wolseley valises and a couple of towels. With the help of a sailor friend. Lieut. Nicholson, R.N.R., we roped it all round. It measured about 10 ft. by 7 ft. 6 in., and weighed complete about 7 lb. The idea was that, having discovered a boat and if need be hewn down a small tree for a mast, we would paddle off from the coast and put up the sail as quickly as possible after sewing the two pieces together. Tip was to be our navigator, as he had done a good deal of sailing in pre-war days.

As Sweet was the only man with a rucksack, we three had to make our own. This meant a good deal of laborious sewing. My own was laid on the foundation of a khaki drill bag originally received

in Mesopotamia with gifts from the ladies of Bombay; this was rein-
forced with an old pair of braces and the necessary webbing sewn on.
It proved a most useful article and stood the journey wonderfully well,
although getting somewhat soiled in appearance.

CHAPTER 6
The First Night

It was not the easiest thing in the world to hold our meetings, ac-
complish our sewing and complete the sail without being interrupted
by other people or giving the show away. Our excuses for keeping
many people out of our room must have seemed rather thin on many
occasions, and certainly gave rise to suspicion in one quarter. One
day the interpreter Napoleon came to the door, but luckily suspected
nothing and departed. Napoleon had been of great service to us after
the wretched Greek interpreter we had had on our arrival, and we
hoped our departure would not get him into trouble.

We instructed our orderly to endeavour to put Napoleon off the
track the morning after we had gone. The rule was that we had to report to him at ten in the morning as well as at night. Very often people
omitted to do so, but in that case, he generally wandered round quietly
until he had seen they were still present. Our confederates amongst
the officers promised to say we had all gone up the hill to work at the
cemetery to which a party went every day, to complete the building
of a wall round the graves of the three officers and three men whom
we had there laid to rest.

In addition, we left a letter supposed to be written by Sweet to me,
talking of our proposed route and saying that he agreed we had much
better go towards Sivas, and giving a number of villages *en route*. This
was supposed to be destroyed and was to be found by accident by our
orderly in a crumpled condition when and not until our escape was
fully realised by the Turks. Our exit was to be made from a side door
into an alley leading off the main street. This door was nailed up, but,
like so many things in Turkey, it was done in a very slipshod fashion
with two boards having only two nails through each. To reach the
door, entrance had to be obtained to a back garden, and this meant
passing through another door which was padlocked every evening. In-
vestigation proved that, though the padlock seemed sound, the staple
might very easily be withdrawn and replaced afterwards.

Six officers helped us enormously on the night we actually started. They were Major Corbett and Captain Raynor, 48th Pioneers,

Captain R. Lowndes, R.G.A., Lieuts. Dooley, Cawley-Smith and Galloway, all I.A.R.O. Three opened the doors while another drowned their efforts by doing some violent bed repairing in a front room, this necessitating much hammering. The others kept a lookout on the sentries in the road or engaged them in amiable conversation in their best Turkish. It had been difficult to decide which night to start. We had no tables giving the time the moon would rise and wanted to arrange to have a good hour of darkness after getting out. Finally, we decided to start on Wednesday night, August 8th, at 10 p.m.

Sweet, who lived in the other group of houses, arranged to come to dinner in our mess, being invited by Captain Martin, I.M.S., who not only assisted us in selecting our food but placed his room at our disposal for storing our kit and assembling in just before starting. Our plan was to wait behind the door in the alley until our mess cook, Prosser, should come and tap on the further side to show that all was clear. This man was in the habit of often going out after dark into the town disguised in an old coat, a *fez*, and a sham beard which he had himself made out of goat-skins. His usual practice was to put the *fez* and beard on in the road and walk straight up past the sentries. On the night in question he got out in some such way and reconnoitred the route we should have to take to get out of the town on to the hill.

Luckily, we were on the edge of the town and a climb of two or three hundred yards through houses would take us out on to a Mohammedan graveyard on the hillside. As we were waiting silently in the dark behind the door, somebody gave a kerosene tin a kick, and the resulting clatter seemed bound to bring some one down upon us. However, nothing happened; but a moment or two later we heard a heavy tread going slowly up the alley.

Our friends, watching, reported that this was the sergeant of the guard and we began to feel anxious. After another minute a tap came on the door. Our orderly had seen the sergeant safely into a small mosque round the corner, and everything was clear. We hurried out in single file, endeavouring to be quite silent but seeming to make an awful noise. I was wearing a pair of rope sole shoes and carrying my boots while the others had put old socks over their boots. In spite of our anything but noiseless departure we were not noticed. We scrambled up the hill and five minutes later were under cover in the graveyard. Here we put our rucksacks and coats on properly and prepared for an all-night trek.

In order to look less like officers and more like local scallywags we had turned our coats inside out and also carried our packs in a blanket over one shoulder. We had decided to wear old khaki, so as to be able to prove we were really British if necessary in case of accidents or bad luck. After taking us a little further, our orderly friend shook hands with us all round, and with a quiet word of farewell and thanks for his invaluable assistance we set off on our adventure.

We had to make a detour round the north of the town across the main valley to get out to the hills on the east. It was a clear, starry night, but even so it was extraordinarily difficult to recognise the hillsides which we knew quite well by daylight. Hardly had we gone a quarter of a mile before a dog began to bark on the main road a little way off. Later on, we did not pay much attention to dogs, as we generally started at least one every night by walking near a village or too close to houses; but this animal, being the first and so near to the town, was anything but pleasant to listen to. We scrambled down a steep bank across a *nullah* and up a gully running into a hill which we had to climb. The main *nullah* we had just crossed ran down towards the road passing the magazine, where by day there was always a guard. However, the dog soon ceased his complaint and quietness reigned.

We were already beginning to feel the weights of our packs and, as the night was warm and our direction led up the stony, pathless side of a steep hill, we soon had to call a halt. In fact, although we did not admit it to each other, these moments were really almost the worst of our whole trip and each secretly thought what an idiot he had been ever to start. Having started, however, there was nothing for it but to continue and after a few minutes' rest we trudged on. A little further brought us out on the top, where we were annoyed to find that the moon was already well up, whereas we had reckoned on at least another half-hour of darkness.

During the last few days, we had carefully timed the moon's rising, and endeavoured to foretell the time for the night of our venture from comparisons with last year's almanac, which was all we had to go upon.

On the top of the hill, we could just make out the big square of the Turkish barracks lying down in the valley, a building which we had passed almost every day during the last year on our way to the football ground or on walks. Sweet wanted to give it a much wider berth than I had intended, and in consequence we were longer in getting down to the Ineboli road which had to be crossed. What was our horror when we did approach it to hear the creaking of country carts coming up towards the town. They seemed to be nearly opposite to us and, as there was little cover and the moon bright, the only thing to do was to lie down in the ditch where we were and hope the carts would pass. We waited some time, but yet more carts seemed to be approaching and the drivers of others had halted almost opposite to us. There was nothing for it but to turn back and try again lower down the road.

After creeping back, a little way on all fours, we made a circle and came out into an open field, heading once more for the road. Here we were dismayed to hear yet another cart coming. There was no cover this time, not even a ditch, so we had to make a dash for it. This succeeded, and we were across the road and some little distance into a field of high crops on the far side before the carts passed. These carts were evidently coming into the town for the following day's market, but we had not counted on meeting any at all. We were now in the centre of the valley, and after crossing the stream made our way over some more fields to the Sinope road which we crossed without further adventure.

We had now reached open country, and after another half-mile rested again. We were all feeling a bit done up and thought we had taken too much kit. On starting again, we found that so far we were on the right track, but from now onwards we were going on a line we had not been on before even by day, and we regretted afterwards we had not for this first night kept straight on down the main Sinope road, along which we could have made good going, although it did not lead due east, which was the direction we had planned. There were guard houses at intervals on this road, but I knew it for the first ten miles, having driven out with my colonel once when he was allowed a carriage to go fishing, this being a special favour which ceased to be granted as soon as the *commandant* of the town got to hear about it.

After several miles of up and down going, we reached the first river we had to cross. Along each side were irrigated maize-fields, but, fortunately, we managed to get through these and over the stream without coming to any houses or dogs, although there were villages and farms quite close. Another ascent met us on the further side and we plodded slowly on. The country was mostly open pasture and plough-land and there were few trees except those beside the streams in the valleys. Eventually, we got to the top of the ridge and a little later found ourselves overlooking another deep valley with a stream running a thousand feet below us. After a steep scramble down, we reached the water and called a halt.

A tin of tongue presented by someone at the last minute was opened and eagerly consumed. It was now about 3 a.m. and we had not much more than another hour and a half to two hours before daylight, when we had to be safely under cover. On leaving the stream, we found we were not far from a hamlet, and roused the attentions of another dog. However, we plodded on once more. We could now see woods in the distance but, before reaching them, had some difficult country to cross. Tip and K. were feeling very done up and, as there were signs of dawn and other dogs taking up the hue and cry, we began to feel a bit anxious. These dogs seemed to be approaching from a village; but we just managed to get away from them, although it seemed that they must rouse the whole countryside.

During our next halt of a few minutes, we heard a cart coming along from the village, and, evidently, the peasants were already starting on the toil of another long harvest day, even though it was only just beginning to get light. Sweet and I had gone on, and on looking back could see no signs of the others. We went back a little way and luckily found them. We had just scrambled up a steep hill and were all fairly well done up. A little further took us to a pine wood, where we decided to lie up for the day. We lay just inside while the cart we had heard approached and passed on up the track we had just left.

Then we turned and went into the wood, only to find, however, that sheep tracks ran everywhere and that the wood itself only extended two hundred yards to the top of the ridge where there were open fields—also, what was worse still, no part of the wood was really thick or offered good cover. Still, now it was too late to go on even if we had had the energy, and the only thing to do was to stay and make the best of it and trust to luck. We looked to each side, but the sheep-tracks were almost as thick in all directions. This meant that at any time, but particularly in the evening, we might expect a flock to come along and that would also mean a man or a boy and a dog.

It was indeed, fortunate for our peace of mind during this first day that we did not know how soon our departure had been discovered. Actually, this was found out within two hours of our leaving. Sweet's absence being first ascertained by Sherif Bey, who simply snorted with rage and fury. What had happened was that our orderly was very nearly caught while trying to return to his quarters: he had to run for it, and in so doing lost one of his shoes. He got in safely, however, and had at once to destroy the other shoe. A few minutes later the Turkish guard came round, searching for the odd shoe, and listened carefully to the breathing and heartbeats of every orderly to see which one had been running. Luckily, however, our friend Prosser had had just long enough to compose himself in bed and was not detected.

CHAPTER 7

On the Hills

We made a breakfast from condensed milk and a small ration of biscuit and some cheese. We dared not make a fire, as people were working on the crops not very far away. After this we took it in turns to keep watch at the top edge of the wood. From this point a fine view could be had across the ridges back towards Kastamuni, although the town itself was hidden in the valley. One track was clearly visible and it was along this we expected to see signs of pursuit, if any; but there was nothing to be seen. The morning was perfect, and the country spread away in the sunshine back towards our old haunts. We appeared to have made at the very least ten miles from Kastamuni as the crow flies, but actually had marched much further owing to the detour round the town and our cross-country up and down route since.

Towards the east more and higher hills could be seen, but we had to be careful of reconnoitring, as there were flock of sheep on the slopes not far away. All of us had sundry adjustments to make in our kit, which we felt we must lighten to enable tis to make better going. My own costume consisted of an old and thin British warm over either a thin shirt or vest with old riding breeches and puttees. The others had regulation tunics, and Sweet was highly respectable, his uniform being nearly new. In the event of our posing as Germans we decided he must be the Herr Hauptmann, as in addition to his better clothes he knew more Turkish than the rest of us.

I set about a ruthless lightening of my coat by ripping out the lining, cutting off the turned-back cuffs and all other small portions that could be spared. We found it difficult to sleep but felt good for another effort as soon as it began to get dark. About three o'clock, we relinquished our observation post, as all seemed quiet, and made another meal. Hardly had we finished before a dog appeared at the edge of the wood and started barking as only Turkish dogs seem able to. A few moments later the expected boy also turned up and stared down upon us after quieting the dog. We thought this meant the village being roused at once, and deputed Sweet to go and spin a big yarn of some sort to the boy. He had scarcely got up before the boy vanished.

The only thing to do now was to pack up and be off at once. This

MAP (SLIGHTLY REDUCED) USED ON JOURNEY TO BLACK SEA

did not take long, as we had purposely remained ready to move at short notice. I abandoned in a bush my rope sole shoes which I had carried so far, and did not regret it, as they were some weight and very slippery to walk in. After creeping along, just inside the wood at the top of the slope, for a short distance, we found we were getting near a farm and could not go further before dark. We could not see the boy, but one or two sheep-dogs were visible not far off and matters did not look at all hopeful. However, no hue and cry followed, and very likely the boy had been as frightened of us as we of him, or he may have thought we were merely out from Kastamuni for a walk—although we had never been nearly so far before.

After waiting an hour at the edge of the wood, we saw the sheep approaching and knew they must be returning towards the farm. We got down the slope back into the wood and as much as possible off their line. There was a little more cover here, but still it was rather thin, and we could easily have been spotted by anyone looking for us. By and by the sheep trooped past, but no dog came near us and once more we breathed freely. To improve our prospects, it now began to cloud over and we had some rain. A dark cloudy night for cross-country tramping was anything but what we required; fortunately, it cleared later on, although even then it was black enough until the moon got up. Before starting again, the question of weight of kit had to be tackled and, although loath to part with any of our food, we decided to discard about two to three pounds each. For this sacrifice most of our cheese and meat was condemned. It seemed likely that the former would not remain good for very long, so that it was not much loss.

We decided to make a start before it got dark, and halt for food when we reached the river which we judged must run in the deep valley we were about to enter. Accordingly, we left the wood at 7.30 and set off across the cornfields. A very steep and stony descent followed, and by the time we struck a road along the valley it was quite dark. We followed this road a short distance until we saw a light in a house a little way ahead. We then turned off and went straight down to the stream, where we proceeded to drink at length and then bathe. During this bathe in the dark, I lost my soap, which was a great calamity and Tip his knife. We dared not strike a light and had to be content to go on without.

After a light meal, we went on upstream. There appeared to be a ceremony of some sort going on at the house with a light, as there was a beating of drums. We crossed the stream a little higher up, taking off our boots and socks for the purpose. Luckily on the other bank we struck a track leading up the further side of the valley, which was very steep at this point.

After climbing slowly up through brushwood in the dark for an hour, we came to more open country. Here there were farms, but we managed to avoid them successfully. The night had cleared sufficiently for us to see the stars, and we were steering a course about due east. A little further on, we got into a thick copse and had great difficulty in finding any track. Eventually, we emerged on to a road running along the ridge beyond which lay the next valley. After a short halt, we got under way once more and made a good distance down the road and along a path we found running down to the next valley.

We had to pass close through a farm and several houses, but luckily there were no dogs. After reaching the next stream and ascending it some way, we crossed over and found ourselves in a maize-field. We gathered some cobs, which were not yet ripe but would do to cook. A few yards further we saw a light in what appeared to be a sheep-pen. This we found was the usual custom in the country. All flocks are collected near the farm at night and a shepherd with a big resin torch sits up on guard. It was now just beginning to get light in the east, so we turned up the hill, and after a long and tiring climb found a tolerably safe hiding-place in a pine wood. Poor K. was very done up and the rest of us not much better, except Sweet, who, physically, was the toughest of us all. For nine hours we had been on the move, but we could not have done more than eight miles in a straight line—though at the time we thought it was much more. We lay down and got two or three hours' sleep before preparing our next meal.

We decided we would risk making a fire, and after hunting about for the most concealed spot boiled water in our canteens and made cocoa. This with a ration of biscuit formed our meal; in addition, we used to allow ourselves a very small bit of chocolate and a little Horlick's milk. The latter by this time had coagulated into one sticky lump, necessitating hard work with the point of a knife before a fragment could be broken off. Luckily, the fire burned without much smoke, and what little there was we endeavoured to mitigate by fanning it in different directions.

Not long after breakfast, we heard two horsemen trotting along a road through the wood and apparently quite close. We thought they were probably *gendarmes* looking for us; but they passed on and did not pause to make investigations in our neighbourhood. Another visitor also arrived, this being a man who was chopping wood, and worked round our knoll for some distance, but never came within sight. Nothing further happened, and we spent a quiet day under the trees. The weather was perfect, and had we had a little more to eat we should have enjoyed it immensely. At five o'clock we made a stew of the maize with a little Oxo; and an hour later, after clearing up all traces of our activities, set off eastwards through the wood.

We soon reached the edge of the wood and found ourselves looking southwards across a valley to a high range of hills. On the lower slopes were several villages; but it was doubtful if people could see us, especially as our khaki was an excellent camouflage for this country: in fact, this had been a great recommendation to the proposal for marching in uniform. However, we endeavoured to keep out of sight; and after travelling across the high ground for a mile reached a spot whence we could see the country eastwards and choose out our route for the coming night.

The main valley had turned somewhat, and now ran eastwards through a rocky gorge which opened out beyond to a much greater width. This seemed to be our best line, and we thought there would surely be a track leading up the valley along the stream. At all events, our water was finished, and it was urgent to fill up our bottles again as soon as we could reach the river. We set off accordingly but had not gone far before someone reported a man coming up the road; we hid for some time, and when all was clear went on again, only to find we were descending to a field where women were still working, getting in the harvest. This necessitated another wait; but as darkness was approaching the women soon left the field.

In order to help out our scanty stock of food and make it go as far as possible, we were always on the lookout for any food we could pick up in the fields and decided to take toll of this cornfield. The wheat was ripe and in a few minutes we all had a good pocketful, meaning to make a really substantial meal of wheat porridge next morning. By the time we reached a path near the bottom of the valley it was quite dark. This track seemed to lead downwards towards the river, and we followed it, expecting to get to the water any minute, but by and by it began to ascend again and then to get rougher and harder to find. This was very trying, as we all now wanted water badly, and so we finally decided to try a rocky gully leading steeply downwards.

Sweet led the way, but, being too eager to get down, or through bad luck, slipped and hurt his leg in falling over a rock. It was very dark in the gully, and two candle ends which Sweet had brought proved invaluable. After climbing and crawling down some way over rocks, we were finally brought up by a sheer precipice falling 200 feet to the river. Tired and disgusted, we sat down to rest, and had to make up our minds to climb out the way we had come, and then either to go back downstream or climb right to the top of the valley and advance and get down again higher up where the valley opened out. The latter course was adopted and, Tip giving us a good lead, we slowly and, in Sweet's case, painfully scrambled back. K. also had a bad time, as he was short-sighted and in such a dark spot it was no easy matter to get along.

CHAPTER 8

Slow Progress

We all felt dreadfully tired as well as thirsty. The past two nights had told on us; and without proper sleep and sufficient food we were not in the best trim for a third night of mountaineering. After getting back to the track, we had to climb up the side of the ravine, which was steep and rocky. Resting every few yards, we eventually reached the top and turned upstream. The point where we had descended the gully must have been in almost the narrowest part of the gorge, and we could see that we should have to move some way along the crest before we could get down to the water. We were still ascending, and after continuing a little further decided to lie down till dawn, and then trust to getting down to the river and hiding before the country people were about. It was hopeless to try to get down again in the dark, even had we possessed the strength.

Thirsty as we were, we got off to sleep; and, when we woke, found it was already beginning to get light. It had got much colder and our thirst had accordingly diminished. I had lost my cap the night before shortly before we camped, and now luckily managed to find it on going back a little way. We pressed on and began to descend again. It took us at least an hour down a very steep tree-clad slope. The stones we set rolling seemed to make a dreadful noise, but actually must have been drowned in the roar of the torrent below. As we neared the river, we found we were quite close to a farm; but no one was about, and we got down without trouble. How we drank, and what a relief it was to be beside water again!

After a wash, we set about getting a meal by preparing our wheat. It took some time to get all the husks off the grain and longer to boil it; but it was very good and filling. Our biscuits had numbered originally about thirty-five each, so that as we had reckoned on a journey of a fortnight to the coast we only allowed ourselves two and a half per day. We made cocoa, in addition to the porridge, and went to sleep under the bushes, feeling a great deal better than we had done for some hours. Our camp was in a most ideal spot. Below this, the river wound down through the gorge, while the steep slopes on each side of the valley were covered with magnificent trees. There were a great many hazel nuts, but these were not yet ripe or we would have gathered a large number.

Later on, we produced our razor and, one by one, for the first time since leaving Kastamuni, made ourselves presentable. I got out the fishing line I had brought, but had no luck, chiefly owing to there being no worms to be seen in the soil on the river bank. The preserved meat seemed to have little attraction for the fish, of which there were plenty, and our biscuits were too precious to be used up in any way as bait.

We started off once more about 6.30, and after some rough going reached the wide part of the valley where fields came down to the river. Here we were soon brought to a stop by seeing people still at work. Retracing our steps, we crossed the stream and started to ascend the northern side of the valley, keeping roughly to our easterly direction. After a steep ascent, we reached a fair track, along which we made good progress. Once or twice we had to wait and hide owing to farm people being about; but after it had got quite dark we got on again without interruption.

On one occasion we passed close to a farm. There was a resin-wood torch burning in the yard, and just as we appeared a woman opened a window and looked out; we expected her to see us, but possibly the glare from the torch was too strong, for she took no notice. By midnight, we had reached some high downland, where there seemed to be a large number of farms. After lying down for a couple of hours, we started off again; but soon lost all sign of our track. Continuing in our direction with the help of the stars or compass, we suddenly found ourselves within range of some village dogs. These brutes devoted their attention to us long and loudly, and there was nothing for it but to get away across the fields as fast as we could.

After a little time, we found a track which presently led into a pine wood. We trudged on through the trees for two hours, the track keeping on the crest of the hill and bending round gradually towards the north. This wood promised good cover for the next day, and as we seemed to have reached its edge we decided to stop here all day. We lay down until it grew light and then moved to the best spot we could find. This day was Sunday, August 12th, and we can only have achieved about 30 miles as the crow flies, although at the time we put it at 40.

Having picked no corn the night before, we had to be content with our small biscuit and meat ration which we carried, helped out with a fragment of Horlick and chocolate. Tip had not been feeling well all night and was now in considerable pain. He said porridge always laid him out, and our brew, which was not very well boiled, had proved no exception. As far as we could tell, it seemed to be appendicitis or something very like it. We discussed gloomy possibilities of giving ourselves up in the event of his not getting better; but he remained determined to push on if he possibly could.

We reconnoitred our route for the coming night and set off again an hour before dusk. From the hill on which we had camped we could see a road leading in the direction we wanted, down a wide valley, and we determined to keep to this for some distance at all events. After forcing our way through brushwood to the foot of the hill, we were held up by hearing carts approaching and had to hide until they had gone past. We used this opportunity for awash and to fill up our water-bottles from a small stream; and then set off again, following the carts down the road.

After marching for an hour, we reached some corn stacks and collected more wheat. It took longer than when gathering it in an open field, but in half an hour we had accumulated enough, and again took the road. We had noticed that, further on, there seemed to be a good number of houses in the valley on our right which we should have to cross. Our direction now led down towards the river and the track passed through a stack yard. We were going quietly forward, when suddenly we were surprised by a number of dogs, which burst out upon us in full chorus from behind a stack. An old man appeared immediately afterwards and quieted the dogs, but luckily made no attempt to question us, and we passed on in silence. At night we always wore *fezzes* and hoped thus to pass as Turks or Greeks.

A short distance further on, we crossed the stream and then were delighted to discover a maize-field, where we gathered a few of the biggest cobs we could find. A moment later someone discovered that beans and marrows were growing on the ground beneath the maize, so we helped ourselves to these also. The beans were of a dwarf French

198

variety, which seems to be the most popular kind throughout the district. Thus provisioned, we set off up a wide valley leading up in front of us.

Poor Tip was having a hard time, and as we had to cross several ploughed fields before discovering any path, matters for him became much worse. He could manage to get along all right on a smooth path, but rough going gave him great pain. Fortunately, the road we now struck had quite a fair surface and we made a good pace for the next two hours, assisted by the moon. Finally, about 4 a.m., we lay down for an hour, until dawn, near the side of the road. We found we had overslept ourselves on waking, as it was broad daylight; so we had to hurry off up a small hill and hide in the bushes. The country round seemed more deserted in this part of the valley and we had got away from cultivated land. As we were all now very done up, we decided to move down to the centre of the valley, which looked as if it must possess a stream. There we intended to hide for the rest of that day and the next. This we thought might give Tip a chance to get right again.

After resting two or three hours on the hill, we scrambled down and eventually emerged in the main valley. Just before we reached it we as nearly as possible walked into two *gendarmes*, who were going up the valley road and crossed our path about a hundred yards ahead of us. However, they did not see us and all was still well. After crossing the main valley and stream, we found a small gully on the further side which seemed to offer us good cover, as well as having a small supply of water. As we crossed the river bed to reach it we came in view of a man and two boys working on an irrigation dam a little higher up. Luckily, they had their backs towards us and did not notice anything.

A little way up the gully, we found a sheltered spot to camp in and prepared a meal, chiefly from the vegetables we had gathered the night before. We made Tip as comfortable as possible, and with the aid of hot compresses succeeded in making him feel easier. Nothing occurred during the day, and, after another stew had been consumed in the evening, we set about making ourselves comfortable for the night. With the aid of fir branches we made a tolerably soft couch. Tip, K. and I for purposes of additional warmth slept side by side under the most substantial part of the sail, while Sweet, who preferred to be on his own, rolled himself up in the lighter piece. We would have much enjoyed a little more warmth at nights and, in spite of putting on the few spare garments we each carried, we were always much too cold before morning.

Our plan now was to follow the road up to the head of the valley and then steer as straight as possible for the Geuk Irmak valley, along which we knew ran the main road to Sinope. It was clear that we could not make fast enough progress at the present rate ever to reach Baffra before our provisions gave out; our boots, also, were getting badly worn and much work was done in repairs at our various halts. Walking across rough country at night had damaged them much more severely than we had ever imagined could be the case.

The following day we spent in resting, cooking, and also shaving and washing. As one or two people had passed along the road in the afternoon, we did not like to make an early start and so waited until it was growing dark. For the first mile the track remained fairly good; then it forked, and we chose the left-hand branch as leading in the direction we wanted most. It was now quite dark and the sky cloudy; but what was much worse, the track got more and more indistinct as we slowly emerged into open country and fields at the head of the valley. Several times we had to halt and spread out to find the path; and then, at last, when we did reach a cart track we almost walked right into a big farm. After pausing to reconnoitre, we decided to try to skirt it on the left and had got halfway round when a sheepdog heard us and started off at full blast. There was a shepherd sitting with a torch in one of the farm buildings, but he took no notice.

Shortly afterwards we found a field of beans to which we helped ourselves, and then had to make a diversion to avoid another house. This led us into a pinewood and we were soon forced to give it up until morning, as we could see no way through in the darkness. We lay down close together and got a few hours' sleep before the first sign of daylight roused us to continue our journey. We had to pass closer than we liked to a farm; but no one was about yet and we got away on to a high ridge covered with brushwood. After making our way for a short time along this, we halted and made cocoa, which with a biscuit formed our breakfast. By this time our biscuits had broken up into small fragments, so that we had to estimate how many bits were equal to a whole biscuit.

Our experiences of the night before forced us to the conclusion that it was hopeless trying to do a good march by night unless on a good track; and we, therefore, decided to cut across a low cultivated stretch of land to the forest covering the opposite ridge and continue by daylight until reaching the Geuk Irmak. It was now about nine o'clock and the peasants were at work in the fields almost all round us. There was no safe way of reaching the woods opposite without exposing ourselves to view, and the only thing was to do the best we could and use all the cover available.

On getting down to a stream from a steep hill, we found we were close to some women and children. The latter saw us, but the women were too busy to notice us and we reached cover in a *nullah* on the further side without any alarm being raised. Our next encounter was with an old Turk. He saw us just before we saw him and was off to ground in some cover before one could say knife. Evidently, he was very much more startled at seeing us than we were at seeing him. After this we were not seen by any other people, and after skirting a harvest field got well into the forest. At two o'clock we halted and having slept for two hours made another stew and prepared to go on till dark. We were in a big forest chiefly of huge pines which were being cut in places for resin.

Our direction was now nearly due north, and every rise we topped would, we hoped, bring us in view of the Geuk Irmak valley. As is generally the case, the longed-for view was very slow in making its appearance, and we had to bivouac for the night without reaching our goal. We had passed a small flour mill, driven by a water wheel. Sweet had investigated it for flour, but it was swept and garnished and absolutely empty.

CHAPTER 9

Bluffing the Peasants

Next morning, we were off at the first streak of dawn, after a very cold night. We were in a narrow valley and look where we would we could not find the track we had seen not long before halting the previous night. The hills were too steep and wooded to make it possible to get along low down by the stream, so there was no other course open except to start climbing again in the hope of meeting the track at a higher level. This we succeeded in doing after toiling up some distance. Following the track, we emerged after a couple of miles on a hill overlooking the long expected Geuk Irmak.

It was too late in the morning and the neighbourhood too populous to make further progress possible, so we bivouacked close by in the wood and hoped to make good distance that night along the main road in the valley. Starting an hour before dark, we were forced to wait for a homecoming couple who were slowly returning along the track we were intending to take. When they were safely off the scene, we had to scramble down through the thickest copse it was ever our misfortune to meet with, and by the time we had reached the river it was quite dark.

As on all such occasions, we took off our boots and socks to cross and placed them on the other side, only to find soon after that there was another branch of the river which we had not been able to see in the dark, so that the process had to be repeated. Even then we were not over dry-shod, as there were now several irrigated fields to be crossed before we could get to the road. Creeping along the small bund dividing two fields, we endeavoured to keep on dry ground; but were not very successful. Finally, we reached a big irrigation *nullah*, which meant another wade. We were now, at last, on the main road; but it had taken us two hours' hard going to get there, which was a great disappointment.

Soon after starting again, we met a couple of men on ponies, driving cattle. At the time we were rather separated; Tip and I escaped observation, but Sweet and K. were not so lucky, for the men stopped and asked who they were. Sweet promptly said "Germans" and gave a few details. The men, however, declared they were prisoners, but did not seem disposed to make trouble, and moved on again after a few minutes, much to Sweet's relief.

After another hour's trek, we felt too exhausted to go further, and lay down, intending to do a little more at dawn. The mosquitoes were a great pest in this valley and we had a very poor night's sleep. We had now come down to a much lower elevation: Kastamuni was 2,500 feet above sea, but this spot could scarcely be 1,000 feet. As soon as it grew light in the morning we were off again along the road, after filling up our water-bottles from the river and investigating another flour mill which proved to be empty. Very soon we came to a picturesque old wooden bridge spanning the stream and, after crossing this, decided to lie up for the day on the hill-side above. The valley became wider at this point and several hamlets and farms were to be seen; it therefore behoved us to get under cover as quickly as possible, since the peasants are very early astir.

We found a good place and lit a fire. This was, perhaps, rather rash, but we felt that it was worth risking a good deal to have something hot to drink. As we had had no luck in getting vegetables the night before, we had to be content with small rations. After an uneventful sunny day, we moved down to the road in the evening, and after filling our bottles with water from the river gathered some maize and marrows from a field close by. We then set off down the road and made very fair progress for the next three hours.

Loaded as we were with several extra pounds each of marrow, we got more tired than would otherwise have been the case. Eventually, the road led us into a village, and we had to walk straight past some people coming towards us. They took no notice, however, and we went on. A little further, there was a light in a flour mill, which was grinding away as hard as it could go, being driven by a small water turbine. There seemed to be no track by which we could avoid going right through the village, and after retracing our steps once or twice we decided there was nothing else for it.

We tramped down the road past several old fellows who were sitting outside a house and were probably interested in the activities of the flour mill. Most likely, by grinding secretly at night, it is possible to escape the government's taxes on flour, but needless to say we did not stop to make inquiries. The road seemed to take us nowhere. After visiting one or two back yards and coming out in another place on top of a house, we had eventually to retrace our steps past the old men to the end of the village which we had first entered. How that road made its way out we never discovered and, in consequence, lost a good deal of time and distance.

After sleeping for a couple of hours in a graveyard, we set off with the first streak of dawn to make a circuit round the south side of the village and reached a hill which promised safety for the day. It took us a long time and many halts had to be made. We disposed of our marrows by eating them raw and decided that they were too heavy to be worth carrying any distance in future. Finally, we reached a snug spot in brushwood high up on the hill and made ourselves as comfortable as circumstances would allow.

In the afternoon, I decided to go to the top of the hill to try to locate our exact position in the valley. After a steep climb I got a splendid view all round and discovered a convenient track for us to follow as soon as it grew dark. A town was clearly visible a few miles further on, and this I felt sure must be Duraghan, although the road leading to it did not correspond with what was shown on our map. However, we decided that it must be this place, as by our calculations we reckoned we must have come every bit of the distance.

Our disgust may be imagined when on the following day we found the place was really Boiabad, a town, 30 miles short of Duraghan. Just after getting back to our bivouac, it came on to pour, but luckily, we managed to get a fire going and a stew made just in time. However, the result was that we started marching an hour later, soaked very nearly to the skin, and with no prospect of being able to get dry in the near future. We came close to the town, as it was getting dark, and after crossing a stream had some discussion as to which road to take. Finally, we selected a track which we thought must lead into the main valley, where we were certain the main road would run on our side of the river.

As a matter of fact, it had crossed to the other side and we did not meet it till next day. We continued along this track till midnight, when we lay down for a little sleep; but it was too cold to be possible in our wet things and in an hour, we were up and off again. A few miles further on, we found we were close to a village through which the track ran and, joyful sight, there were several corn stacks close by. These promised a warm shelter until dawn; but it was not to be. The usual village dog had already heard us and although we remained stock still he would not cease his frantic barking. One old peasant had already been roused up and came slowly towards us.

Our only course was to go straight on; and we went right into the village, past several houses, through a cow pen, over a hedge and so on to the moor beyond. Just as we got clear some sportsmen let off a shotgun. No pellets came near us and it was probably only meant as a warning to robbers! Luckily, we were not followed and got away over the hill, steering east. After some distance we rested again, until morning should show us our whereabouts. We were evidently some way from the river and a good height up.

As it began to get light, we moved off towards the river, hoping to find a snug hiding-place near the water. No such luck was in store for us, for just as we reached a slope overlooking the river we saw a small village at our feet, and the village dogs saw us almost at the same moment. Wearily we retraced our steps uphill, and when out of range of the dogs held a council as to our future efforts. It was clear that while walking by night we were covering very little distance, and that at this rate the food we carried would be exhausted long before we reached the sea. We decided, therefore, that our only hope lay in bluffing the country people that we were Germans and buying food where we could.

Accordingly, we made for the first house we could see, where a miserable peasant and two women were working. We explained that we were Germans surveying, and produced our maps and passport in support of this contention. They did not doubt us; but they had no food to sell and, indeed, looked as poor and wretched as people well could. However, they referred us to their master, who was the headman of the locality. We crossed a few fields and were then met by this gentleman, to whom we told the same story. He led us into his house and providing us with seats gave orders for food to be prepared.

In the meanwhile, Sweet carried on a conversation to the best of his ability. It appeared that our host was one Ahmed Chaoush (sergeant) who had been fighting against us in Gallipoli but now had a year's sick leave. He took in our story, but asked some awkward questions, such as why we carried no revolvers? Sweet had to pretend not to understand and, luckily, Ahmed did not become suspicious. We gathered from him that the town we had passed in the night was Boiabad and that was several hours' distance in front of us. This was a cruel blow, and only showed us how much slower we had been than we thought. In the meantime, the *chaoush* had produced some small pears which were soon disposed of. Finally, after much anxious speculation as to whether or no our host intended to give us a meal, real signs of preparation appeared for that eagerly expected event.

A few minutes later a small circular table was produced and several dishes were brought in. These consisted of cucumber sliced up in milk, small wads of boiled flour in milk, yoghourt or curdled milk and *chapatties*—a feast such as we had hardly dared to hope for. Turkish fashion, we sat round, each armed with a wooden spoon and dipped in the same dish, emptying one after another. It is etiquette on such occasions to wait until the next man has taken a spoonful so that all may get the same number in the end, but I fear we were not always so scrupulous and ate as fast as our usual habits would allow.

When the table and dishes had been cleared away, Ahmed was given a little English tobacco and told it was the best German variety. Soon after we bid him a grateful farewell, and, although he was unwilling to take anything, succeeded in getting him to accept some money. We felt that to accept his hospitality and humbug him without any payment would scarcely be playing the game. He directed us towards our road, for which we had to descend again to the main valley and cross the river.

On the further side we were delayed by a large irrigation *nullah*. When across this we found a good many blackberries and some onions in a field. The latter we seized upon with avidity, as being the first we had met with. There was some doubt as to which of two roads we should take, but it was decided to pursue one which some women had pointed out as the right road to Duraghan. This led straight away from the river and began to climb steeply. After a couple of hours, we had ascended some distance and decided to bivouac till the afternoon. The sun was pretty hot, but we were now high up and on top of a small hill from which the surrounding ranges could be clearly seen. It was evident that we had not come in the direction we had intended, but, on the other hand, we were now heading direct for the sea.

After some discussion and poring over the map, we decided that our only real chance of reaching the sea lay in making a bee-line across country as nearly as possible in a north-easterly direction, buying food where we could and walking by day. If we had gone on we should not only have had to skirt Duraghan by night, or make a big detour by day, but the distance down to the sea would have been very much greater. In addition, it would have been much hotter for walking, with the extra hardship of mosquitoes at night.

CHAPTER 10

Reaching the Coast

We made it to be 30 miles in a straight line to the sea from the spot where we now lay and hoped to do the distance in three days. After the *chaoush's* hospitality at breakfast we scarcely felt inclined for another meal till the afternoon, when we made tea, and then packed up, intending to follow up a track beside a stream which flowed down from the range we had now determined to cross. Descending our hill, we came to a small village, and thought it would be just as well to see if we could purchase any provisions before going further. We asked some children for eggs, whereupon a Turkish matron of an unusually agreeable type came out and after a little parleying brought us quite a royal supper. This consisted mainly of an excellent tomato stew, *chapatties*, yoghourt and fruit.

Taking into account what we had accumulated from Ahmed Chaoush, we had now got quite a good stock of *chapatties*. The amusement afforded by bluffing these good people had considerably raised our spirits, but all at once the good dame serving us staggered us completely by saying casually she had seen us in Kastamuni. We assured her it must have been other people, as we had no connection with Kastamuni and were real Germans from Angora.

Just before leaving a man appeared who eyed us very suspiciously, and we were glad to get away without waiting to make his acquaintance. We had hardly gone a mile before an old man ran to meet us with his cap full of apples. We seemed almost to be entering on a triumphal progress and were tremendously amused. Several houses and a large village were passed without events but a little further on we found several men with mules resting a short distance from the road. They called to us, and probably wanted to continue their journey in our company, but it was sailing nearer the wind than we cared for and, pretending we had to go on at once, we did not stop to hear anything more from them. Just before dark we passed through a very picturesque gorge, where the stream ran through a deep narrow gateway between two enormous masses of rock, and beyond this found a nook to sleep in for the night where we should be protected from the wind. This had been a truly great day, and its success seemed to confirm the wisdom of our new policy.

Early the following morning, we were once more pursuing our path, which now became fainter and steeper as it rose towards the rocky ridge towering above us. Towards eleven o'clock, we reached some poor houses not far below the crest. Hoping to be able to purchase food, we stopped and made inquiries, but all the chief people seemed to be away at some market and there was nothing to be had. We continued on our way and after another hour's tramp came to a cattle trough by the side of the path. As there was water flowing here, we decided to halt till the afternoon, and found a snug spot a few yards up the hill.

In the afternoon, after washing and shaving, we were nearly discovered by a man who appeared to be a *gendarme*. He came riding down the path and stopped to water his horse at the trough but passed on without noticing anything. Soon afterwards we were again marching, still upwards towards the crest of the mountain ridge. We must have been now over 4,000 feet up and hoped when we reached the top we should actually see the sea. An hour's trek took us to a poor village standing very high and, probably, in winter almost always in the clouds. An ill-clad woman informed us that she was a Greek who had only just arrived from Kastamuni. She seemed to have a pretty clear notion as to what we really were, but said nothing and, eventually, got us yoghourt and some *chapatties*.

Our direction was now about north-east and we were making for Tel Kelik, a small place marked on the map, a little on the northern side of the watershed. Most of the peasants seemed never to have heard of it, and we had some difficulty in getting on to a path leading in the right direction. As it grew dusk, we found ourselves in a second village at almost the same elevation; there was no one about, but eventually a man turned up who said he was on his way home to another village. The village women in particular were most suspicious, declaring that there was no food anywhere; and it was not until some little while later, when the colour of our money had been clearly shown, that anything was forthcoming. We had intended to spend the night in a village hut if possible, as the only alternative was sleeping in the mist, which at 4,000 feet was a cold and dreary prospect.

However, after some parleying, we were led to what proved to be the travellers' rest hut. Our story was absorbed with due interest, a large fire lighted and some food brought in. We lay down on mate on the floor, rejoicing in the warmth and, if undisturbed by smaller visitors, felt we should have a really good night's rest. Several village worthies looked in during the evening to see the *Almans* (Germans) and we hope were not disappointed.

A young soldier just returned on leave from Constantinople helped to procure some butter and syrup for us. The latter is a poor substitute for treacle and seems to be made from raisins. This reception in a travellers' rest hut was the limit reached by our bluff; it gave us much satisfaction to think how annoyed our Turkish friends in Kastamuni would be to know of our being entertained in such a manner.

We had a splendid night, although lying on the floor, and in the morning obtained a little more food and some butter through our soldier friend. After a hasty meal we hurried off with our first acquaintance of the previous night as guide to put us on the right road. We were soon at the highest point of the range, although as yet the sea was not in view. A little further on, after having bought a large knife from our friend, we bade him goodbye with many expressions of gratitude. Tel Kelik was now quite close, and it was fortunate that we were not compelled to march through it, since we found later that there was a Turkish detachment stationed in the village.

Leaving the Tel Kelik valley, we climbed the hill on our side and an hour later—at 9.30—were delighted at finding the sea stretching out before us in the sunshine. It looked about fifteen miles off, but the mere sight seemed to raise our spirits marvellously, and we were, perhaps, almost as elated as Xenophon's men when the same sea greeted their gaze at Trebizond. We were now in a copse and decided to halt till evening. To celebrate the occasion, we made a late breakfast of buttered eggs, the eggs having been bought at a cottage we had passed during the morning. The next work in front of us was to make something of the coarse flour which we had procured two days previously from the Greek woman. Sweet got to work and, using some of the butter and our last tin of condensed milk, turned out a very fine dough. Baking was the chief difficulty and, after trying to make an oven, in the end we had to be content with making small *chapatties* on our diminutive frying-pan turned upside down and on the lid of a canteen. The results were very satisfactory, although consisting largely of fragments.

At four o'clock in the afternoon, we set off again and by dark had gone a good distance, and, after finding a sheltered spot for the night, collected a quantity of dead bracken to make ourselves as comfortable as possible.

We were off again early next morning, and had a steep scramble down through a wood, and eventually, to a stream at the bottom of a deep valley. Here there were a number of blackberries which we took advantage of, and then climbed the further side, coming out at last on the top and finding nothing now lay between ourselves and the beach, which must have been only three miles away at the nearest point. A moment later a sailing boat was seen close in to the shore and two or three others soon after. We were overjoyed at this, as it meant that boats were still being used along the coast and that there was no truth in all the stories we had heard in Kastamuni to the effect that no boats were now plying.

There was a small wooded hill projecting into the sea a little west of where we now were, and from its summit there would be a good view of the coast in each direction; on the other hand, we knew we could not be far from the town of Jerse and going west meant getting still nearer to it. Also, there were several farms and open country between us and the hill, and we were now very anxious not to be seen at all if we could help it. In the end, we decided to stay where we were for the day and go straight down to the shore in front of us late in the afternoon.

The wood we were in was very thick and, try as we might, no good spot for a halt could be found which would also give us a clear outlook on to the coast and any boats sailing along it. We had to be content to do without further observation of the sailing boats and bivouacked amongst the trees. Tea was made and a frugal meal of biscuits followed: our cocoa was now all exhausted, and greatly did we wish we had brought more of it in the place of some other things.

Recaptured

In the afternoon, we sewed together the two halves of the sail and cut a handle for our axe head so as to be as ready as possible in the event of discovering a boat. After making a stew from some beans we had gathered in a field on the hill that morning, we packed up and set off, full of hope and excitement. The question of going across to the wooded hill arose again when we got clear of the wood, but it was thrown out, and, bitterly did we regret it next day. Turning down to the shore, we crossed the road and, eventually, reached the beach just as it was getting dark.

There were one or two small houses just on our right above the shingle, and we were reconnoitring carefully when a big rowing boat was seen coming along close to the beach, rowed by some eight men. It went a quarter of a mile further along, and the boat was then pulled up by the men and others who appeared from the houses. It was too dark to see what they were, but for some unknown reason we did not suspect that they were men of a guard at this place or connect the houses with a place shown on one of our maps as being somewhere near here. We debated whether to go along the coast when it was quite dark and reconnoitre, or whether to wait for dawn.

In any case, it seemed hopeless to think we could push off the boat which had just been pulled up: it was far too heavy and they had brought it up a long way. Finally, we decided to wait till dawn and then go along and see what we could find. As soon as it began to get light next morning, August 23rd, we were up; our excitement was increased by seeing a small boat moored a little way from the beach. This had mast and sail and was just the size of boat we were hoping for. We crept quietly down to a track along the shingle. Sweet was in front and reported seeing a peasant near the first house. We walked quickly on finding that there were rather more tumbledown houses than we had expected.

However, it was too early for people to be about and there seemed no reason to suspect danger. We were hurrying on towards the boat we had seen, when we passed the end of a tumbledown boat-house and, to our dismay, found a Turkish sentry standing just inside. He stopped Sweet, while we three hurried on a little further. Sweet told him we were Germans bound for Samsun, the next port along the coast. However, the old man insisted on telling his *chaoush* or sergeant.

Meanwhile Sweet had rejoined us, but there was no chance of getting away, as by this time three or four others of the guard had turned out. The sergeant had us brought back to the guard-house, where the next scene of the pantomime began. Sweet, as had been previously arranged, was to play the part of a German officer, while we three were orderlies. Accordingly, we carried his pack for him, jumped up and down and saluted and, generally, behaved in a manner calculated to show our subservience.

Meanwhile, the *chaoush* who was in charge of the guard at this place—a village called Kusafet—was evidently not at all sure of his ground and suggested we should go with him to Jerse. We replied we were going in the opposite direction and wanted a boat with which to reach Samsun. The boat which had been moored off the beach had now been brought to shore and was landing some stores for the guard. We spoke to the skipper of this boat and, finding he came from Trebizond and knew a little English, hoped he would be amenable to helping us. Our idea was that having got on board for Samsun we could persuade him for a consideration to take us on to Trebizond, which was in Russian hands.

He went upstairs to confer with the *chaoush*, but whether he gave us away or not we were never quite sure. He came down advising us to go to Jerse and see the *commandant* there. This man, he assured us, knew no English or German, and was very ignorant and would believe our story. The *chaoush* wanted to make us march to Jerse, but we refused and, eventually, set off in the boat under the escort of the *chaoush* and two other armed soldiers. Before leaving we had obtained some *chapatties*, and a little raw fish which was better eating than we had expected.

On the way we suggested to the skipper that with the help of the crew we could easily overpower the guard and then set sail east; but he would not agree, and with the probability of the crew of five joining the guard we should have stood no chance at all. Hugging the coast, we reached Jerse in two hours, finding a small Turkish town built on a slight promontory. On the way, we passed the wooded hill we had talked about so often the day before. We should have been quite safe on this hill and, what was more, should have seen two or three boats in which we could probably have got away without much trouble.

On reaching Jerse we found ourselves moored beside a small patrol boat of the Turkish Navy, one of the crew of which said openly we were English. However, Sweet had gone ashore with the *chaoush*, and we were left hoping for the best, but fearing the game was up. Half an hour later we were summoned to join Sweet and were conducted with him to a police station. Here Tip was made to speak on the 'phone to a German officer at Sinope. He could think of nothing to say but *"Sprechen sie Deutsch,"* to which the Teuton eagerly responded at the other end. After shouting this down the 'phone several times Tip threw down the receiver, declaring it was out of order! Another man coming into the station declared he had seen two of us at Kastamuni.

We were then taken to the *commandant* of the town and agreed it was useless to try to bluff any longer, since they believed us to be English spies and it was only a matter of getting hold of any German for our whole story to fall to the ground. We, therefore, admitted that we had escaped from Kastamuni, saying we had been so long prisoners that we wanted to get home. The *commandant* was one of the best types of Turkish officer it had been our fortune to meet and was most polite. We were searched, and our maps and compasses and diaries taken, except from K., who managed to smuggle his map through. My original compass, not being recognised as such, was not taken.

Sweet told us that on first landing he had seen the *commandant* of the local *gendarmerie*, whom he had no difficulty in bluffing, as the skipper had foretold. Sweet told him we were on our way to the Caucasus to help in preparing a coming offensive for the Turks. He took all this in and Sweet was congratulating himself that our troubles were over. After giving Sweet coffee he said, no doubt, we would now like to be going on our way to Samsun. Sweet agreed, and they were just coming back to rejoin us when the *yuzbashi* mentioned that there was a colonel who was *commandant* of the town and that he would probably like to see Sweet before he left, the fat was then in the fire.

Sweet proffered our passport, but the colonel was suspicious and a Turkish naval officer whom he called in confirmed his ideas that we were British. The colonel told us later that there were two mistakes in our passport, which otherwise he evidently thought was quite good. He had our names and had been warned of our escape some two or three days after we had left Kastamuni.

The *yozbashi*, finding how thoroughly he had been bluffed, was now equally frantic in his wrath. We were said to be going off that day to Sinope and he was already preparing to handcuff us together in pairs. Luckily, the colonel turned up in time to prevent this. Most of our money was now taken and a receipt given to us for it. A little later we were told we were not going that day and were given a better room in the police station. The *chaoush* was very pleased with himself and told us he was going to accompany us to Kastamuni. He, also, it appeared, had been warned of our escape and, having passed through Kastamuni recently, probably suspected us more quickly than he would otherwise have done.

The colonel came in to see us and endeavoured to find out as much as he could from us as to which way we had come and how we had got food, but we told him very little. We got some food sent in and finally lay down on the floor for the night. Tip was now suffering again from his previous complaint, and we insisted that a doctor should be brought. However, no one was forthcoming. Next morning we were allowed to go into the bazaar to buy a few things needful, and on our return were told to get ready to march at once. A small donkey was brought up and on this we loaded our kit.

Tip was still feeling very poorly and had a bad time on the march. After some eight miles, mostly along by the sea, we reached some Turkish barracks which had evidently been only recently put up. They were wooden buildings, but, fortunately, cleaner than might have been expected. We were put into a small corner room in the officers' quarters and were much amused to find that no less than three sentries were posted to guard us; one outside the door, and one outside each window.

The officers consisted of a fat and surly *yuzbashi* and an Arab lieutenant, a huge man who was most genial and friendly. He told us his home was near Mosul, but he refused to believe that the British were in Bagdad and evidently thought we were trying to bluff him, the ignorance pervading all classes in Turkey as to what is happening in the outside world being colossal.

CHAPTER 12

Rescued

We had several visits from the Arab officers, and they very kindly gave us a share of their food, which consisted chiefly of a vegetable stew. The following morning, we were given a bread ration for five days and told to get ready at once. Tip was not fit to move, but they would not listen to us and dragged him out. We found a small pony had been brought, so Tip mounted this and we set off with a guard of a sergeant and eight privates; our former friend, the *chaoush* from Kusafet, was not coming with us after all and in his place, we had a truculent quick-tempered fellow who looked as if he would be any-thing but an agreeable companion on the march.

The men were evidently in the best of spirits, a visit to Kastamuni being a great event for them. In addition, they carried a good deal of tobacco, which they doubtless expected to sell again at a large profit on arrival. A great deal of tobacco is grown in the coast districts, more particularly near Samsun. We set off at a very easy pace and after pass-ing the German wireless station soon had a halt. The guard had two donkeys which carried their kit, but the *chaoush* would not hear of us putting our packs on them as well. After another halt in a village, we reached a *caravanserai* early in the afternoon, where the guard prepared their food, the man who owned the donkeys acting as cook to the *chaoush*.

This fellow had not even the disreputable uniform which the aver-age Turkish soldier possesses but was clothed in thin black stuff. His efforts produced boiled rice over which a little melted butter was poured. This was taken to a raised corner where he and the *chaoush* proceeded to shovel it into their mouths from the same bowl, eti-quette prescribing that the two parties should take spoonfuls strictly in turn. An hour later we were off again and began to ascend the lower slopes of the mountains we had crossed a few days previously. Now, however, we were on the so-called main road. It was one of the worst roads it had been our lot ever to have seen, and we wore truly thank-ful we were not travelling in carts. Long stretches were strewn with blocks of stone, which had been, apparently, left there promiscuously by some contractor who had not finished his job, like so many others in this country.

An hour or two later, after ascending some little distance, we stopped for the *chaoush* to get his pony shod. This animal he had com-mandeered at a village we had passed through, and now fancied him-self to no small extent as a mounted man. After a long wait the shoe-ing was at last accomplished and we set off once more. To our delight the *chaoush* had also procured a second pony, and on this we were allowed to load our packs. About eight o'clock we reached a small vil-lage where we were to spend the night; an empty log hut was found and a fire made in the large open hearth. We were given one side of the chief room while most of the guard slept on the rest of the floor.

With some eggs we had bought we made a very good supper and, thanks to the fire, were as comfortable as the circumstances would allow. We were now high up and it would have been very cold to bivouac in the open, as we must have been surrounded by clouds during the night. Before going off to sleep we considered the chances of escape. There would be little chance after another day or two when we had got further from the sea and were halting in larger villages, so that the present night seemed the only practical time, should opportunity offer. However, we soon came to the conclusion that it was quite impossible, as not only was there a sentry in the narrow passage outside the door but one or two of the *askars* in our room were told to keep awake in turns. The only exit was the door, to reach which we should have to walk over several of our guard.

First thing in the morning, August 27th, we were off again up the road. It was a glorious day and nothing happened beyond the usual halts every hour or so. We discussed our escapade once more, again deciding we had had a good run for our money, but that we had not been cautious enough when we did reach the coast. We went over afresh the various routes possible and alterations in plans which we would have adopted with the experience now gained.

It was about nine o'clock and we had been on the march fully two hours when suddenly with a cry of "*Askar*" shots rang out from the nearside of the road. For a moment we were too startled to know what to make of it. Then K. and I made a dive down the "*khud*" side, as the open road seemed anything but the best place to stay in. The first shot had bowled over the man in black who was riding a donkey in front. We had been told so much at Kastamuni about the bandits infesting the hills that we quite thought we might have fallen amongst a party of them and that to be taken and held to ransom would be a worse fate than returning for a few months to the civil prison at Kastamuni or Angora.

On going a little way down the hill, I saw a man whom I at first thought to be the *chaoush*, but as he beckoned to me saying "*Venez, venez,*" I saw that this was one of the new arrivals. He wanted me to go off down the hill with him, but after descending a little way I explained there were other officers on the road and I must go back to them. In the meantime, he was very voluble and excited, but I could not gather who they were or what had brought them. On arriving back on the road, I found K. and Tip; the fighting was now over, and three of the brigands were collecting the *askars'* rifles and ammunition.

The guard had put up no show at all and the nine of them were all disarmed and standing like sheep within two minutes, thanks almost entirely to the efforts of the three now collecting their arms, since my friend had been too far down the bank to have done much firing himself. The question now was whether we were to go with these fellows. K. was all for going off at once, but Tip and I hesitated as to the position we should be in, if caught again by the Turks before getting away. Our new friends would, of course, have been shot as outlaws, and we should very likely have shared the same fate. We took them aside and at length made out that they were adherents of the old Turk party and had no use whatever for Enver and his government.

They said they had come specially to rescue us and had a boat ready to put off for either Trebizond of Sevastopol in three or four days' time. After realising this, a process which took some time, as our knowledge of the language was very sketchy, we decided to throw in our fortunes with our new friends, as it seemed a heaven-sent chance of getting out of the country and almost too good to be true. We had seen nothing of Sweet since the firing started and now began to shout for him and search on each side of the road.

Our new friends set the old guard on to look for him, but not a sign of him could we see and no response came to our calls. After searching and shouting for an hour, we finally had to give it up, and leaving the guard in the road set off with our new acquaintances, whom we will now style the "*akhardash*"—or comrades—as that was the name they always used for themselves and their supporters.

As far as we could see, Sweet must have dashed away when the first shots rang out, thinking no doubt that this was a splendid opportunity of getting free again. It was very hard luck for him, especially as he had all along been one of the keenest and most energetic of the party. The old guard watched us go without emotion; they were apparently used to surprises of this sort. The *chaoush* remarked that we should now go to our homes, and we often wondered what happened to him when he got back to the barracks and reported.

He would be sure to say his party had been greatly outnumbered and were only disarmed after a prolonged resistance, but, nevertheless, he was probably reduced to a private. Besides the man in black who had been killed, two of the others had been wounded. Considering the rate at which the *akhardash* started firing, at a range of only twenty yards or so, the wonder is they did not hit many more; probably after inflicting a few casualties to start with they afterwards fired high on purpose. The guard, beyond firing one or two shots, seemed to have made no resistance at all. They were completely surprised and totally unready for such an occurrence.

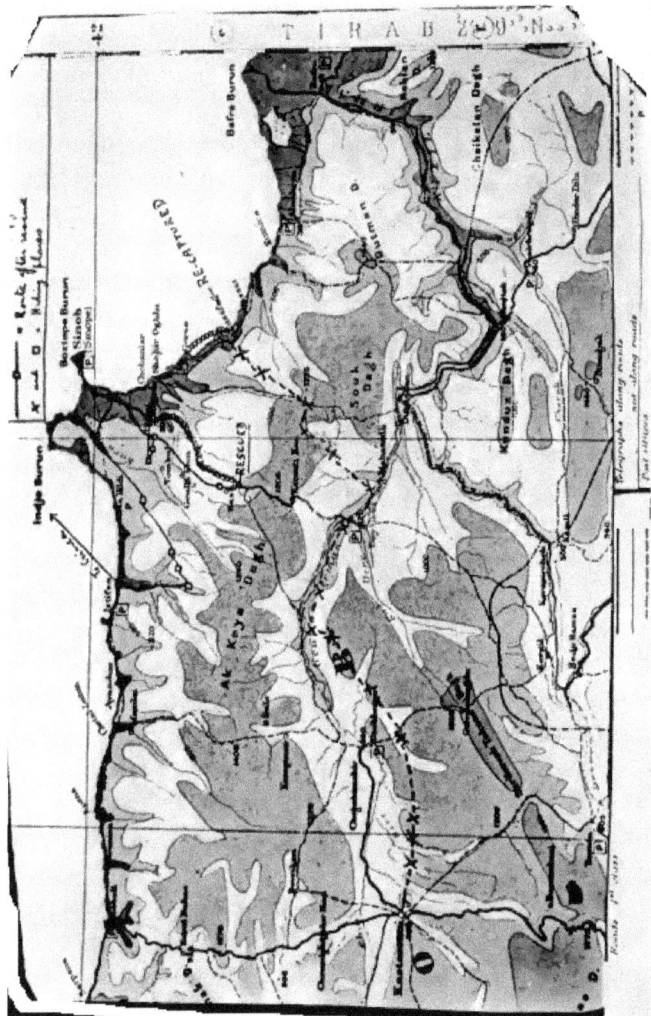

MAP (REDUCED) SHOWING ROUTE OF ESCAPE

Tip had an unenviable experience. He was riding his pony when the shooting began and had our rucksacks festooned round his saddle and over his legs so that he could not dismount in a hurry and found himself in a helpless position in a small storm of bullets. Finally, he was dragged to the ground by the tallest of the *akhardash*, who proceeded to kiss him with much fervour! This man, whose name was Musa, became our great friend. He was a tall lithe fellow and was always ready to do everything he possibly could for our comfort during the following weeks.

The leader, whom we always rather suspected of having played the part of the Duke of Plaza Toro in the actual scrap, was one Bihgar Bey, a most evil-looking gentleman. In fact, none of the four at the time we first saw them presented an appearance likely to inspire any confidence but resembled more the types one sees portrayed as those of the greatest criminals. Bihgar Bey, we learnt later, was one of a dozen implicated in the murder of Mahomed Shevket Pasha, (*grand vizier*, 1913), some years previously, but as he alone when caught was not in possession of arms his sentence was only one of transportation, while all the others were put to death.

The other two were Keor, an old Armenian who looked as if he had led a very hard life, and Kiarmil, a little man who had been a sergeant-major in the Turkish forces during the late Balkan war. Their looks, however, entirely belied them, as will be seen from our subsequent experiences, when on all occasions they went out of their way to lessen the hardships of our life in the woods. During the following days we found that they had been able to pay a certain sum yearly to avoid military service up to a few months previously, when all such privileges had been cancelled. They had then been forced either to serve or become outlaws and had chosen the latter alternative.

After living in the woods supported by more law-abiding friends, of whom they seemed to have a great number dotted about the country, they had decided to leave for Russia, and made arrangements with a man in Sinope to embark in his boat when all their party had been gathered and all arrangements completed. In the meantime, a *gendarme* at Sinope, who was also of their political views, had given them news of our recapture and march back to Kastamuni. They determined thereupon to effect our rescue, and the evening before had made a forced march of over twenty miles.

At first, we could not understand why they had taken on such an enterprise, seeing that it could only hinder their own plans for getting away, and would probably make it much more difficult for them to leave at all, as the Turkish authorities would be sure to take a good deal of trouble to prevent our getting out of the country; but they seemed to have a profound contempt for any number of *gendarmes* and no doubt considered we should form a good introduction for them to Russia. Whatever their reasons, it was a very plucky act for four of them to take on a guard of nine, although at the time when the man in black was bowled over it seemed a horribly cold-blooded business.

CHAPTER 13

In Hiding with the Turks

Throughout the following weeks our new friends did all they could to make us as comfortable as circumstances would permit, and we can never be sufficiently grateful to them for thus enabling us to leave captivity and reach home. They would never listen to any offers of payment, saying they did not wish to be taken for men who had rescued us for money.

Going back to the morning of our first acquaintance, we left the guard standing in the road while we, with all their ammunition and four of their rifles, retraced our steps along the road towards the sea and then branched off down a side track, finding a secure hiding-place in a thick wood about a mile further on. We thought it might be as well to impress the guard with the idea that we had been taken off by the "brigands" against our will, and therefore got them to tie our hands together and behaved as if we did not want to go with them at all.

When out of sight, we undid the cords and marched on again as really free men, Bihgar Bey continually cheering us by saying, "*Allons, enfants de la patrie,*" which, considering his position as an outlaw, was distinctly humorous. It was wonderful the inspiring effect the change from captivity had upon Tip who had been so seedy during the last few days; now he began to recover rapidly and succeeded in marching all the following night without any ill effects.

We had taken Sweet's kit with us, thinking we might meet him and that in any case it would be of no use to leave it with the guard. After sorting it out, we took one or two articles each and made our rescuers some small presents from the remainder. Bihgar and Kiarmil went off to fill our water-bottles and returned a little while later, after announcing their approach by clapping their hands. This we found was the method always adopted by the *akhardash* when meeting each other in woods or by night.

It was arranged that two of them would accompany us down at nightfall to a secure hiding-place, while the other two were to go in the opposite direction to meet friends from Boiabad who were also joining the party and, as far as we could make out, were bringing a good deal of money with them. In the end, we set off about half-past seven under the guidance of Keor, the old Armenian, while the other three set off again towards Boiabad. They had told us that we should reach our hiding-place in three hours, Bihgar Bey making our mouths water by describing it as a place of milk and honey, where we would be provided with meat, butter, eggs and cheese, all of which since we left Kastamuni had seemed the greatest luxuries.

Keor started off at a trot down a path through the wood. He was carrying his own rifle and one of our late guard's weapons, as well as four bandoliers full of ammunition and a bag on his back. We three each carried a rifle but hoped there would be no more cold-blooded shooting of the type that had effected our rescue. Keor's pace must have been about five miles an hour, and we soon had to request him to go slower, as I had a dicky knee which would be likely to give trouble going downhill at a trot over a bad path with daylight almost gone. Our packs with some of Sweet's kit were now a good weight, so that with a rifle in addition we were well loaded.

After being told that we should reach our goal in three hours we felt fairly confident of attaining it in five, especially as we kept ap a good pace and the recognised halts were not observed. Keor several times missed his way, but always found it in the end. After a couple of hours, we reached a river and wended our weary way down its bed, first on one side, then crossing to the other side and then back again. There was no path and we floundered along amongst the boulders in the darkness. Whenever we halted, which was not often, Keor always said it was now only one hour's march further.

About 3 a.m. we were going along a rough track beside the river bed when suddenly my bad knee gave way and I took a complete toss, rifle and pack going all over the place. There was nothing for it but to go on, so tying up the knee with a *puttee*, I hobbled on—the others nobly helping me by carrying my rifle. We were now all pretty well done and signs of dawn began to show in the east. Keor was very anxious to get in, saying there would be a great many *gendarmes* hereabouts the following day. At length we left the river, climbed a small rise, and passed close to some cottages, where the usual dogs soon started a chorus. This led to one or two shots being fired, probably with the idea of scaring off robbers, but, apparently, we were not actually seen. Finally, we dragged ourselves up a steep track, and got to ground in a thick copse. We were worn out; it was now a quarter-past five and we had done nine and a quarter hours instead of the three we had been promised. Still, we were free—and nothing else mattered. We put on what extra garments we had and were very soon asleep.

A few hours later Keor disappeared and returned shortly afterwards with what seemed to us a splendid breakfast: fried eggs, *chapatties* and yoghourt. Apparently, we were close to the house of an *akhardash*, from whom all this had been procured. Although some children came near us during the day, we were not discovered, and remained quietly where we were till nightfall. Then we tramped off once more, but only to halt at a very short distance further on under some trees near a house, which was probably the one our breakfast had come from. Here we were met by a boy of fifteen, by name Aziz, who came to us through the trees with a loaded rifle slung over his shoulder. Our friends always carried their rifles with a round in the chamber, but with the bolt not pushed home. We were continually expecting some accident to happen from this practice, but luckily nothing did.

Of the rifles belonging to our four rescuers, two were short Lee-Enfields which had been captured on the Gallipoli peninsula, and had found their way to the bazaar in Constantinople, where they had been retailed for £T.10 or nine pounds sterling: now, however, they assured us that the price had gone up to £T.20. Musa had a Turkish Mauser, made in Germany, while Keor possessed a Russian rifle. Aziz met us with an old Greek weapon, but much to his delight was given one of the rifles which had belonged to our guard. He was a very bright boy, and intensely excited and jubilant over our rescue and the discomfiture of the guard. In every case, the muzzle piece was removed so as to lighten the weapon, a bayonet, apparently, not being considered worth carrying when fighting *gendarmes* in the mountains.

In addition to their rifles, some of our friends carried Caucasian daggers. These are straight, with a very fine sharp point and double-edged blade about fifteen inches long. They were used for cutting brushwood, rigging up shelters in the woods, killing sheep, or chopping up meat, as required. Whenever we halted, Keor used to spend much loving care over his bandoliers of ammunition, seeing that each round was clean and not too loose in its leather loop.

After a few minutes under the trees a woman brought us a frugal supper, after which we set off accompanied by Aziz to find a hiding-place for the following day. A short distance brought us to a small Turkish house where a good deal of conversation took place between Keor, Aziz and the owner. Finally, we were taken into a maize-field and camped under a tree in the centre. The maize was seven or eight feet in height, so that we were well concealed. Our host brought us some bedding, consisting of a couple of old mattresses and quilts.

During the following days we had a pretty thorough experience of the delights of such bedding and came to the conclusion in the end that we should have been happier without any. However, in the present case it was not so bad and we had a comparatively undisturbed night. In the morning food was brought us by our host, which consisted mostly of a vegetable stew and coarse bread. The day was uneventful.

We spent another night in this field and moved on once more the following evening. Keor declared it would only take us half an hour and I trusted it might not be far, as my knee was not much better yet. It amused us to think what a trio of crocks we seemed to be. Tip had been ill off and on most of the time since we left Kastamuni. K. had been very unwell that day and suffered a good deal on account of his short sight; and I was dead lame. A few minutes after starting we met another of the *akhardash,* a very good fellow named Kasim, and conversed with him for a few minutes in the shade of a corn stack before proceeding.

It was a fine moonlight night, and we again passed the German wireless station, which was now below us and between us and the sea. In not more than an hour, we got close to the place appointed and after a long wait were conducted to a spot which seemed very secure, as it was in the centre of a thick copse with no houses near. Another youth turned up here and, apparently, was the son of our new host. For the next three days we stayed here, this boy bringing us food twice a day and telling Keor all the local news.

It was now we heard that Sweet had been retaken or had had to give himself up and was being marched back to Kastamuni. Later when Bihgar Bey and the others rejoined us they declared that Sweet had gone back with an escort of no less than 60 *gendarmes.* The idea of such a number being necessary tickled them immensely and they evidently considered it a great compliment to the disturbance they had caused, though they were genuinely sorry for Sweet and would have made an effort to rescue him had it been possible.

Our menu was rendered more attractive now by our being able to get a little butter and some fruit. As we had to keep still all day, there was little to do except speculate as to the composition of the next meal, and with having only two meals a day there was a considerable interval between these events. K. spent some time in making up his diary and checking dates. Our friends could never make out what he was writing about, and would say, "Here there are trees and mountains but whatever can a man find to write about?" Indeed, they never could make K. out very well.

Tip was far the most popular; for one thing the fact that he was an aviator roused their imagination, and in addition his good humour under all circumstances made him a great favourite. They always addressed him as *Kaptan*, but only called K. and me, by our surnames. The want of tobacco in the early days had not affected K. and me, as we did not smoke, but Tip had had to go very short; now, however, the *akhardash* seemed to have inexhaustible supplies and were always ready to roll cigarettes for Tip—an art which he never succeeded in mastering.

One day Keor informed us that some of the *akhardash* including Aziz had raided the German wireless station the night before, killing all the Germans and taking a lot of money. This was absolutely untrue, but he seemed to believe it and had evidently been told the story by the boy bringing our food.

CHAPTER 14

Continued Delays

On the afternoon of September 2nd, the third day in this wood, Bihgar Bey and Musa arrived, and announced that the friends from Boiabad had also come and that we should move on towards the sea. One of the newcomers had arrived with them at our lair, this being a stout fellow whom we always referred to as the Fat Boy: he was in fact the only pure Turk amongst them, the others all being of Circassian extraction. As it grew dark we moved off picking up some others of the *akhardash* shortly afterwards and took a line which would bring us towards the coast while at the same time approaching Sinope.

After some hours, it became evident that they were not very sure of the way, with the result that in the early hours of the morning they decided to stop where they were and reach the appointed place the following evening. At dawn a countryman stumbled upon a sentry guarding a path near which we lay. He was thoroughly scared and was allowed to go, after having evidently sworn never to tell of anything he had seen.

As morning dawned, rain came on and we moved under some bigger trees, where Keor very soon had a shelter rigged up, cutting down ash saplings with a dagger and using our sail as a cover. It was not a very efficient protection, but better than nothing and luckily on this occasion the rain did not last long. Next evening, under the guidance of a new comrade, we were conducted a little way further, finally halting in a maize-field until such time as some unwelcome guests had left our new host. This was an old Greek as poor as he was dirty, but he had evidently agreed to hide us until the boat was ready and we were much indebted to him. Finally, the Turkish visitors left the old man and he came to meet us.

The first thing he did was to go off with one of the *akhardash* and procure a sheep for us. We had not tasted any meat for about ten days and looked with great interest at the fine animal now procured. The old man then brought us bedding, and we are not likely ever to forget it. We remained in his care for nearly a week, and every day seemed to increase the interest which these mattresses took in us. At daylight, the old man cleared a space for us in a neighbouring thicket, and we moved in there. All the others except Bihgar departed, saying they were going to prepare food for the voyage. Left alone with Bihgar the time hung somewhat heavily. He looked after us like a father and by our calling him this he was highly delighted. He played picquet with Tip and did his best to learn a little English. The old Greek sent a messenger into Sinope for us, and we thus got hold of a few small note books and some playing cards, which helped to pass the time.

After a few days in our first clearing, we moved to another, a short distance off, this being considered rather safer. There were a good many houses round about and people passed by a path running within 50 yards of where we lay, so that we had to keep very quiet. After three or four days here, we began to get a little impatient, Bihgar Bey being somewhat indefinite; but at last one night, after going off at dark to meet some of the others, he came back and woke us up at midnight and told us to hurry up, as we were off. We hoped we might get right down to the coast and find the boat ready, but this was not to be.

After a second meeting under the tree in the maize-field and a farewell to the old Greek, we set off down a lane and past some houses where the inevitable dog was soon aroused. However, no one came out and we got out to a field near the main road, where, after a wait

BIHGAR BEY

of an hour, we were met by Kiarmil, whom we had not seen since the first day. At this point, the other had also met us and had with them a pony laden with bread and a little cheese, which were to be our rations on the voyage. The party now consisted of twelve of the *akhardash* and a boy with the pony, the latter not intending to leave the country with us.

We learnt that they had had a long fight with the *gendarmes* the day before, one being killed on each side. Apparently, the *gendarmes* had rounded them up in a village where they were preparing the food which they had now brought. There were, they said, 80 *gendarmes*, whereas they had only eight! Anyhow, our guide of a few nights before, a swarthy, powerful looking man, had been killed, but in the end, they had succeeded in getting away from the *gendarmes* or driving them off. The story, naturally, lost nothing in the telling and we never quite knew what to believe. At first, from their accounts, it sounded as if they had deliberately invited a scrap, and it was some time before we found out that they had been almost surrounded. They also brought the news that hundreds of *gendarmes* were being sent to Sinope from Kastamuni, but as there were never many at Kastamuni we were somewhat sceptical about this also. Crossing the main road, we found we were close to the sea, and a little further on entered a copse where we spent the rest of the night.

At dawn we went still further in, and sentries were posted. Meanwhile, the pony boy had gone off on his steed to Sinope to interview the boatman, and we waited till the afternoon, hoping that we might hear the boat was coming to pick us up that night. Our hopes were dashed again when the boy returned with the news that the boat and its proprietor were not in Sinope but had gone round the coast to the next port to the west. The *akhardash* decided it was too risky to stay where we were and, therefore, we moved again at nightfall. After following the main road, a little way on towards Sinope we left it, climbing slowly and going farther away from the sea. After some hours they found that they had missed the way again, although we were close to our destination, which was the inevitable *akhardash's* house.

Making across some fields and hedges, we gained a lane, but soon had to leave this, as carts were heard coming along. Luckily, Turkish carts make their presence known a long way off by their perpetual creaking, so that we were all safely under cover by the time they passed. A certain amount of misunderstanding now arose, Bihgar not seeing eye to eye with another of the *akhardash* who knew best our whereabouts, with the result that we nearly split up into two or more groups in the darkness.

However, we eventually all got together again, and reached the house of our new host or rather the field surrounding it. He came to meet us and escorted us to a wood close by. Here we slept till dawn and then moved farther into the trees. This old man was evidently a more influential "comrade" than most of those we had met so far. His house was a good deal larger than the average and he was treated with great respect. Another more humble supporter also appeared, and between the two we were provided with food. Late in the day, the old man departed for Sinope, and our hopes again ran high that he would be successful in arranging for the boat. Disappointment was once more in store for us on his return about six o'clock.

The leading three or four conferred apart with him, and it was not until afterwards that we were told that the Turks were so bent on preventing us leaving the country that they had had all boats pulled up, masts and sails taken out and guarded, and that no boat was allowed to put to sea from Sinope to eastwards of Kusafet, the place where we had been recaptured. The *akhardash* said that, this being the case, we must try elsewhere, and they proposed to march off towards Iyenjak, a little town about 30 miles westwards, where the restrictions imposed at Sinope would probably not be in force and where they hoped to get another boat. They said if this failed they would then go east towards Samsun, a distance of fully 100 miles across rough mountainous country.

We were beginning to wonder if they ever would get afloat. On August 27th, when they had rescued us, they declared everything would be ready in three or four days. It was now September and our early sailing seemed more unlikely than ever. In addition to this our boots were nearly worn out, and physically we were not in particularly good condition. It looked as if they would have a much better chance of getting off without us. so, we decided to offer to go off on our own and leave them free. We explained that it was a hanging matter for them if caught, whereas it only meant a few months in prison for us. They realised this only too clearly but would not hear of our leaving them for an instant, and declared they would get a boat, however much it might cost.

Kiarmil, upon whose person all the wealth of the party had been concealed in various places when it was thought we were about to embark, now began to disgorge his treasure and divide it up again.

227

Musa appeared to be by far the richest of the party and seemed to be quite a country gentleman. He told us he would lose his house, cattle and land worth thousands of pounds. These would all be confiscated by the Turkish authorities, but he confidently hoped with the next change of government to return to the country and get it all back again with a little more besides. Some of the others were in a similar situation in a lesser degree. They had succeeded in changing most of their money into Russian notes which had somehow found their way into Sinope and Jerse, and these transactions had delayed the preparations a good deal.

After a supper which included a little meat and was therefore noteworthy in itself, we set off again on the march, but found we had left behind one of our party who had had fever. At the start, we made good progress along a road, but then turned off to follow a river down the valley. To find the track was not always easy. Many fences had to be partially demolished to allow the pony to get through, and no effort was ever made to repair the damage or conceal our tracks. After crossing a good deal of cultivated land, we reached the river bed and began the type of march we knew so well, crossing continually from one side to the other, stumbling along over boulders and rocks. About three o'clock in the morning, we reached a thicket in a lonely part of the valley where the sides had narrowed considerably. They decided to halt here till the next night, much to our relief. Cross-country marching by night is never a very easy mode of progression, but when an attempt is made to use a stony river bed as a road it becomes a prolonged torture.

No incident marked the following day, and just before dark we were off once more. As dawn was breaking we reached the neighbourhood of yet another *akhardash's* house and went into hiding in thick brushwood which was soaking with dew. Just as we had got settled down, Bihgar for some reason decided that we three would be safer elsewhere, and much to our disgust hustled us off to an equally wet spot in a thicket on the opposite aide of the road. He was always prone to worry and fuss a great deal more than the others, and later on in the day, in a rash moment, I expostulated with him, going through a little pantomime to show how he had acted in the morning.

The effect was startling and a great deal more than I had bargained for. He began by fervently kissing my hand, declaring he was our servant and that everything he did was for our benefit. I hastened to stop the flood of protest and affection which I had unwittingly let loose, but it was some time before he was calm again. That evening we moved on, having been fed during the day by the local *akhardash*. We were now under the command of the fellow we termed the Fat Boy, Bihgar having gone off with some of the others to interview another friend regarding a boat. This man never worried at all and would shout to men on guard over the crops as if he were a countryman returning home late.

The fires all over the countryside at night in this district were used for scaring wild pig from the maize and other crops. In nearly every field would be a small perch for a man, who would keep a blaze going beside him and make various noises to scare off the intruders. Most of them had old guns of some sort and frequently a shot would be heard. The subject of pig formed a perpetual joke; the *akhardash*, as Mussulmans, declaring it was not good to eat, whereas we always offered to show them how good it was if they would bring us one. Another source of never-ending merriment was the prophecy that Tip would be taken prisoner when flying in France and again be sent to Kastamuni.

Towards midnight we reached a big wood and, under the guidance of a new supports, found a sheltered spot beneath lofty trees. The character of the country had altered a good deal since we had reached the coast. Here the rainfall was evidently a great deal heavier than it was at Kastamuni and the climate milder, with the result that all sorts of trees abounded and the vegetation was much thicker. This was the first spot considered safe enough by our friends for a fire and they soon had a fine blaze going. We lay down in the warmth and were quickly asleep.

Our comfort was short-lived, however, as it began to rain heavily. A small oil silk sheet which had belonged to Sweet kept me dry for a time, but it soon became necessary to move, as the fire had nearly gone out and another had been started further away. Tip evinced a wonderful power of being able to sleep when lying in a puddle and soaked through. The *akhardash* were experts at fire-lighting, under all circumstances, and skilfully arranged the logs to protect the inside of the blaze from the rain. In the afternoon we moved on under the guidance of two sturdy lads, one of whom with the aid of an axe cut a way for us through the brushwood and made a track up the steep hill, along which the pony struggled heroically. On reaching higher ground we found a path and followed this a little further to a water trough, near which we camped, another fire being lighted at once.

Our guide of the night before turned out to be a Turkish soldier on leave, but he showed little surprise on finding out who we were. The other lads had also been in the army and, as far as we could make out, had been sent to their homes on account of the shortage of rations in Constantinople. They bore us no ill will and evidently thought that the Gallipoli campaign showed them to be the better soldiers of the two. They knew nothing about our having taken Bagdad and were quite ignorant of all other war news. The following day was fine at intervals, generally just long enough to allow of our drying our clothes before it began again.

Our diet had been limited to coarse Turkish bread, of a most indigestible and half-baked variety, with potatoes and meat which we cooked by toasting small pieces on long sticks; but now the bread ran out and for two days we lived almost entirely on potatoes. The erstwhile soldiers also brought us a number of small pears. For washing we had the trough, but while the rain continued and for some time after each shower a small stream flowed down beside our camp.

The next event of interest was the arrival of a visitor who brought with him a sheep. We were told that this man had been employed in the *gendarmerie* but was now also leaving for Russia and intended to sail in ten days' time. He suddenly wanted our party to postpone their departure, so that he might join us, but this was not agreed to. To show his good faith, he had brought the sheep as a present and no time was lost in turning it into mutton. A long pole was cut and supported horizontally on two Y pieces driven into the ground beside the fire.

The sheep's carcase was scientifically balanced and tied to the pole and the roasting process then began, the pole being slowly turned in the supports. We made use of our canteens and anything else we could get hold of to catch the dripping: butter had been scarce and any substitute was greatly in demand. Our experience in this connection was that coarse, indigestible bread became much less harmful when any butter could be had to eat with it.

CHAPTER 15

Three Days on the Black Sea

There had been a certain amount of going and coming amongst the *akhardash* during the days we spent in this wood, but on September 19th Bihgar Bey arrived and declared everything was arranged. A boat said to be quite new had been purchased for 400 *liras*. This sum had been paid in hard cash, gold and silver, a fact of more interest than might appear since at that time not a single coin of any description was to be seen in the bazaars in Turkey. Notes had been issued down to 1 *piastre* and below this postage stamps were used.

We again offered to contribute a share to the cost of the boat, but they would not hear of it. Nearly all of them had some gold coins, English sovereigns being as numerous as Turkish *lira* pieces. The following day, September 20th, our *gendarme* friend again appeared, bringing another sheep, which was cooked without delay in the same manner as the first. We were to leave that evening at six o'clock, go down to the coast and embark the following evening. At last everything seemed to have been definitely arranged and our spirits rose accordingly.

A dark night march followed over some bad going and as we got lower down we entered the inevitable river bed. This lasted for an hour only and we then climbed a hill and found ourselves in a small copse immediately above the sea.

Since our recapture at the coast we reckoned we had covered about 150 miles, while our trek from Kastamuni to the coast must have been about 200 miles.

In the morning the pony boy was sent along to interview the boat owner, and on his return, we were told the boat was to come along at dark and we were to embark at eleven o'clock. The day passed un-eventfully, and there was nothing to be done but to lie still and hope that no misfortune would upset the scheme at the last moment. On these occasions the *akhardash* posted one or more sentries round our hiding-place and great care was taken to make no noise. As it grew dark Bihgar told us to go to sleep and said he would awaken us when the boat came. No sign of the boat had been seen and they were evidently much wearied. It looked as if even now something had gone wrong. The pony boy was despatched again and returned hours later to say that the boat had left as arranged.

Meanwhile, we had gone to sleep and did not wake until dawn. An awful presentiment seized us that another failure had occurred. However, as it grew light, the sentries who had not seen the boat the night before discovered it a quarter of a mile away across a stream with a fire lit on the beach above it. This had, apparently, been the signal, but for some reason had not been seen. No time was now lost in getting down to the boat. The pony boy galloped off, presumably to his home, and we trust never aroused the suspicions of the authorities. The sacks, containing the bread for the voyage were carried down and put on

BOAT IN WHICH THE PARTY CROSSED THE BLACK SEA

board, and a kerosene tin and keg from the boat taken to the stream to provide the water supply.

Meanwhile, others had been ballasting the boat with boulders from the beach. Just as the water was being brought back to the boat an old sentry emerged from a tumble-down house on the beach, which our friends had, apparently, thought to be deserted. He had scarcely taken in the situation before he was disarmed and tied up near the house. His Mauser rifle and ammunition were all taken from him, and in exchange he was left with an old Greek rifle, but without a round to put in it. The last of the party pushing off the boat leaped on board, and with thankful hearts we felt we really were off at last.

Our vessel was the usual type of coastal fishing boat, with a single big sail. She was about twenty-four feet long and between two or three tons displacement, but, whereas we had been expecting a new boat, we now found a very old one with mast and rigging that looked anything but trustworthy, the only sign of any recent attention being a little fresh paint here and there. However, we had left Turkey and had a boat and that was all we wanted. The question of navigation and handling the boat we left to start with to the *akhardash*, of whom several said they were accustomed to sailing and knew all about it; but we relied on Tip's experience to help us along if our other friends failed.

The first thing that engaged our attention, when the boat had been pushed off, was another vessel of the same type which was very slowly making its way close in along the coast and was now quite near to us. The result of a short palaver amongst the *akhardash* was that they rowed quietly up to this boat, not a rifle showing and all except the four rowers sitting down as quiet as mice. On getting up to the new-comer they all jumped up and levelled their rifles at the unfortunate crew in true pirate style. The crew had no course left but to accept any orders they were given, and after a few minutes' violent yelling and gesticulation their captain and one other were transferred to our boat, while Musa and the Fat Boy took their places in the other. Both boats now sailed off in company.

There was a good breeze from the east and they had decided to make for Sevastopol; but it soon became evident that they had little idea of the direction as a course N.E. was taken, whereas Sevastopol lay rather to the west of the point at which we left the coast. Other diversions, however, put questions of direction in the background for some time. To start with, the spar in our boat very nearly broke in two and had to be lowered and patched with two small pieces of wood and some old nails, a makeshift which gave little promise of being a permanent remedy. This was not accomplished without a tremendous hullabaloo, in which Bihgar played a prominent part. Arms were waving and all seemed to be yelling instructions to all the others. During the process the end of the rope suspending the spar ran through the pulley at the top of the mast, and it became necessary to get it back again somehow.

The captured captain of the second boat made a noble effort, swarming up the mast and holding on to the shrouds like a monkey; but the boat was rocking about a good deal and after several vain attempts he had to give it up. This necessitated the mast being unshipped and causing more frantic excitement, especially when the moment arrived to put it up again. But, in the end, the feat was successfully accomplished and both boats sailed off in company. The breeze was strong and the sea choppy. Several of the *akhardash* at once became *hors de combat* and remained nearly motionless at the bottom of the boat for the next three days.

It was a glorious morning, and, as we watched the coast receding, we were more than repaid for all the discomfort of the last few weeks. The Sinope headland stood out away on our right, and it was not till late in the afternoon that we were out of sight of the mountains. A small boat crossed our course soon after starting, but there were no signs of any pursuit or commotion on shore. We wondered what stories of our doings would reach our friends in Kastamuni and were pretty sure that the Turks would tell them we had come to an unhappy end at the hands of the "brigands."

We now attempted to get our friends to steer a course more nearly north instead of north-east; but they would not do so, as they were in a terrible state of apprehension lest they should reach Rumanian territory occupied by Germans. K. produced our chart—the largest map of the Black Sea we had been able to find at Kastamuni—but it was only some three or four inches long and coming as it did from an "Ancient Atlas" showed the Greek colonies in 500 B.C. and nothing more modern. We were not sure of the exact position of Sevastopol but did not allow our friends to know. Whatever was urged had no effect and the course remained N.E.

When dark came on, it soon became evident that neither our captured mariners nor the *akhardash* had the least idea of steering by the stars; and, finally, about midnight. Tip discovered we were going about due east. We thought it was high time we took charge, and therefore

234

MAP (ACTUAL SIZE) OF THE BLACK SEA

arranged to take watches, one of us sitting up beside the steersman and keeping the direction a little west of north. The boat had no cabin, but the stern was decked across and we were allowed to keep this to ourselves.

All the first day there had been a good breeze, but it became much feebler at night. With dawn the wind grew stronger again, and we were making a good pace in company with the second boat when, at nine o'clock, signals of distress from her were noticed. She was about 300 yards from us at the time and it was impossible to make out what had happened. Pandemonium at once reigned on board and we thought by the commotion that our companion must be sinking. After much shouting, our sail was lowered, the oars got out and the vessel slowly brought up to our comrade in distress, only to find that the latter had broken her rudder. Much shouting now took place on both sides.

Any thought of steering with an oar was never entertained and they decided to abandon one boat. As the captured second boat was so much the better of the two, an attempt was made to substitute our rudder in her, but without success. The result was that she was abandoned after transferring her crew, sail and spar, and part of her cargo to our boat. We were now packed very tightly, having a total of nineteen on board. Some of the ballast had been thrown overboard, but not enough to compensate for the additional load. Had we realised at the time that the second boat had a valuable cargo of kerosene, the price of which was fabulous in Turkey, we should have made some attempt to salve her or, at all events, have set her on fire. This information was not divulged till afterwards, but even so it is doubtful if she would not have sunk before drifting ashore or being discovered by another boat.

All went well, despite the crowd, until about midday, when the wind dropped altogether and rowing had to be resorted to. The boat was arranged for four oars and it was in this capacity that the captured crew proved of the greatest service. They were relieved at intervals by some of the *akhardash*. We calculated our speed when rowing at about two miles an hour, whereas for the first 24 hours it must have been at least double this. I plotted our course as nearly as possible on the diminutive map, and it was annoying to see how much further on we should have been had we started in the right direction the day before.

Our rations were the coarse bread, together with a little honey and butter which we had preserved for some days; but as neither of the latter could be said to be good they were not of much value. Some of our Horlick's milk was still left, and this helped matters along.

The morning of the third day broke with windless serenity and rowing went on uninterruptedly. The sky was perfectly clear, but at midday we noticed some very small clouds straight ahead which seemed stationary. We held on our course, trusting that the clouds meant land. At 6 o'clock that morning, as far as we could make out from the chart, we were at least seventy miles from the nearest point of the Crimea.

During the afternoon the question of rations and water was discussed, and we decided that if land was not in sight the next morning to take over all the remaining bread and water and distribute it ourselves, as the *akhardash* had not the least idea of rationing and used to eat and drink as the inclination prompted them. We had not liked to interfere before, but now it was a matter of necessity.

The sun set in a glorious blaze, and just at this moment there was a commotion at the forward end of the boat and the word went round that land was sighted. It was anything but clear, but we took the word of the sailors for it and everyone became much excited. Just before this event, Keor had made a fire in the bottom of the boat, making a hearth with some of the stone ballast and using some floor boards and any other bits of wood he could find as fuel. On this was cooked some meal which had been brought in from the abandoned boat; sea water was used to boil it and a very useful sort of porridge resulted.

CHAPTER 16

The Crimea and Home

At dawn on the fourth day, September 25th, the land was very clear and we could see a lofty headland which ran steeply down to the sea. An hour or two later, we could make out houses and then it became clear that we were approaching some seaside resort. All through the previous two days after we had taken charge of the steering, the *akhardash* had continually inquired whether the "road" was "good" and they were now more than satisfied that we knew the best way over the sea. Fortune had been with us, in giving us fine weather and clear skies by day and night; otherwise we might have reached a very different destination. Rowing on steadily, it was soon clear that the place was quite extensive and probably much frequented. Several large buildings could be seen and something which looked like a pier or jetty, to which we now steered. It was not until one o'clock that we finally reached this spot and landed, to find ourselves opposite the baths.

ALUPKA

For days we had talked of the delights of a good hot bath and now we had come straight to the very place. We were met by a Swiss who was bathing. He hurried off to dress, but before he could return we were accosted by several other people, notably a retired Russian general and an American diplomat who lent us clothes and escorted us to the baths. After getting really clean once more, we were taken to a *pension* and made the guests of the hospitable Russian ladies to whom it belonged. They told us the place was called Alupka and was one of the most popular seaside places in Russia. Meanwhile the *akhardash* had been escorted into the town. In the morning they had begun to don their bandoliers and handle their rifles, but we persuaded them that they would be looked upon in a more friendly manner on landing if they abandoned these weapons.

It had taken us 78 hours to cross the 180 miles of sea, but actually we must have sailed well over 200 miles. We found that, comparing our position on the third morning with the spot we had marked on the map, we were only some twenty miles out, which, as amateur navigators, we considered quite good work.

At the *pension* we were given lunch, and wine was produced in our honour by our new friends. We shall never forget their kindness, and the extraordinary feeling of being amongst all the amenities of civilization once more after two years under other conditions. In the afternoon, we were taken to the municipal office and there interviewed by a very businesslike and intelligent lady who seemed to combine the duties of commissioner of police and most other municipal departments. Our friends told us that there was some difficulty in establishing our identity, since the *commandant* of the town—who a few months earlier before the Revolution had been an actor—was very suspicious and inclined to believe we were really Germans.

In fact, some splendid stories were going about. According to one, a boat-load of Turks under the command of three German officers had attacked the town, one of the Germans being wounded. Tip had been to see a doctor and this no doubt lent colour to the idea. At all events, the *commandant* told off a sentry to shadow us about wherever we went. The *akhardash*, we found, had been accommodated in the central police building, where they had been given plenty of food and seemed to be receiving visitors. We bought them some fruit and tried to cheer them up, as they had imagined they would be received with triumphal rejoicings and were somewhat crestfallen at being treated more like prisoners.

ALUPKA BATHS

Our first object was to get in touch with the nearest British consul, so as to put their case before him and get matters explained to the Russian authorities; but no one seemed to know where the nearest consul was to be found. We got telegrams sent off to our people at home addressed to the Embassy at Petrograd. It was hopeless at this time to try to get private telegrams through, and for mails from home we found they were even worse off here than we had been in Kastamuni. It was strange, indeed, being in a spick and span town, with well made roads and everything clean and up-to-date, after the filthy dilapidation which characterises everything in connection with the Turk.

Some people we met seemed rather annoyed that we had not struck a mine, as they assured us there was a large minefield through which we had passed. We discovered, later, this was quite wrong, but in any case, our boat was of much too shallow draft to be in much danger. Others told us that we were fortunate to land where we did, as had we gone a little further east we should have come to the estates of some of the grand dukes who at that time were interned under armed guards, with orders to prevent anyone approaching from land or sea! We were told that everyone was on rations and that food was getting scarce. One of the most striking contrasts to Turkey was the magnificent fruit on sale, grapes, pears and peaches, all evidently cultivated with great skill.

As we emerged from our interview with the lady commissioner, we were summoned to halt in order to be cinematographed by the representatives of some Moscow firm. All the educated people we met in Russia were kindness itself to us and made our journey through the country very pleasant. It was pathetic to be asked, as we were, to tell people in England that not everyone in Russia is bad and worthless. All classes, we found, had welcomed the Revolution when it started, thinking a new and brighter era had dawned; but it very soon became clear that the pendulum was swinging much too far in the other direction, and no one would dare to prophesy what might happen next. Fortunately for us, there was no actual internal fighting taking place at the time and we got through the country without trouble.

The following day we left Alupka by motor for Yalta, a port a little further east. The road led past some of the grand dukes' estates and Livadia, the *Tsar's* Crimean palace. The scenery all along was magnificent, the pineclad hillsides sloping steeply down to the blue, with white houses or palaces. Yalta itself was one of the most charming spots it had been our good fortune to see and is easily equal in beauty

YALTA

to any of the Riviera resorts. From here we were to travel by night by a transport back past Alupka, reaching Sevastopol on the following morning, but before leaving a surprise was in store for us.

As we had some time to wait, we went into an hotel, with the officer conducting us, for tea. This, however, we found was the headquarters of the local committee of soldiers and workmen, and a few minutes later we were asked to go into their meeting hall to receive their congratulations. This promised to be rather awkward, as we knew no word of Russian; but fortunately, a schoolmaster who knew French was introduced to us. As we entered the room, the soldiers and sailors present all clapped vigorously. There were about 30 or 40 present and it was necessary, as on every possible occasion in Russia, to shake hands all round.

The schoolmaster then gave a harrowing account of our imprisonment in Turkey and told them how we had eventually escaped and reached Russia. He appeared to say that we had been manacled in chains and endured the worst possible fortune as prisoners. After a suitable expression of thanks conveyed through the schoolmaster, we shook hands again all round and returned to our tea. This was our only actual meeting with a revolutionary committee, and we are bound to say they seemed to have no love for the Turk or any wish to leave their Allies in the lurch by concluding a separate peace.

The transports steamed only at night and kept close into the coast for fear of possible submarines; so that the chances of our being picked up by one on our way over had been very remote.

The *akhardash* travelled with us to Sevastopol, and on arrival there we met the British Naval Representative, Commander Sage, R.N., who looked after us for the next few days. As he spoke Russian fluently and was in touch with all the highest authorities, we had no trouble of any sort. The *akhardash* were handed over to the Russian Staff authorities, who provided them with good quarters on a ship in the harbour. We three lived with Commander Sage on an auxiliary cruiser, the *Almaz*, which had previously been used as a private yacht by the grand dukes. The *akhardash* had for some time wished that we should all be photographed together and we, too, were anxious to have such mementoes of our time with them.

The Russian Staff very kindly arranged it and we had two groups taken, one with our original rescuers with their rifles and bandoliers, and one with all the others included. Unfortunately, Keor, the old Armenian, was ill in hospital and could not be present. As some days

THE THREE OFFICERS WITH THREE OF THEIR RESCUERS

had elapsed before the photos were taken, our friends had obtained new clothing and hats and, therefore, did not present the picturesque appearance to which we had become accustomed. As regards some recompense for all their services, we could not get them to accept anything more than what they had spent on our food during all the time we were with them, but the Russians paid them the exact sum they had given for the boat, so that they were not out of pocket on that account. As souvenirs, they had given us each one of their long Caucasian daggers, and we in return got wristwatches for them and a suitably inscribed cigarette case for Bihgar Bey. We left them in good hands and have often wondered since what has been their fortune. No men could have acted more pluckily in rescuing us in the first place or taken more trouble over our comfort and welfare during the weeks we spent with them in the hills and woods; and never shall we forget how much we owe than.

After some days in Sevastopol, we said goodbye to them and went round to Odessa on the *Almaz*, where we made arrangements with the British consul for our journey home. At Odessa we were entertained at a most convivial dinner by the British and American Club. Like all dinners in Russia, it proved prolific in speeches, a start being made with the king's health, in the middle of the fish course, by an enthusiastic American. From these speeches we learnt how wholeheartedly the great American nation had entered the struggle and the efforts they were making in Russia, more especially with regard to improving the railways.

Coming out of the obscurity of Turkey, these things were new to us, although by reading between the lines of the Turkish papers we had been able to get a fair idea of the general position on the actual battle fronts. Another speaker told a pitiful story of the position in Rumania and of the appalling, lack of medical stores and awful ravages of disease in the army. A visit to the races and opera helped to pass two very enjoyable days before saying goodbye to Commander Sage and our new friends, and leaving for Mogileff, the then headquarters on the Russian front to which we had been summoned by the British Mission.

On our way we passed through Kieff, a magnificent town, peopled very largely by Poles. Here we met some forlorn British gunners who did not know what was to be their fate, but were soon, I trust, back in England. After a day in Mogileff we went on to Petrograd. Travelling even at this time was very comfortable on the Russian lines, for those with passes such as we possessed, except for the temperature of the

THE THREE OFFICERS AND THE AKHARDASH

carriages. In some it was impossible to open any window. The result was that we all got heavy colds, although during the past six weeks we had kept fit while sleeping out in the open and occasionally getting soaked through.

Petrograd was cold, wet, and dreary, and we spent our time in rushing about between the various departments before we could get passports and tickets through to Bergen. We, eventually, accomplished this by hard work in three days, and were then told we were fortunate not to have been kept at it for a week. It was necessary to borrow mufti to travel through Sweden and Norway. Clothes in Russia were practically unobtainable, but, fortunately for us, two naval officers at the Embassy came to our rescue by most generously giving us the necessary garments. We were also indebted to the Red Cross Depot at the Embassy for other assistance in the way of clothes.

Tip and I left on October 14th, and after an interesting trip through Sweden and Norway reached Aberdeen ten days later.

K., on the other hand, returned to the Black Sea. It had been hoped, and we had done our best to arrange, that an attempt should be made with the assistance of the *akhardash* to release some of the other officers at Kastamuni. Unfortunately, this plan never materialised: for one thing our friends were moved further inland from Kastamuni before any attempt could be made, and when everything was settled on our side the Bolshevik rising had commenced and brought all plans to a standstill. K. reached England two months later, after having made a trip over to the Turkish coast in a Russian destroyer, and worked in every conceivable way to bring off the scheme for the rescue of the other officers. His persistent but unsuccessful efforts bring the account of our adventures to a close.

CHAPTER 17

Friends in Captivity

This story would not be complete without recording the deaths of Captain R. J. Tipton, R.F.C., and Captain R. T. Sweet, D.S.O., 2/7th Ghurka Rifles.

Tipton, after very few days at home, reported again for duty and would not rest content until he had obtained leave to fly and fight over the German lines. For this purpose, he had refused his majority. On March 9th he was severely wounded in a fight with a Hun whom he brought down. With great courage and skill, he brought his own machine back and landed safely, but the injury he had received proved fatal and he died three days later.

Tipton thus went back to fight at the earliest possible moment, feeling it his duty to the other officers left behind in Turkey, who were bound to be suffering for our escape. Although the youngest of our party, he was our leader on the long journey to the coast; and to his unfailing good humour and tact we owed much more than we realised at the time. Although in pain for many days, he kept cheerfully on and would never give in.

Few men have been more beloved by all with whom they came in contact, and his gallant death has left a wide blank in the affections of all who had the privilege to know him.

Sweet, whose gallantry at Kut had earned him the D.S.O., was imprisoned at Angora, after being brought back from the coast, and exhibited to the other officers at Kastamuni for a few minutes on the way. He shouted to them to take a few days' provisions and try their luck, that it was quite easy to get away, and that he meant to start again the first chance he had. In reply they cheered him, much to the disgust of the Turks.

After two dreadful months in the civil prison at Angora, he was taken to the officers' camp at Yozgad, a place 4,000 feet above the sea amongst the hills, in the very centre of Asia Minor. Here he remained till a few weeks before the armistice with Turkey was announced, when he fell a victim to the influenza scourge and died of pneumonia.

In our escape Sweet was always the most indefatigable, and on many an occasion spurred us on when we three had no energy left. His knowledge of Turkish was invaluable and enabled us successfully to bluff our way along during the days when we were posing as Germans. It was only the merest accident that parted him from as when the *akhardash* arrived, and it is hard to feel that so small a thing should have ultimately resulted in the death of such a brave officer.

The first officers who died in Kastamuni were Lieutenants Reynolds, of the 103rd L.I., and Lock, of the I.A.R.O., attached 104th Rifles. Reynolds had been unwell during most of the journey up and, undoubtedly, had not got over the hardships of the siege; he succumbed within a few days of our arrival. Lock, who had been an indigo planter in Bihar, went down with peritonitis very shortly afterwards. Both officers had done well in Kut and were greatly liked by all who knew them. Their death in a strange country, after the worst of our troubles seemed to be over, was all the sadder to think of.

The third officer who died was Commander Crabtree, R.N.R., of the S.Y. *Zaida*, which struck a mine while patrolling the Adana coast. He, along with three other officers from the same ship, was sent on to Kastamuni. At Angora he was ill, but the Turks considered him fit enough to travel, and sent him on in a springless country cart over the 140 miles of rough road to Kastamuni. Riding in a cart over this road is bad enough for a fit man, but in his case, it must have simply jolted him to death. At all events, he arrived dying, and never regained consciousness.

Another sad death occurred amongst the officers after they had been moved to Changri from Kastamuni. On Christmas Day, 1917, Major Corbett, 48th Pioneers, died suddenly from an aneurism of the heart after some strenuous tobogganing, which had been allowed as a special concession.

Major Corbett was one of those officers who assisted our party to escape and would himself have come with us had he considered there was any small chance of success. To the camp at Kastamuni he was invaluable as staff officer to the lower group of houses, always energetic and cheery and turning his hand to something. Carpentry formed his chief occupation when not playing games.

He was one of those men whom we felt we simply could not do without, and his loss may well be imagined in the camp at Changri, where conditions had been rough and painful in the extreme.

Appendix A

GARRISON OF KUT
HEADQUARTERS
MAJOR-GEN. C. V. TOWNSHEND, G.O.C.

16th Infantry Brigade, MAJ.-GEN. DELAMAIN.
{ 2nd Dorsets.
66th Punjabis.
104th Rifles.
117th Mahrattas.

17th Infantry Brigade, GEN. HOGHTON.
{ Oxford and Bucks L.I.
22nd Punjabis.
103rd Infantry.
119th Infantry.

18th Infantry Brigade, GEN. HAMILTON.
{ 2nd Norfolks.
120th Infantry.
110th Infantry.
7th Rajputs.

30th Infantry Brigade,
MAJ.-GEN. MELLIS
{
2 Coys. Royal West Kents.
3 Coys. 4th Hants T.F.
2/7th Ghurka Rifles.
24th Punjabis.
67th Punjabis.
76th Punjabis.
}

DIVISIONAL TROOPS

17th Coy., S. & M.
34th (Poona) Signalling Co.
Sirmoor Sappers (Imperial Service).
1 Squadron 7th Hariana Lancers.
48th Pioneers.
63rd, 76th, 82nd Batteries, R.F.A. 18 guns, 18 pdr.
104th Battery, R.G.A. 2 4" guns.
84th Battery, R.G.A. 4 5" guns.
Volunteer Battery. 4 15 pdr. guns.
" S " Battery, R.H.A., left behind 2 14 pdr. guns.

Naval Detachment. 4 4·7" pdr. guns.

H.M.S. *Samarra*: 2 3 pdr. guns; 1 13 pdr. gun.
Machine Gun Battery (6 guns).
Supply and Transport, including Jeypore Transport Train, Wireless, Royal Flying Corps, Depot and other details.

MEDICAL SERVICE

One British General Hospital.
One Indian General Hospital.
3 Field Ambulances.

	Strength of garrison at beginning of siege.	*Strength on surrender.*
British Officers - -	301	277
British Rank and File	2,851	2,592
Indian Officers - -	225	204
Indian Rank and File	8,230	6,988
Indian Followers -	3,530	3,248
Total -	15,137	13,309

Losses: Killed and died of wounds, 1,025.
Died of disease, and missing, 803.
Arab population of Kut (?) 3,700.
Animals (horses and mules) before killing for food, 3,000.

Appendix B

Copy of translation of pamphlets thrown over from Turkish trenches towards our line during the earlier part of the siege and picked up between the two old lines when these had been evacuated on Jan. 21st.

Oh dear Indian Brethren,

You understand the fact well that God has created this war for the sake of setting India free from the hands of the cruel English. That is the reason why all the Rajahs and Nawabs with the help of Brave Indian soldiers are at present creating disturbances in all parts of India and are forcing the English out of the country. Consequently, not a single Englishman is to be seen in the N.W. Frontier of India districts of Saad, Chakdara, Mohmand and Kohat. Brave Indian soldiers have killed several of their officers at Singapore, Secunderabad and Meerut cantonments. Many of the Indian soldiers have on several occasions joined our allies the Turks, Germans, and Austrians of which you must have heard.

O heroes! our friends the Turks, Germans and Austrians are trying merely for the freedom of our country (India) from the English and you being Indians are fighting against them thus causing delay. On seeing your degraded position, one feels severely ashamed (lit. 'blood in the eyes') that you have not got fed up of their disgraceful conduct and hatred towards you.

"You should remember how cruelly were Maharajah Ranjit Singh of the Punjab and Sultan Tipu treated by the English govt., and now when our beloved country is being released from their cruel clutches you should not delay the freedom of your country and try to restore happiness to the souls of your forefathers as you come from the same heroic generation to which the brave soldiers of the Dardanelles and Egypt belong.

You must have heard about the recent fighting in the Dardanelles when Lord Hamilton was wounded and Lord Kitchener cowardly ran away at night taking with him only the British soldiers from the Dardanelles siege and leaving behind the Indian soldiers who on seeing this murdered all their officers and joined the Turks.

Nearly everywhere we find that our Indian soldiers are leaving the British. Is it not a pity that you still go on assisting them?

Just consider that these and we have left our homes and country and are fighting only for *rupees* fifteen or twenty; a subaltern 20 or 25 years old is drawing a handsome amount as salary from Indian money while our old *risaldar* and *subadar* majors are paid nothing like him—and even a British soldier does not salute them. Is that all the respect and share of wealth for the sake of which we should let them enjoy our country?

For instance, see how many of you Indian soldiers were killed and wounded during the Battle of Ctesiphon and there is nobody to look after the families of your deceased and wounded brothers. Just compare the pay a British soldier draws with that which you get. Brethren hurry up, the British Kingdom is going to ruins now. Bulgaria gave them several defeats; Ireland and the Transvaal are out of their possessions of which perhaps you already know.

H.M. the *Sultan's* brave Turkish forces which were engaged at the Bulgar frontier before are now coming over this side in *lacs* for the purpose of setting India at liberty.

We were forced by the British to leave our beloved country for good and had to live in America, but on hearing the news of our country being freed from English hands we came here *via* Germany and found our Indian brethren fighting against H.M. *Sultan*.

Other nations are trying to restore us freedom from the British, but it appears we do not like to be freed from slavery, hence we are fighting against our friends the Turks.

Brethren, what is done, that is done, and now you should murder all your officers and come over to join H.M. *Sultan's* Army like our brave Indian soldiers did in Egypt and the Dardanelles. All the officers of this force and Arabs have received orders from the *Sultan* that any Indian soldier, irrespective of any caste, a Sikh, Rajput, Mahratta, Gurkha, Pathan, Shiah or Syed, who come to join the Turks should be granted a handsome pay and land for cultivation if they like to settle in the *Sultan's* territory. So, you must not miss the chance of murdering your officers and joining the Turks, helping them to restore your freedom. Dated 28th December, 1915.

Printed and distributed by the Indian National Society.
Translated from originals in Urdu and Pushtu or Punjabi.

Appendix C

Comparison of rations issued in Kut at the middle of April, 1916, with full service rations.

BRITISH

Normal Field Service.	In Kut.
Bread, 1¼ lb.	4 oz. (from April 17th).
Fresh meat, 1¼ lb.	1¼-1½ lb. (horse and mule).
Potatoes and vegetables, ½ lb.	Nil. (except ság).
Bacon, 3 oz.	Nil.
(or butter 1½ oz. twice a week).	
Tea, ⅝ oz.	Nil.
Sugar, 3 oz.	Nil.
Salt, ½ oz.	Nil.
Jam, 4 oz.	Nil.
Cheese, 3 oz.	Nil.
Ginger, —	⅓ oz.

INDIAN

Normal Field Service.	In Kut.
Atta (wheat meal), 1½ lb.	4 oz. (barley meal).
Ghi, 2 oz.	½ oz.
Dal, 4 oz.	Nil.
Meat, 4 oz.	9 oz. (horse).
Gur, 1 oz.	Nil.
Potatoes, 2 oz.	Nil.
Tea, ⅓ oz.	Nil.
Ginger, ¼ oz. Chillies, ⅛ oz. Turmeric, ⅛ oz. Garlic, ¼ oz. Salt, ½ oz.	½ oz.

Appendix D

Rations at end of Siege
All except meat and ginger dropped by aeroplane.

British.	Indian.
Bread, 3 oz.	Indian atta, 3 oz.
Sugar, 1 oz.	Gur, ½ oz.
Chocolate, ½ oz.	Dal, 1 oz.
Meat, 1½ lb. (horse or mule).	Salt, ½ oz.
	Ginger, ⅓ oz.
	Meat, 9 oz. (horse).